It Would Be
So Nice
If You
Weren't Here

It Would Be So Nice If You Weren't Here

MY JOURNEY THROUGH SHOW BUSINESS

CHARLES GRODIN

VINTAGE BOOKS

A Division of Random House, Inc.

New York

FIRST VINTAGE BOOKS EDITION, SEPTEMBER 1990

Copyright © 1989 by Charles Grodin

Library of Congress Cataloging-in-Publication Data
Grodin, Charles.
It would be so nice if you weren't here : my journey through
show business / Charles Grodin.—1st Vintage Books ed.
p.   cm.
Originally published: 1st ed. New York : Morrow, c1989.
Includes index.
ISBN 0-679-73134-2
1. Grodin, Charles.   2. Motion picture actors and actresses
—United States—Biography.   3. Theatrical producers and
directors—United States—Biography.   I. Title.
[PN2287.G74A3   1990]
791.43′028′092—dc20
[B]   90-50151   CIP

To my parents,
Ted and Lena Grodin

Acknowledgments

I wish to thank my representative, Owen Laster, for his encouragement over the four-year period it took to write this book.

I'd like to express my appreciation to Lauren Weiss, at the William Morris Office, who helped so much in getting various permissions, which at times seemed as demanding as writing a book.

Barbara Shalvey typed, retyped, and retyped the manuscript with an absolute minimum of sighs.

I want to thank my daughter, Marion, whose good heart and generosity made her quickly accept the proofreading task. Only later did she say, "I've got to watch out for those good-heart and generosity impulses."

I found my editor Lisa Drew's guidance and suggestions impeccable. When I first met Lisa she was so sensitive and enthusiastic I wondered if it could last. It did.

Bob Shuman, Lisa's assistant, took care of every issue that fell in no specific category but lay everywhere, every day for months. He, like the others, should win some kind of award for kindness.

And finally, I would like to thank my wife, Elissa, who listened to my various issues with the compassion, patience, intelligence, and understanding that I cherish.

Preface

This is a book for people who are aspiring toward something and finding it a lot harder to achieve than they ever imagined.

I remember crying once as a little boy (I forget why) and thinking that if this was how hard life was going to be, I wasn't so sure about going on. And then, one day, oh, my God! I went into show business.

I knew when I decided to go into this profession that it was tough, but I had no idea how tough.

This is the story of what I did to keep going when the overwhelming message was: Stop . . . Go away . . . We don't want you . . . Get lost . . . You're no good . . . and worse.

Contents

Candy Bergen and I were filming the movie *11 Harrowhouse* in a castle outside London. We were sitting in a room off the main hall where the cameras were being set up. After a few minutes an Englishwoman appeared. I don't know who she was, but she acted as though she had a duchess-or-something title. She said: "Did someone ask you to wait in here?" "No," we answered, a bit taken aback. She responded: "Well, it would be so nice if you weren't here."

It Would Be
So Nice
If You
Weren't Here

As Likely As a Man
Walking on the Moon

$\mathbf{A}$ friend's thirteen-year-old daughter was to play a part in a school production of the musical *Bye Bye Birdie*. She was told that because of the number of students in the class, the rules were that someone else would be playing her part after the intermission. I was never replaced at intermission, but . . .

Maybe the only way harder than show business to make a living is selling poetry door to door, so I guess you have to wonder why so many people go into show business. Some people's families are in it, and they simply follow the family business. My father, I. Theodore Grodin, had his own store. He sold wholesale supplies to cleaners, tailors, and dressmakers—materials to make suits, hangers, buttons, zippers, and about a hundred other things cleaners, tailors, and dressmakers need. My father's father, whom I never knew, was Charles Grodin—he changed it from Grodinsky sometime early this century. He rolled cigars in his home. My mother, Lena Grodin, helped my father in the store, took care of our house, cooked all the meals, washed all the clothes, and generally made sure anyone could eat a meal off any floor in the house. My mother was also capable of putting a comic slant on just about anything. Whenever I would call down from my upstairs bedroom, "Is the front door locked?" my mother would call back, "Who's going to steal you?" It never reassured me, but I did admire her talent at putting a little spin on her answer to a nervous question. She also had an uncanny ability to predict how stories on the radio and television were going to turn out. What amazed me even more was Mother's capacity to know where absolutely every single thing in the house was at all times for decades—without a miss.

"Mother, do you know where that rubber ball is I was bouncing last month?"

"It's in the little basket in back of the filing cabinet next to the coal bin."

My mother's father, when I knew him, was an old Russian Jew with a long white beard who always wore black suits and a big black fedora. He came from a long line of rabbis in Russia. He arrived in Pittsburgh, Pennsylvania, around the turn of the century. Sometime in his thirties, he decided to spend all his waking hours studying the Talmud. From father and mother, going back to Russia, no show business anywhere in the family.

I've always heard that most people become performers because they crave more attention than the regular world will give them. Like many other children, I didn't feel particularly noticed. I was always colder than anyone else. I used to sit on the dining-room floor on top of a heating vent. Everyone had to step over me to walk upstairs. I regularly called for family meetings to discuss . . . anything. But the demands on everyone's life were such that I heard responses from Mother and Dad like: "Talk? What do you want to talk about? This kid just wants to talk." No meetings were held to discuss my unannounced issues. You could say I wanted more attention. This is probably the deeper reason why I went into show business. But that was all unconscious. Here's the conscious story:

I was born in Pittsburgh in 1935. I followed my brother, Jack, by six years. Jack was an almost obsessive student. He became an attorney, a CPA, and head of his own firm. Because of our age difference, my brother's main adjustment to me (whenever he looked up from a book and noticed me hanging around) was to amuse himself. When the Japanese bombed Pearl Harbor, I was six, he was twelve. I asked him if the Japanese were going to come to Pittsburgh. He smiled and said yes. I asked if they'd come to our house. "Yes, they will," he answered again.

Shaking a little, I said quickly: "Well, I'm going down to the basement. They wouldn't come down there, would they?"

"Uh-huh," he answered, with a gleeful look.

He also used to like to chase me up the stairs, his hands grabbing at my ankles, barking like a dog about to bite me. Today, he never teases or barks, and he's one of my closest friends.

When I was four we moved to a house near the very large Highland Park Zoo in the East Liberty section of Pittsburgh. Our block sat alone at the top of a hill and bordered the park. There were clusters of smallish connected houses in groups of three on our side of North St. Clair Street, and on the other side, single large homes with beautiful lawns. It was like having a richer neighborhood right across the street. The camaraderie between the kids on both sides eliminated any ritzy attitude from the richer side or any possible resentment from us.

My Chicago cousins, Fred and Elliot, would stay over in my room with me, unaware that we lived so close to a zoo. The roar of a lion in the middle of the night opened their eyes a lot wider than you would think eyes could open. I, myself, never really got used to the roar of a lion in Pittsburgh. Is he roaring from inside or outside his cage? Is he out? Is he coming to get me? You know he's not, but who needs any of it. And this was considered a nice place to live!

Some nights I would lie in bed, kept awake by what seemed like the almost constant laughing of the hyenas. I would try to entertain myself by thinking of jokes I could finish telling just before the next hyena laugh.

There was one lasting effect of living near the zoo. Until I was at least ten, when I heard on the news that guerrillas were massing in the mountains planning a violent overthrow of some government, I thought they meant zoo gorillas. I would hear the report, pause a moment to get a mental picture, consciously think it real odd, and decide I didn't think it would happen . . . but if it did, I'd deal with it then.

From the time I was about seven years old until I was thirteen, after grammar school I attended Hebrew school, preparing to be Bar Mitzvahed. The classes were held in the large Margaretta Street Synagogue. One day when I was about eight I explored the building. I was down on the bottom floor opening every closed door—a broom closet, an empty classroom. Suddenly I opened a door, and there was a room with a small stage. On the stage was a piano player and a short, stocky, pretty woman singing "The Man I Love." I had never seen a live performer before. I was awestruck. The whole idea that someone on a stage was singing a song somehow took my breath away. It was as though I had entered into a fairy tale. Opening that door, by chance, opened a door in my mind about performing. And then, because it was so out of my world—so exotic—I quickly closed the door and forgot about it . . . as far as I knew.

My brother remembers our mother asking me to sing for some neighbors. I remember asking my mother to ask me to sing for them. What we both remember is that by the time I got around to doing it, it was for a few people in our living room, and because of my nervousness, I was singing from the dining room—unseen. I sang "Don't Fence Me In." The neighbors were polite.

When I was twelve years old and in the seventh grade at Fulton Grammar School, a beautiful orange-brick building, the teacher told us that a man was going to speak in our classroom as part of the vocational-counseling program. He was going to talk to us about show business. It seemed a little odd since hardly anyone was thinking much about their vocation, and certainly (as far as I knew) none of us twelve-year-olds was thinking about show business. This guy showed up that afternoon. He was slim, had sandy hair, and looked like someone who was just routinely doing his job. After he told us his name, he jumped right in: "How many of you would like to be in show business?" Several kids raised their hands. "How many of you would like to go into the theater?" That got a few hands. "How about the movies?" Many more hands shot up. My hands stayed on my desk. I was just watching, startled that all my pals, out of the blue, suddenly seemed to want to go into show business. The vocational counselor casually counted hands as though it were some kind of scientific experiment. When he had completed all his counting, he looked up from his papers and peered at the class for a long moment. Then, in a voice suddenly filled with rage, he shouted at all of us twelve-year-olds: *"You don't know what you're talking about! Do you realize that nobody in show business makes a living?! Do you realize that there's no work for anyone?!"* He was furious at this class of children, just livid. This guy had obviously been an actor who had run into many, many brick walls, and his mission in life, it now seemed, was to warn everyone that there was only disaster out there. After he finished his outburst, he said good-bye politely and left. If anyone in that seventh-grade class was crazy enough to later go into show business, they couldn't say they weren't warned.

His visit had no effect on me, however, because, in spite of my jokes for hyenas, the idea of me going into show business was as likely as a man walking on the moon. Both impossible.

My only actual experience with acting came at Fulton School in the graduation play when I was thirteen. Our English teacher, Miss McCallum, a tall, slim, energetic woman with glasses, by accident assigned me the leading part of Don, the janitor boy, in *Getting Gracie Graduated*. She later admitted she hadn't realized that Don was the lead, but gave me the part because I always asked a lot of questions, and so did Don.

I learned all my lines and everyone else's, so if anyone faltered, I sidled over and whispered their lines to them. People commented that I was good (I was prepared, anyway). All the attention made me feel a lot better than I was used to feeling.

Aside from asking a lot of questions, I was an all-around talker—so much so that when I was ten years old I was impeached as president of the fifth-grade class for talking too much.

When not talking, I was given over to an unusual amount of daydreaming. Our eighth-grade teacher, Miss Purcell, an iron-maiden type standing about five feet tall, with steel-rimmed glasses that matched her personality, was regularly yelling at me: "Grodin, you're somewhere between oblivion and limbo. Come back to us, boy!"

I was usually daydreaming about my main interest in life—sports.

I tried out for a sandlot football team. Today I am six feet one and weigh about 180 pounds. At thirteen I was five feet one and weighed about 120 pounds. I had to stand at the foot of a hill in Highland Park wearing a T-shirt and blue jeans—no protective equipment. On top of the hill stood a much bigger fellow with full football equipment. He charged down the hill at me. If I could tackle him I could be on the team. He ran right up my body over my face, but I tackled him, and was told I'd made the team. I resented the unequal test. It's the first instance I can remember of a lifelong tendency to question rules. I decided not to sign up because of the unfairness (also possibly because of the cleat marks on my face).

I played for a basketball team at the Y. We called ourselves the Marauders and wore purple uniforms. I think we were in the wrong league because we would win games 51–4, or 49–2. Occasionally, there were closer games, but not too often. Our team was made up mostly of our Fulton School basketball team, led by the magical Jack Fagan, who used to dribble by me as though I were invisible. I wasn't on the starting team. In fact, I was mostly on the bench. I'm not sure why I hadn't developed as a player as well as my buddies, but it hurt.

One day, Bill Gorin, a friend of my family and the head of the athletic department at the Y, took me into his office and closed the door. Bill was among other things, a weight lifter. To paraphrase an old joke, he had muscles in places that other people don't even have places.

Bill paced around the office for a few moments. Finally, he said, "Chuck, you seem to do a lot better playing against the little kids. What do you think?"

I said, "I was hoping no one else noticed that."

"Why do you think that is?" Bill asked.

"I have no idea," I said.

Bill nodded sympathetically, and I nodded back. The conversation came to an end as we both sat there nodding.

The meeting only increased my desire to improve myself as a basketball player. I would measure myself with a yardstick against the door at home, stretching as much as I could in an effort to grow taller. I was beside myself with excitement whenever I thought I detected even one thirty-second of an inch of upward movement on my five-feet-one-inch frame. It was tough to detect too because I measured myself about six times a day. I also persuaded my mother to allow me to construct a basketball ring and net above the doorway between our dining room and kitchen. I would actually dribble through the dining room and shoot baskets. As I look back now, it seems remarkable that my mother, a most practical person, would have allowed this. Recently, in an effort to understand her thinking better when writing this, I called her.

I said, "Mother, do you remember letting me put up a basketball ring and net in our dining room?"

There was a long silence on the other end of the line as she searched her memory of almost forty years ago. Finally, she said, "Yes, I do." Then, as though the memory astounded her even more than me, she asked with vehemence: "Would you let *your* son put up a basketball ring in *your* dining room?"

"No," I said.

"Would you let *your* son shoot baskets in *your* house?" she asked, her indignation rising.

"Absolutely not!" I exclaimed, equally indignantly. "So why did you allow it, Mother?"

She quickly answered: "To get you off my back."

I said, "To get me off your back about what? What did I want?"

"You wanted to play *basketball*!" I laughed. Then so did she.

When I hung up I thought about it further. It suddenly struck me: Where was my father in all this? My father was a startlingly strong character in about every way, so why didn't I remember what he had to say about his dining room becoming a basketball court? I called my mother again.

This is how she responded to my question: "Your father never noticed anything in the house. He was always outside on the sidewalk with the neighbors, betting." My father liked to bet on sporting events—all sports, anywhere. ("Who do you like in the Iona-Hofstra game?" I can hear him ask.) My mother said, "He didn't care which side he bet on, as long as there was a bet. He would have said something about the basketball if you ever broke anything."

For my part, I doubt that I ever dribbled through the house when my father was home. I think he would have told me to dribble out the back door, keep on dribbling, and don't come back.

High school was one of the best times of my life. We had elections for class officers every six months. Each time I was elected president of my class, and eventually of the whole graduating class of Peabody High. I'm not really sure why that was, but I've always liked people, and I guess since we were all together for four years, my classmates could tell. Being elected president eight times by the kids I went to high school with remains to this day near the top of the list of the most exciting things that have ever happened to me.

Of course, I always acted pretty cool about it. In fact, I had dreams and nightmares about winning and losing, mostly losing. The first time I won, I wasn't even there. They just had home-room elections one day when I was home sick with a cold. A classmate, Lois Wesoky, called and said to my mother, "Tell Chuckie he was elected president of his home-room class." My mother called the news up the stairs to me, and I just lay there, staring at the ceiling, feeling a surge of warmth. And I wasn't even there, I thought. Around the sixth time I won, our home-room teacher, Miss Morrison, said casually, "Charles, I believe you've won every time." I just as casually responded, after a moment's pretended thought, "Hmmm, I think that's right." (I'm sure I had a nightmare about losing the night before.)

As class president, it was my job every morning to either read the Bible to the class or assign someone to read it. There was a problem with that. I was always a little on the slow side getting out of bed in the morning, and it wasn't that unusual for me to hear the nine o'clock school bell ring its terrifying alarm as I was racing into the building—not the classroom. The classroom I entered around 9:02. The students would all be seated, and Miss Morrison would be looking toward the door. As I burst through, she never said, "You're late," but only, "Charles, have you assigned anyone to read the Bible this morning?"

"No," I'd gasp. She would then hand it to me, and I would try to get my breath back throughout "The Lord is my shepherd, I shall not want."

As class president, I would regularly go to Mr. Bower's (the principal's) office. Unfortunately, about 50 percent of the time I wouldn't be there to discuss school issues but, rather, the fact that I had been kicked out of class. Mr. Kennedy, a genial, bushy-haired man with a surprising trigger temper, was the activities director and teacher of economics. He was constantly throwing me out of class for asking too many questions. I don't mean I asked this endless stream of questions. I mean if I would ask *one* question after Mr. Kennedy felt the issue had been covered, he was irritated. I would ignore that and ask again. When Mr. Kennedy was once more dismissive, it would then go something like this:

ME
Mr. Kennedy, I don't understand why [such and such].

MR. KENNEDY
I've covered that.

ME
Well . . . why did [such and such]?

MR. KENNEDY
I'm not discussing that further.

ME
Well . . . how can you not discuss it further? I don't get it, and I don't think the rest of the class does either.

Then I'd look around and ask the class: "Right?"

THE CLASS
(*Yelling out*)
Right!

MR. KENNEDY
Grodin, why don't you take it up with the principal!

Then I'd go to the office of Mr. Bower, who would always look at me quizzically as I entered, wondering if I'd gotten kicked out or if I was there to make my case once again for my major presidential policy: *more school dances!*

I not only wanted more school dances, I wanted dancing during the lunch hour. After lengthy conferences, Mr. Bower let us do it. He came to see that all this dancing led to more romance, and nice Mr. Bower just wasn't against that. Mr. Kennedy, on the other hand, instructed me that the proceeds from the dances would be given as a gift to the school when we graduated. I felt that was up to the class to decide, which was another reason Mr.

Kennedy was constantly kicking me out, as we debated that issue right there in economics class. So I didn't learn all that much about economics, but I did get to know the principal better. I'm sure we were the dancingest high school of the fifties. We danced to the dreamy music of the Four Aces and the Four Freshmen mostly, and by the time we graduated we were in such a good mood, we *did* give all the dance proceeds to the school.

My run-ins with Mr. Kennedy were far from my roughest in high school. One semester, when I was fifteen, a big, strapping fellow suddenly appeared. He was a student teacher from the University of Pittsburgh who'd come to take over parts of our gym program for a while. He was around twenty, but he seemed like a full-grown man. One day when I was playing on one side in a softball game, he was on the other. But he was also the umpire. When he called one of our guys out on a close play, I questioned whether he should play and be an umpire at the same time. After the game, in the locker room, he came over to me, lifted me off my feet (I was still very small), and held me against a locker. Looking like he wanted to kill, he said, "If you give me any more trouble, I'll punch your face in." I told him again that I didn't think he should play and umpire, and suggested that he do whatever he wanted to about my face. As he glared at me, other fellows started to come over. He slowly lowered my feet to the ground. Shooting me a terrible look as he walked away, he obviously realized his punch would do him more harm than it would do me, at least in the long run.

I believe I antagonized certain people then and occasionally over the years because of my refusal to subjugate myself. I might be inadequate, I might be wrong in my opinion, but I never thought I did anything that should cause me to be treated as less than an equal. I wasn't accepting condescension, patronization, or autocratic behavior of any kind. Of course, an autocratic person seems to view someone who presents himself or herself as an equal as a challenge to his autocracy. I always felt that the president of the United States should get no more or less respect than a doorman, and both should get a good amount, as we all should. This attitude has made me popular with doormen but sometimes less so with "important people."

Once, years later, at a gathering at Gracie Mansion, the

home of New York's mayor, Mayor Koch said to me: "Call me Ed."

I responded, in his same friendly spirit: "Call me Chuck."

Some people in my group thought I was rude. I didn't.

Also years later, at another gathering, never having met any royalty before I asked the Duchess of Gloucester (a cousin of the Queen of England) what the main focus of her life was.

She looked at me as if I had just asked her to go skinny-dipping. After recovering herself, she said, "My family." Then she said, "I shouldn't ask you such a question, but since you asked me, what is the main focus of your life?"

I said, "Talking to friends."

That was the whole exchange. Amazingly, the world didn't come to an end.

I was a member of a lot of organizations in high school, one of which was the Mask and Wig Club—even though I could never be in a play because I wasn't free to rehearse, since I sometimes had to work in my father's store after school. When the time came for the high school graduation play, a strange thing happened: The teacher, Miss Owen, a short, bulldog-looking, pugnacious woman, wanted me to be in it. I told her I couldn't because of my after-school work obligations. Miss Owen got angry, as though she didn't believe me. Finally, I said to her, "Why do you care so much about me being in the play? You've never seen me act. What makes you think I'd be any good?"

She looked at me oddly for a moment, and said: "I know you'd be good, and so do you." It was particularly strange since I had done no acting in high school, and I seriously doubted she'd ever heard of *Getting Gracie Graduated*. I was so startled by the angry way Miss Owen spoke that I had no room in my mind for what I thought.

My only participation with the Mask and Wig Club came when we were being taught makeup. Miss Owen had me apply makeup to a girl who was half a year ahead of me in school. No big deal, except that this girl was the major crush of my young life. Her name was Judy Gotterer, and the sight of her reduced me to speechlessness. Earlier, I had asked her for a date, after almost having a nervous breakdown trying to figure out exactly what to say. I ended up tapping her on the shoulder as she stood facing her locker in the crowded hallway after school. When she turned around, I said: "You wouldn't be free on Saturday night, would you?" She said, "No." That was her whole answer: "No." I nodded and walked away—crushed, but deeper in love than ever. In those days, if a girl was six months older than a guy, it just wasn't happening. So I had to confine my relationship with Judy to hoping I'd catch a glimpse of her in the hall from time to time. Since there were sixteen hundred kids in the school, the glimpses were few and far between.

I never saw Judy at a dance, which made her even more elusive and remarkable and unattainable and . . . oh, well. I even knew she liked me, because I had heard that she thought I'd be good for her fourteen-year-old sister, Susie. There seemed to be enough encouragement in the air that, in desperation, I actually dug out my birth certificate at home, got an ink eradicator, and, by changing a five to a four, made myself a year older. I found Judy the next day and produced my certificate casually, as though this type of presentation was an everyday occurrence. She just as casually glanced at it and said easily: "The date's been changed."

I looked at it as though I had no idea what she was referring to, said only, "What? No, it's . . . I . . ." and slunk away in abject defeat.

Now, in this newly formed makeup class, here was Judy, and Miss Owen was asking me to put makeup on her face. My hands on Judy's face! I touched her as delicately as a brain surgeon for about fifteen seconds, while her eyes gazed up at me and my heart beat wildly. Then Miss Owen suddenly shoved me aside and applied the makeup like someone giving artificial respiration to a face. That was my entire involvement with the theater in high school . . . and also with Judy Gotterer, for that matter.

My father called his store The Grodin Company. One of my friends used to tease me, saying that since the store was basically run by just my father, how could he call it The Grodin Company? But my dad, who had had to quit school when he was nine years old to help support his family, worked so hard he was like a whole company.

We had a tug of war throughout my high school years—me wanting to go out and play ball, and he wanting me to work in the store. I felt that if he needed help he could easily pay someone fifty cents an hour to come in, which he often did. I had started kindergarten when I was four, grammar school at six, had of course been in school from then on, and from seven to thirteen went to Hebrew School three times a week for two hours. All that school of different sorts left precious little sports time, so at fourteen, Bar Mitzvahed and free after school for the first time, I was reluctant to dive full force into The Grodin Company. I wanted to help sometimes, but too often when I went it would only be to count up grosses of buttons for later sale. I was very edgy working in the dry-goods field. Our relationship reached such a level of frustration for my dad that he eventually suggested that on any major issues we should communicate through letters, even though we lived in a small six-room house. It was at least as tough a standoff as the Russians and Americans had, maybe a little tougher because the countries occasionally discussed their differences.

I Saw a Movie

I had no idea what I wanted to do after high school. I had some vague half-interest in majoring in journalism at the University of Pittsburgh, but I wasn't even really sure what journalism was.

As graduation from Peabody was nearing, I decided it would be a good idea to take an aptitude test the school offered to students who were confused about what to do with their lives. The test results indicated that I should pursue a career as an accountant. The fact that I had no interest whatsoever in being an accountant seemed irrelevant to them. I'm still puzzled at the results since my memories of algebra class are mostly of me with my head down on the desk in complete despair. I also spent a semester in geometry baffled as to what the hell everyone was talking about, and why. When it was suggested I take a course in trigonometry, I felt like running, screaming into the night. I instantly disregarded the test's advice and headed toward graduation, still with no real plan for the future.

Graduation day came, and to my father's absolute shock, there was his wayward son (whom he had always seen as trying to avoid work—he wasn't much impressed with the sports desire) up there onstage as the valedictorian. I was making a speech about our past, our present, our future. Like most speechmakers, it was easier to talk about ideas than to actually know what to *do* after graduation.

At one point there were five of us on the stage in front of about a thousand people, when the four students sitting to my right suddenly stood up. We had rehearsed these proceedings earlier, but I had absolutely no idea why my classmates were suddenly standing. I stood too. They all turned to their right. So did I. They then started to walk off the stage. I took about half a step to follow, when I heard Miss Morrison, who had the look of a practical saint, whisper loudly from the third row of the audience, "No, Charles, not you!" I quickly sat down, my heart pounding. I watched my four classmates leave the stage and join the choir for a number. I hadn't remembered that from our earlier run-through. I hoped the audience just thought I had been incredibly polite when I stood with them. No one mentioned it later, but it was my first experience of being up on a stage feeling frightened.

After graduation, which was in February, I decided to go to the University of Pittsburgh for journalism in the fall. I was more frequently helping my dad out in the store now, and also had a job in a local Buick dealership called Kenn Buick. I was what they called a car jockey. We had to move the new Buicks from one end of the warehouse to the other. The problem was that these cars started to move as soon as the motor was turned on and the car was in "drive" or any gear. Until that point, I'd never seen a car move on its own without giving it some gas, so I dented quite a few fenders and was soon called over by my boss on a Thursday and told I wouldn't be needed on Friday.

"Should I come in on the weekend?" I innocently asked.

"No, not then, either," he said.

"Well," I said, "I guess I'll see you next week."

"Look," he finally said, "we're going to try to get along here at Kenn Buick without you."

I wasn't very upset because I didn't see my future in the automotive industry. It was the first time I was ever fired. It wouldn't be the last.

I was now biding my time waiting for September. And then one day I saw the movie *A Place in the Sun*. In it, Montgomery Clift was hitchhiking on a highway, and a beautiful young Elizabeth Taylor came by in a white Cadillac convertible. She gave some exotic foreign honk and disappeared off into the distance. Later in the movie Elizabeth Taylor fell in love with Montgomery Clift. Never mind that also later in the movie Montgomery Clift murdered Shelley Winters and got the electric chair. A poor boy is on a highway, and Elizabeth Taylor comes driving by and ends up falling in love with him. Montgomery Clift made it all look pretty easy—the acting, getting Liz to fall in love, the whole deal. I wanted to be in the movies.

Aside from sports, it was the first time I ever really wanted to do anything. It was a strong, romantic feeling. There I was, seventeen years old, about to study journalism at the University of Pittsburgh, and I saw this movie and figured, Well, I don't know . . . go into the movies? How do you go into the movies?

I went to my father and said, "Dad, I want to be an actor."

He looked at me as though I'd said, "I want to be a zebra," and I'm sure he was stifling an urge to ask me to write him a letter, but he said only: "What?"

My father was just getting over an incident that had happened about a year earlier. In the family business we had a 1949 green Kaiser Traveler; the backseat folded into the floor and was used for deliveries. It was very important to the business, so my father protected it.

One of his ways of protecting the car was not to lend it to me, except on rare occasions, such as to take my driver's test, which I failed the first couple of times. On my third try, I passed the test. That day my father was standing in front of his store anxiously looking up the street, waiting for me to come back. As I drove up, I yelled out the window: "Dad! Dad! I passed! I passed!" and crashed right into a parked car.

He had just gotten over that when I hit him with: "I want to be an actor." I hadn't been in a play since *Getting Gracie Graduated* at thirteen, and I never talked about being an actor, so he really didn't know where I got the idea. I didn't think it was the right time to mention Elizabeth Taylor.

He was stunned. He had wanted my brother to go into the business, and my brother had gone on to law school. In spite of all the chaos and tension between us, my dad still hoped I would go into his business, and here I was saying, "I want to be an actor." After he caught his breath, he suggested I get involved with theater activities at the Y. "It could be a nice hobby, an avocation. Get it out of your system." But no, I wanted to do this as my life's work. Not only did I want to be an actor, but worse, I wanted to be a drama major at the University of Miami in Florida.

In the fifties, the University of Miami was considered a playboy school. I wanted to go there because my best friend, Jack Krongold, had gone there half a year ahead and said there was a good drama department, and there was a dean down there from Pittsburgh, Dean Alter. Jack said that if I came down, maybe after a semester I could get a scholarship.

My father felt it was a disastrous choice. He knew that just about no one going into acting made a living. But because of my passion in wanting to do this, he decided to stand behind me . . . which meant he would pay for me to go. It has always touched me that he did that, knowing how against it he was.

My father had rheumatic fever as a boy and never really recovered. He was sick all his life, in and out of hospitals, even regularly in oxygen tents. But when he was out of the hospital he worked very hard seven days a week. He would walk across a bridge in the wintertime to where his store was in downtown Pittsburgh so that he could get a less-expensive parking deal. He always wore a fedora indoors, even at the dinner table. My mother would tell him to take it off, and he'd always just grumble something like, "All right, what ya want, my hat!" and leave it on. He insisted on sitting at what he considered the head of the kitchen table, even though he always had to shove his chair in real tight against the table if anyone had to open the refrigerator during dinner—which everyone did. Then, as he shoved his chair in, he'd mumble something like, "Awright, the refrigerator, waddaya need, what?" As time went by and he grew more exhausted, he would hold his head up with his left hand as he ate. Even though it made things heavier, he still kept that hat on. He used to laugh uncontrollably at *Amos 'n' Andy* on TV as they mispronounced words, which he did too on occasion. One time he played in a softball game between the grown-ups and the kids. He batted once, wearing his suit, vest, tie, and, of course, his hat. He popped out to short.

To me, he mostly snarled his observations. There were a number of reasons, I guess, not to like him, but I was crazy about him. I never saw anyone so sick work so hard, and to me that overwhelmed every other single fact about him. I got as used to seeing my father sick as I did to seeing my mother healthy. Neither made an impact on my young mind: They just were. In spite of his regular trips to hospitals and oxygen tents, and holding his head up with his hand while he ate, I was in a state of complete and utter shock when he suddenly died. I was told it was going to happen seven hours before it did, and it had never entered my mind until that moment. He was fifty-two. Even as I write this now, thirty-five years later, I find that I would quickly like to change the subject.

Friends, Romans, Countrymen

In September, two and a half months later, I prepared to leave for the University of Miami to study acting. I had gone from being a fun-loving, easygoing, congenial young fellow to being a withdrawn, removed, silent character. I was in a deep depression, and should have been in therapy, but at that time it was widely thought to be something reserved for people in mental institutions. I felt so bad about what had happened to my father that I wouldn't allow myself any pleasure. Once someone pointed out a beautiful view, and I was unwilling to turn my head to look.

I drove down to Miami with my friend Jack and a third fellow I'd never met before from nearby Mount Lebanon named Joe Grosso, an extremely likable but jumpy guy whose family was regularly pursued by the police for the type of activities that are even now only legal in Las Vegas and Atlantic City. Jack was a considerably more sophisticated teenager than I. In fact, Jack may have been the most sophisticated teenager anywhere. He had a car and girls and was always a couple of years ahead of the rest of us in the social department. He was really more like an older brother to me, whom I looked to for guidance. But our relationship had been subtly changing in the last year. I think the combination of being class president (Jack's comment had been: "I identify with you so much I feel like they're electing me") and losing my dad had made me more and more uncomfortable in a backseat role to anyone. I felt I had to grow up in a hurry. About a hundred miles into our fifteen-hundred-mile trip to Miami from Pittsburgh, we got into a seemingly meaningless dispute over the color of the car in front of us. I said it was dark green, Jack said black; or maybe it was the other way around. Amazingly, our intense relationship came to an abrupt end right there. We drove on in silence as Joe Grosso kept looking back and forth between us wondering what the hell was going on.

The three of us roomed together, as planned, in an apartment off campus in Coral Gables. Jack and I were polite to each other when we spoke, which was hardly ever. The break in our friendship sure didn't help the overall environment for me at Miami. (About twenty years later, Jack and I had a reunion and a good time. We avoided any mention of cars.)

The University of Miami had a sprawling campus filled with palm trees and artificial lakes with little bridges over them. Having only seen Pittsburgh, it struck me as close to Wizard-of-Oz land. Shortly after arriving at the university, all two thousand incoming freshmen were told to go to a large auditorium for an orientation session—to find out how the university worked, what the curriculum offered, and a lot of general information such as how Guild Hall got its name. Pamphlets were distributed. We were told we would be tested on this information the next day. It was all done fairly casually, it wasn't a course, and it wouldn't go on any grade transcript.

The following day we were given written tests, and a few days later we assembled once more. Out of the two thousand of us, six had done outstandingly. The university official then went on to say that out of a potentially perfect score of 40, so-and-so had gotten a 26, and how about a nice round of applause. The students applauded indifferently. He then announced the names of two people who had gotten 28; perfunctory applause followed again. Another had gotten a 30, and another a 36. In spite of themselves, the students were getting caught up in it all now, and the applause was building. He then said that one person out of all the incoming two thousand freshmen had gotten a perfect score of 40, and asked that when he called out that person's name, "Let's have a rousing round of applause." He then called out: "Will Charles Grodin please stand up!"

I was astonished. I stood and sat quickly, and received an ovation and more than a few curious looks that seemed to say, "Some people will study anything!" I had no idea I had studied hard enough to get every question right. I had gone to Miami against my father's and everyone else's advice, and I knew I had something to prove, mostly to myself. On leaving Pittsburgh, I vowed to my mother that if hard work had anything to do with doing well in a profession where almost no one succeeded, then I wouldn't fail on that score. Without my even realizing it, the penchant to work hard began with that relatively meaningless orientation test—and really hasn't stopped to this day.

In spite of mastering the orientation test, I was startled to discover a piece of information I had missed: New freshmen weren't permitted to study acting. I explained that this was really the only reason I was there, and, probably because of the desperate look on my face, got myself assigned to a basic acting class among all the other courses I was required to take.

One course I particularly remember was semantics. I was sitting in the classroom, with my left leg jumping up and down uncontrollably in a spasm. I had written a paper about what I felt was the barbaric nature of funerals, at least the kind I had just seen, beginning with the viewing and ending with watching my father being lowered into the ground and dirt being thrown over him. The teacher gave me a high grade and said it was a heartfelt paper. Unfortunately, it was heartfelt and legfelt.

Our semantics class was told that at some point later in the semester we would each be required to give a five-minute speech without notes—a terrifying prospect. The next day the instructor, a bouncy Italian fellow, walked in with an official from the university and announced that today was the day some of us would be required to get up and speak. All the students were truly frightened by the idea. The teacher said that if no one volunteered, he would select someone. Since we had earlier been told we would be given notice, I felt we had been tricked. Suddenly, as the teacher was going to pick some poor soul, my hand went up, I think involuntarily. We were in a large hall. I went up to the podium, angry at the teacher for torturing the class this way, and proceeded to tell a story about being on a hunting trip in northeastern Pennsylvania with my girlfriend. I had never been in northeastern Pennsylvania, I had never been hunting, and I didn't have a girlfriend. (No one said it had to be a true story.) I told of how we were attacked by a bear who dragged my girlfriend away. I went to get help, but neither the bear nor my girlfriend was ever found. The teacher, the school official, and the class all stared at me up there, mouths open, eyes aghast. I finished my speech, took my seat, and the class kind of dribbled away after that. No one asked me if it was true. No one approached me at all. Why I did that, I have no idea. Retaliation at being unfairly treated? A story about a sudden, heartbreaking loss? I don't know. After that, I was always pointed out on campus as "the guy who had the bear thing happen."

After a couple of months in the acting class, we all had to get up and do something. I picked the monologue from *Julius Caesar* that begins, "Friends, Romans, countrymen . . ."—Marc Anthony's speech. In other words, I went from Don, the janitor boy, in *Getting Gracie Graduated* to Marc Anthony in *Julius Caesar*.

Walking to class the day I knew I had to perform, I was oblivious to everything around me. It was as though I were moving in a cocoon. I was so nervous I just wished the ground would open up and swallow me. It was a kind of tension I had never experienced before; it was so disorienting I had trouble even feeling my feet beneath me. This was performing to be judged! And Shakespeare yet! By someone who not only wasn't a performer but who knew absolutely nothing about Shakespeare. I felt like I had really taken a wrong turn in the road to end up in this mysterious, horrifying situation.

When the teacher called my name, my heart began to pound. I got up from my seat shaking and walked slowly to the stage, all the while looking at the floor. Once on the stage, I looked at the teacher and the class, who looked back at me expectantly. It was a moment I was to experience many times over the years. The feeling was: Oh, my God, how did I get into this?! I took a deep breath and shouted out: "Friends, Romans, countrymen, lend me your ears!" The actual shouting out of the words amazingly seemed to send a signal to my body to stop shaking. I later learned that the body doesn't know you're acting. So I figure that when my body heard the words "Friends, Romans, countrymen" yelled out with such authority, it decided to relax a little to hear what I had to say.

When I finished, the class and the teacher, Professor

Fred Koch, who was the head of the University Drama Department, were all smiling at me. Everyone seemed impressed. I think it helped that the speech was about injustice. It seems that just about anybody can get their teeth into matters of right and wrong—and it clearly seemed very wrong that Caesar was stabbed by all his buddies, which is what the speech is about.

Professor Koch was enthusiastic. He said that if I worked hard, there was no telling where I might go. I nodded and quietly thanked him. Inside, I was ecstatic. In my wildest imaginings I could not know that those would be the last real words of support I would hear for years.

Living the Part

I never performed anything else in the remaining months of the semester. I didn't have a lot to feel good about, and I was afraid that if I got up again to perform I might fall on my face. The fear that the words of support would be withdrawn kept me sitting and watching for the rest of the semester.

I was lonely, and my depression continued. Miami was stunningly hot . . . and this was the wintertime. I remember sitting on the edge of my bed staring into space, numbed by the heat.

I was always very interested in girls, and here I was in the playboy school of the world, but I was so withdrawn and depressed that I couldn't even begin to think of having a date. I was very young, heartsick, and homesick.

So I came back up to Pittsburgh during the Christmas vacation and got an appointment to audition for a scholarship at the Pittsburgh Playhouse School of the Theater. I figured I'd do my "Friends, Romans, countrymen," and maybe it would work again. The Pittsburgh Playhouse was located in the cultural center of Pittsburgh, an area called Oakland. It was only a few minutes from the University of Pittsburgh, where everyone in my family still felt I should be studying journalism or anything other than what I was doing. I walked toward the Playhouse, looking at the building. It was so forbidding to me; it looked like a cathedral of some kind. It was a *play*house, and in it were all these actors. And actors to me meant people who could do dialects, maybe wore beards, and did Chekhov and Ibsen and Shakespeare. Maybe even T. S. Eliot and Christopher Fry—writers that I'd never even read and couldn't possibly understand. I was basically just a depressed kid waiting for Elizabeth Taylor to drive by and carry me away.

Sitting alone in the back of the theater, waiting for me to begin, was the head of the school, a heavyset man with thinning hair and piercing eyes named Bill Putch. (Bill Putch, years later, would marry the actress Jean Stapleton—Edith from *All in the Family*. Also about thirty years later, I would co-star with Jean Stapleton in a very successful cable production of Jules Feiffer's play *Grown-ups*.) I shakily walked out on the stage. This was a regular-sized stage in a regular-sized theater, far bigger than the one I had been on in *Getting Gracie Graduated* or in drama class at the university. This time, in order to be heard, I really cut loose into "Friends, Romans, countrymen," and again my body stopped shaking and started listening. And once more this injustice thing seemed to work, because when it was over Bill Putch seemed to be saying I'd won a scholarship. I was in a daze. I felt like such an impostor. I thought, This is all I can do, this "Friends, Romans, countrymen." Wait till they find out that's it.

Bill Putch and I went back to his office, where he took out a piece of paper, drew three objects, and asked me to tell him what they resembled. He was giving me some kind of a Rorschach test. Of course, he was an acting teacher, not a psychiatrist. Evidently I had done something that had caused him to want to check my mental condition. I know I must have appeared nervous, but other than that I thought I was coming off as fairly normal. Apparently not.

I felt that the main thing I had to do to fit in and not lose the scholarship was to appear to be a complete theater guy, a guy whose every thought was about theater, and he would think I was one of *them*.

So when he showed me a circle he had drawn, I said, "Well, that circle, what's that remind me of? That's very much like the Arena Theater, a theater in the round they have down at the University of Miami."

"Uh-huh," Bill said. "What about this?" He pointed to something that looked like one of a thousand things or nothing.

"Well," I said, "that's very much like the proscenium arch of the theater downstairs where I did the 'Friends, Romans, Countrymen' thing."

"Uh-huh," he said.

And then the third object, which again could have been absolutely anything. "Well, that reminds me of a curtain—you know, a curtain in a theater."

Bill looked at me skeptically for a moment. "That reminds you of a curtain?" I nodded tentatively.

There was one of those uneasy silences you hope you never run into. Finally, he said, "Well . . . you come back in February, you can start school here."

I walked out on a cloud: I had been given a scholarship to study acting. That had to be a good sign. Thank God for "Friends, Romans, Countrymen."

I came home a couple of months later and started to study at the Pittsburgh Playhouse School. There were only about twenty students in the whole place, so it was hard to hide. About three weeks into the term it became clear to me, and unfortunately to everybody else, that I wasn't very good at anything. I just wasn't. They used to bring over teachers from Carnegie Tech (now called Carnegie Mellon). It's a local university with a nationally acclaimed Drama Department. I didn't go there after leaving Miami because I was so singleminded in the pursuit of the study of acting that I had no patience with all the other courses a university required.

Edith Skinner, a tall, thin, austere woman with glasses, who was one of the foremost teachers and authorities on "good American speech," came over from Carnegie Tech. Her dedication to having everyone master "good American speech" was as intense as that of a scientist trying to rid the world of a dread disease, which was how she saw "bad American speech"—something from which I evidently suffered in abundance. "Good American speech" to me, on the other hand, sounded like an English accent. Many of Carnegie Tech's drama majors graduated sounding like Englishmen, which didn't lead to a heck of a lot of work in America. I would say a few sentences for Miss Skinner, and she would write furiously, page after page of notes of criticism for just my few sentences of "bad American speech." Finally, she said, "How can you ever expect people to pay money to see you as an actor, given how you speak? Nobody should speak like that; it's just not good American speech, it's terrible."

In spite of Miss Skinner's passion for her cause, I couldn't put my heart in working toward "good American speech." I thought that Montgomery Clift and Spencer Tracy didn't sound anything like what she wanted; they didn't have English accents or anything close—they just sounded like regular people, like themselves, which was what I had in mind. But I kept quiet, because I thought that if I caused any trouble, they might take away my scholarship, which was feeling shakier as each week went by, anyway.

My other problem was that our acting teachers were telling us basically to learn our lines, get out there, and do it . . . which is a good idea if you're a great actor. I, of course, didn't know anything, but their approach struck me as superficial, more like pretending.

Right around this time the Actors Studio was in full prominence in New York: "the Method," living the part. Marlon Brando was considered the genius actor of America, and he was a method actor. Lee Strasberg, the head of the Actors Studio, had gone to Moscow and come back with his own version of the work of the famed acting teacher and director Konstantin Stanislavski. That was what I wanted to do, what Konstantin Stanislavski, Lee Strasberg, and Marlon Brando were saying: Live the part. That seemed to be something of which professions were made. Besides, it seemed to me even then that if you weren't deeply involved with the character and the situation, you would always suffer from the nervousness of being in an unnatural circumstance—standing on a stage in front of a large group of people. So when we would do scenes in class, instead of learning the lines, getting out there, and doing it, I would try to live the part. Of course, I had no *idea* how to live the part. I would walk around thinking and, unfortunately, sometimes softly saying: "I've got to live the part." Some of the faculty and a few of the older students would stare at me for a while and then say, "Look at that fool, look at him! What's he doing there? What are you doing, trying to live the part? Ha, ha, ha." The ridicule was all good-natured—at least I tried to take it that way—but it made me withdraw even more into my shell.

There was a tiny theater connected to the school, and downstairs there were two large theaters to which the people in Pittsburgh would come and pay to see the productions. The plays on the main stages were cast with professional actors or experienced actors who lived in the area. Sometimes some of the smaller parts were given to students from the school. Eventually, I got a part in a main-stage production of a play. I guess they thought it was okay to give to me because it was a very, very small part. The play was *My Three Angels*. I had to enter and stand in the doorway for the last two minutes of this play. I had a dark tan and wore an all-white navy lieutenant's uniform. I came in, and the audience went, "Ooooooh!" every night, "Ooooooh!" I thought, I'm certainly not living any part, but this is great. This is really something! When the play ended, one of my teachers said to me: "No, no, you were terrible!"

"Really? Why?"

"You turned your head too much."

If someone were talking to my left, I'd look left; if someone were talking to my right, I'd look right; if someone talked behind me, I would turn around; if someone dropped something, I would look down. I guess there was a little too much acting in those head turns, but I didn't know it, and no one bothered to explain it. I was quickly learning that there wasn't anything I couldn't do badly. "You turn your head too much, your speech isn't good, you're just a bad actor." Again, this was all done in a kind of good-natured ridicule, if there is such a thing. And again I didn't respond, because I thought they were probably right. But I figured that while it was all fairly nerve-racking, it wasn't that surprising since I was so raw. It never even occurred to me to leave and go someplace else since I had a scholarship, and since I'd already quit college to go there. It seemed like it would be kind of nice to graduate from something, especially since I was this valedictorian in high school. Besides, I was getting to perform, even if just in front of a class, and I figured this was the time to be bad. At least I wasn't asking anyone to hire me.

There was a wonderful actor at the school named Doug Robinson, who, incidentally, was not part of the group that enjoyed making fun of me. Doug was a couple of years older and obviously more experienced, and would almost always play the lead in the student productions. I was so far down the ladder of who was considered good that if they had done *The Charles Grodin Story*, Doug would have played Charles Grodin. We were now going to do a student production of the comedy classic *Charley's Aunt*. Doug would of course play the part that Jack Benny played in the movie and Jose Ferrer played on Broadway: the man who dresses up as a woman. I never saw Jack Benny or Jose Ferrer in the role, but years later I did a production of *Charley's Aunt* for cable playing Doug's part. I patterned a lot of what I did after his beautiful performance, and had a very successful experience.

In our student production after all the young parts were given out, there were a couple of pretty good-sized older parts to fill, and suddenly I was fifty-year-old Sir Francis Chesney, the father of Jack, one of the boys. I was nineteen years old and I was to wear a top hat, tails, and spats. I thought, All right, it's too old for me, and all of that, but here's a pretty good-sized part and here's a chance to try to live it. If I could just live the part of Sir Francis, I could really answer these people who were making fun of me. This is not just standing in a doorway and turning my head too much: I can step out there and really do something. So I began to concentrate like crazy on living the part of Sir Francis Chesney. I got hold of the script and said to myself, Okay, the first thing Sir Francis says when he enters is: "Jack, my dear boy." So my plan was that I was going to say this line, "Jack, my dear boy": "*Jack*, my dear boy. Jack, *my dear* boy." I was going to say it so often that maybe I'd start to become a little *like* Sir Francis. "Jack, my dear boy. Jack, my dear boy." Day after day, I'd say it. I'd lie in bed at night: "Jack, my dear boy. Jack, my dear boy." I was hoping that maybe one morning I'd wake up and I would miraculously *be* Sir Francis Chesney.

But nothing happened. I was just this young kid walking around saying, "Jack, my dear boy."

Then I got an idea while watching Jackie Gleason on television. He did this character called Reginald van Gleason who wore a top hat, tails, and spats. With my hope gone of living the part of Sir Francis Chesney, I was starting to get very nervous. So, I figured I would do an imitation of Jackie Gleason. I had to do something. It was a big part, and the potential for my failing out there was also big. The Gleason imitation might be something; I figured maybe no one would notice that's what I was doing, and maybe somebody would even like me, and that would sure help, as the abuse was getting through my protective armor. I could always tell, because my posture would suffer.

Opening night of *Charley's Aunt* arrived. It was performed in the student theater of the Playhouse, which had a tiny stage. There was the set, and behind that a painted piece of scenery with trees and sky on it, but no crossover. (A crossover is the space behind a set where the actors, out of the audience's sight, get in position for their entrances and where they go when they exit.) Without a crossover, when someone had to enter from the right, the only way to get there was to crawl on your hands and knees below the window to the door, where you would stay and wait for your cue. I had to do this, so I crawled on all fours, with my high hat and tails and spats, keeping very low so the audience wouldn't see my hat sticking up at the window as I crawled by. Also below the window were the props they were going to put onstage in the later scenes.

I crawled over and I waited for my cue to enter. To calm my nerves and in a desperate last-minute effort to become Sir Francis and not me—anyone but me—standing there, I started muttering softly to myself: "Jack, my dear boy. Jack, *my* dear boy. Jack, my *dear* boy. Jack, my dear *boy.*" I heard my cue, burst onto the stage, and cried out: "*Jack, my dear boy!*" The audience laughed. I stood there and thought, Hey, they liked that! (This was at a time when I would review myself after every line.) I strode into the room and said a couple more lines, and I got another laugh—even bigger. Then they were laughing and laughing and laughing so hard at each line I said that I started to think to myself: I'm going to be a star! I shook hands with a couple of the other characters, sat down in a chair, and said a couple more lines, and—BOOM!—they were absolutely screaming with laughter! They were going crazy! The other actors didn't know what to do; they were just staring at me. I was sitting in a chair thinking to myself, I'm going to be a living legend!

When it was time, I stood up. "Good to see you. Take care. Keep in touch. Nice to see you." Over and out. By the time I left the stage, the place was going berserk. It was bedlam out there! As I crawled on all fours under the window to get back to my dressing room, I was thinking, They're going to name a theater after me! I came off the stage, and I was totally flush with the triumph. I couldn't believe it! I looked at all the people standing there offstage, and they were pointing at me. I had whipped cream all over my clothes. It was one of the props that had been lying backstage, and I had gotten it on me as I crawled past. When I went onstage I got it all over everything—on the chair, on the other actors, on the gowns . . . everywhere.

My moment of triumph was shattered. The actors backstage were laughing hysterically, with their hands over their mouths so the audience couldn't hear. I was turning more and more into a figure of ridicule. That moment was the culmination of all the good- and bad-natured teasing and abuse I had been receiving at the Pittsburgh Playhouse, and I think at that moment it also became clear that I was going to have to develop a conscious system of survival in the profession I was, of course, not even in yet. I decided that since no one else seemed inclined to, *I* was going to really try to give myself a break.

So I thought, Well, that whipped cream was probably responsible for most of the laughter I got out there, but maybe not *all* of it. Maybe a tiny little bit of it came from practicing "Jack, my dear boy" in my never-ending effort to live the part. Maybe. Just maybe. I had to hold on to that possibility to be able to go forward in the face of all the wrong kind of laughter.

You Work Sixteen Hours a Day, You Pay Us Fifteen Dollars a Week

One day, as we neared the end of the term at the Playhouse before summer break, a man appeared who was to play a big part in my life. Richard Scanga, a hefty fellow with a sunny disposition, was the head of the Duquesne University Drama Department (a university in Pittsburgh known mostly for its outstanding basketball teams). He came to our school to audition us to be apprentices at the Rabbit Run Theater in Madison, Ohio, a summer theater where he was going to direct. He handed me a scene that called for a lot of emotion. It must have sounded pretty real, as Bill Putch came running in to see what was going on. Dick Scanga asked me to be an apprentice, because he had stumbled onto something I could act—frustration.

The deal was you'd pay them fifteen dollars a week, and they'd let you work sixteen hours a day. Fifteen dollars was for room and board. The room was six bunks in an old, deserted garage. My mattress smelled so bad, I said, "I think there's something like a dead rat in the mattress." As usual, by speaking at all, I was instantly looked at as difficult. I mentioned it often enough so that after about ten days they took the mattress apart . . . and found a dead rat.

Most of the time my job was to clean out the theater and help build scenery, paint sets, find props—anything they asked me to do. I drew the line only once. One of the producers of the theater, a skittish character named John Hruby, asked me to dress up in a rabbit suit and mingle with the audience prior to the show. A little local color. I said I couldn't. I tried to explain that the suit was okay, but it was that big rabbit head that went over my regular head. "I'm claustrophobic," I said.

"Well, you just put it on," Mr. Hruby said. "You'll be fine."
I put it on. I wasn't fine. "No," I said.
"You'll be fine."
"I can't," I said.
"You'll be fine."
"I can't!"
"You have to!"
"I won't!"
"You won't?"

"Right, I won't. I can't. I won't." There was a long silence. Apprentices never disagree. Mr. Hruby glared. What happened? Nothing. He let the whole thing drop. He walked away, shaking his head as though I were the most difficult young man he'd ever run into.

A few days later we were having our dinner, which always seemed to be half a dinner: one small hamburger patty, a boiled potato, something green—no seconds. I was talking to one of the other apprentices, a girl named Patricia Murphy, who also had come from the Playhouse. I looked away from Patty for just a moment, and when I turned back she was gone. She had fainted and slid quietly off her chair and under the table. She came to quickly.

A few of us apprentices got together and discussed whether we should even be there. The conditions were rougher than anyone had imagined. But I had nothing to measure it against. Maybe this was just the way it was when you were starting. Long hours, short food supply, you had to clean out toilets and sleep on dead rats. Who knew what it was like anywhere else? I mean, I was considering quitting Rabbit Run, but I didn't want to quit show business, and at that point I had no way of knowing if Rabbit Run *was* show business. In a way, it was like the old joke about the guy whose job it was to clean up elephant dung at the circus. He hated it. When a friend suggested he leave, he said:

"What, and quit show business?!" After some hesitation we decided to stay to see what would happen next.

One week we did a big musical. There were more than twenty parts, so everyone was needed to be in the show, and I was actually given my own song to sing called "At the Drop of a Hat." It went something like: "At the drop of a hat, I will pick up my feet, and I'll dance just like that." I was a little surprised to get the part, but I was having a great time with it. Of course, I worked on it night and day in the tradition of "Jack, *my* dear boy/Jack, my *dear* boy." I was always singing the song. I was even picking up a couple of dance steps that went with the number. I loved it. I thought, This is wonderful—I'm singing! I'm dancing!

I was on my way home one night—home to the garage—and as I walked by another garage, I heard someone singing, "At the drop of a hat, I will pick up my feet . . ." I thought, Hey, I'm really going over big! Everyone is singing my song! This is great! I love show business. It's all right—the rat, the whole thing.

I went back the next day to rehearse, and the director, Dick Scanga, said: "Come here, let me talk to you a minute."

"Yeah, what?"

"Let's have Jimmy Reilly do 'At the Drop of a Hat.'"

"Jimmy Reilly?"

"Yeah. Let's have Jimmy Reilly do it."

"Why?"

"Let's have Jimmy Reilly do it."

"Okay," I said, deciding not to pursue the reason any further.

That was the first time I was ever fired in show business. It was very delicately done. It was never really explained. As good a time as I was having singing, I never heard myself, and, well, I was just left to draw my own conclusions.

After my experience in the musical, I was moved to the offstage area as the unseen voice of the gondolier in the play *Time of the Cuckoo*. It was a very romantic play set in Venice. In the story, they have gondolas going down the canals, and my job was to stand offstage and, at certain times during the play, call out as melodically as I could, with an Italian flair: "Goooooon-da-lah!" After about the third night's performance, I thought to myself: Hey, this is something, too! You can try to be great at anything. So, I started to work on my "Gondolas" day and night. I started to "go for it" a little bit. I went for something like: "Gooonnn-daaalaaaaah," stretching it out with as much of a musical sound as possible. After the show, people would come around and say, "Are you in the show?"

And I would say, "No, I'm the offstage gondolier."

"Oh, very nice!" they'd say.

"Really? Thanks a lot. I appreciate it."

By the time it got to be closing night of the week's run, I thought, I'm *really* going to go for it. This is the last performance, and I'm really going to go for something extraordinary here. So when my first cue came, I went for a high falsetto, meaning to be breathtaking: "Goooooonnn-daaaaaaaa-laaaaaaah!" And my voice cracked . . . badly.

The audience went into hysterics, and the spell of the play was broken.

Backstage, I dropped flat out on the floor. I was in anguish with embarrassment. I saw a pair of large shoes walk over and stop next to my face. I looked up, and there was the man who ran the theater, Will Klump, a very tall gentleman (at least, from my vantage point) with an extremely somber expression.

I looked up at him for mercy. I wanted to say something, but I couldn't think of anything to say.

He was looking down. I was looking up. We gazed at each other for a long moment. No one spoke. Eventually, he walked away. I lay there waiting for my next cue, intending to leave a little of the music out.

I don't know if it was a conscious plan on management's part, but I didn't appear on- or offstage for the next couple of weeks. I was given stagehand duties. I may have still been a little bit thrown by my "Gondola" experience because when they put me up in the lighting booth for the next play, I didn't do so well there either.

The director, Dick Scanga, climbed up a steep ladder to my perch in the middle of a performance and with a strange look on his face asked, "What time of day is it now in the play?"

"Afternoon," I answered confidently.

"That's right," he said, barely containing his frustration. "So why is blue moonlight coming through the living-room window?"

I'd have to rate that as one of the tougher questions I'd ever been asked. Dick shook his head . . . and I hope that not everyone in the audience saw moonlight turn to sunlight over the next few minutes.

I was backstage again for the next play, *Rope*. I held a drum on my lap for two hours and rolled hard beans around in it to simulate the sound of rain. I acquitted myself satisfactorily— meaning it rained when it was supposed to.

Then I began to play some small parts. It just turned out that the next few plays required more young people, and I was free (in every way).

By the end of the season I was playing bigger parts—very nervously, not effectively, but I was "out there," and nobody was asking for their money back . . . as far as I'd heard, anyway.

An Amazing Thing Happened

I went back to the Pittsburgh Playhouse after that, expecting more abuse but determined to graduate. I got the part of Howie, the milkman, in a student production of *Our Town*. When the young girl, Emily, dies and then comes back and sees her town, I guess the audience is supposed to see the town and people as Emily sees them in her memory, or something. I wasn't really sure, even though I loved the play. Anyway, someone said that I did appear as though I were a memory as Howie, the milkman. I wasn't sure what that meant either, but I knew it was a compliment. It wasn't the kind of compliment you could turn into money at the bank, but it was good to hear, whatever it meant.

Eventually I got a certificate that said I graduated. I walked out of the Playhouse, happy to be moving on. It wasn't until years went by that I started to really *feel* the abuse that had been inflicted there. I was always grateful for the scholarship and the chance to get up and act, so it took me a long time to realize how unproductive, and even destructive, most of that experience was. I have no idea what's going on there now, or if they even have a school. I saw that same harmful pattern at other schools over the years—people who had never had professional acting careers very aggressively telling young, vulnerable people how bad they were, and not really helping them. I always tried to be respectful about it, but early on I stopped blindly buying everything anyone was saying. It was crucial to think for myself. The amount of misinformation being put out in acting classes—or anywhere, for that matter—staggers me. They ridiculed the Method at the Playhouse because they could neither do it nor understand it. Ridiculing "nervous" work was bad enough, but the lack of an overall feeling of goodwill and support was the worst. I don't think it's a coincidence that over a period of decades a relatively small amount of people emerged from there to have any kinds of careers at all.

I got a chance to do another season of summer stock at the Little Lake Theater in Washington, Pennsylvania, about sixty miles outside Pittsburgh. This was a beautiful little theater-in-the-round in a peaceful country setting. It seemed to draw full houses on a regular basis. The pool of talent here was the same as for the main-stage productions at the Playhouse. My only other experience with these people was as the lieutenant in *My Three Angels* when I turned my head too much. I arrived at the theater and casually announced, to anyone who asked, that after this summer-stock season I was going to Hollywood. This statement was always greeted with a sudden stillness followed by an attempt at a subtle looking me over to see if I was nuts. Obviously, I had hardly distinguished myself in my two years or so in the so-called business; I had yet to be paid a nickel, although at Little Lake I believe we were paid twenty dollars a play. But Hollywood? This was the point where anyone who knew me figured I would head for the Y and the avocation idea, and maybe go to journalism school or someplace where they trained people to go into a profession in which you could get hired on a reasonably regular basis. But Hollywood? Professional acting? The unemployment rate has always been at least 88 percent, and the average income about nine hundred dollars a year. I mean, it *is* referred to as a tough field.

If it's not already evident, and it may not be, I should point out that whatever my multitude of shortcomings may have been, I never lacked in determination. Judging by my surprise at the results of the University of Miami orientation test, I was determined before I even knew I was determined. This, by the way, didn't manifest at all in my personality. I appeared to be exactly the opposite of what is commonly thought of as a go-getter. I was the quiet, determined type. The only way anyone would even know I *was* that committed was that I'd still be there after most anyone else would have left. I knew I hadn't gotten anyone excited about my ability, including myself. I didn't expect to star in the movies. I just said I was going to Hollywood. In my mind at that time, it was either Hollywood or New York, and Hollywood was where the movies and Elizabeth Taylor were. I figured I'd go out there and study some more and, if the movie studios weren't too far away from where I was, well . . .

I played the young boy next door in the first play that season, a light comedy called *Kiss and Tell,* and I was adequate. The people who knew I was heading for Hollywood in a month shook their heads in wonderment.

I was next to appear in the Philip Barry play *Holiday,* playing the alcoholic younger brother of the leading lady. It was right then that an amazing thing happened. It amazed me almost as much as it did the people who were watching the saga of my "career." I suddenly was good! I'm not sure what happened, but for the first time I actually was able to, if not "live the part," maybe live it enough so that it looked like I was living it. Some theatergoers actually began to call the theater to find out when I might be appearing again.

The same pal who had teased me earlier about my father calling his company The Grodin Company came to see me in *Holiday.* He came backstage afterward and said I was good. Then he put his arm on my shoulder, lowered his voice a bit, and said, "Between us, are you making up some of those lines as you're going along?" I'm sure he didn't realize the compliment, but was just checking to see if I had some angle up my sleeve. He was always looking for an angle. Once, when we were fourteen, he said, "I have an extra ticket to the hockey game. I'll give it to you, but if you catch a puck you have to give it to me." I had never been to a hockey game, and as far as I knew, catching a hard rubber puck would be like catching a brick at a hundred miles an hour. I was certain that if one ever came in my direction, which would have been miraculous since the stands are protected from that, I would hardly try to catch it. I said, "Sure, if I catch a puck I'll give it to you." About halfway through the first period, a puck somehow came screaming off the ice and cracked the wood on the empty seat next to me. I picked it up. Without a word, my pal put out his hand, and I gave it to him.

After *Holiday*, I was the boy in a comedy about the movies called *Boy Meets Girl*. Here was my first comedy lead, and I seemed to get a laugh with just about anything I did—and there was no whipped cream on my clothes, either. A lot of stunned looks were being exchanged by the people around the theater. They were just shocked at my being received like that. I wasn't too casual about it myself. It was startling. While the success in *Holiday* was clear, to have it in a comedy lead where I heard the laughter throughout the evening was tangible, ongoing proof that something brand new was happening for me. I'm not sure why I was suddenly effective. These were the best parts I'd ever had, and little by little I was getting used to being "out there." Maybe all the hard work was starting to pay off. But it was nothing I could have been too confident about, because in the next play, *The Philadelphia Story*, where the young man's part was a little less interesting, so was I. "Mediocre" would have been a fair description. So I hadn't suddenly mastered a craft, but whatever lay ahead, they couldn't take *Holiday* and *Boy Meets Girl* away from me.

By the end of the season I had a strong booster, a man named Don Hall, who was connected with the theater. Don, a cheerful man, was a successful printer who had formed acquaintances with a few people connected to the movies, and he kindly gave me some letters of recommendation. (Don was the most enthusiastic supporter a young person could have. I seemed to be his pride and joy. Unhappily, he died about ten years later of complications from gallbladder surgery a few years before I became recognized.) I read Don's letters and, with the confidence they gave me, headed for Hollywood.

Hollywood, Here I Come!

It was, however, a great distance in more ways than one from the nonunion Little Lake Theater in Washington, Pennsylvania, to Hollywood, California, home of the movies. In fact, my confidence seemed to diminish the closer I got to Hollywood, reaching its lowest point on the day I arrived for my first appointment with the casting director at Warner Brothers Studios. My tension level wasn't all that different than it had been on that walk to class at the University of Miami for my first "Friends, Romans, countrymen." It was going to take a lot more, it seemed, than *Holiday* and *Boy Meets Girl* for my nerves to be able to deal with the higher stakes and expectations of a movie studio.

Huge portraits of movie stars were framed in glass cases on the lawn as I walked up the path at Warner Brothers looking for the casting office. Even though two years had passed since I had taken that Rorschach test at the Playhouse and felt compelled to act as though my every thought were of the theater, I was still what could kindly be called stunningly naïve. It seemed to me at that time, looking at the movies and at photographs of young stars in Hollywood, that the farther your hair came down over your forehead, the better your chance for success. With that in mind, I showed up on my first day at Warner Brothers with my hair combed straight down over the old forehead. I thought that if I could get that hair only an inch or so above my eyebrows, I might be put under contract immediately. I drew some odd stares as I entered the place.

The first letter of recommendation had gone to the head of production of the studio, a man named William Orr, the son-in-law of Jack Warner, who, with his brothers, ran the studio. He sent it on to the Warner Brothers casting director, Hoyt Bowers. After making my way through an armed-guard station and a couple of receptionists, I presented myself at his office. His secretary shot a quick look at my hairline and politely asked me to take a seat. I sat down and felt so inadequate that I had to fight an impulse to say, "Look, I'm sorry . . . I don't have any business being here . . . sorry to have bothered you," and leave. Instead, I said nothing and just thought it. Looking into Hoyt Bowers's office, I caught a glimpse of him looking back at me, then turning to another man with a deeply bemused look. Eventually, I was told to go into the office. Mr. Bowers was a veteran casting director who had seen so many hopefuls come and so few stay that he greeted me with a politeness that couldn't quite conceal an attitude of "no interest whatsoever." Even though I'd been in the "business" almost no time at all, I was already expecting nothing else. I was told to come back on another day, which I did, and was sent to a room where there was a group of some twenty other aspiring young people who were all asked to choose a scene from something to audition for the head of Talent. At that time, Warner Brothers and several other studios kept a group of young people under seven-year contracts. It was pretty heady just to be sitting there. It was not that long ago that I was the apprentice who couldn't handle an offstage gondola.

As the head of the Talent program, a middle-aged man, spoke to us, he ran his hand through the dyed-orange hair of a young fellow who sat at his feet. I looked around to see if any of the others thought this odd, but they acted as though at every gathering there was always a middle-aged man running his fingers through the orange hair of a young fellow. It was all kind of dreamlike.

Those of us who didn't know what scene to pick were assigned scenes. I was told to do a scene from *The Hasty Heart*. I was to play the part of Yank, and my partner was to play the part of a Scottish fellow, Lachie. Yank was an American with a bad stutter. My overwhelming nervousness on the day of the audition didn't help me stutter, but, instead, I went right past stuttering into an imitation of the other actor's Scottish accent. The head of the Talent program stared a long moment at the end of the scene. His only comment on my "work" was: "Yank doesn't have a Scottish accent."

"I know," I said.

He waited for some further explanation. I had none. Then, seeing my extreme nervousness, he most good-heartedly suggested I choose another scene.

I picked a scene from *Tea and Sympathy*, which was a hit play at the time, a story about a young, sensitive boy and his relationship with the wife of the headmaster of a boys' school. In the play, the boy is accused of being a homosexual. In playing the part, I made a conscious effort to "lighten" my quality in an attempt to conform to the acting conventions of the time in playing homosexuals. It seemed to go okay. Well, at least there was no Scottish accent, although this time there was a little genuine nervous stuttering.

The head of the program said, "Very nice," and told me to have my agent call him.

"Very nice. Have your agent call" translated, in my twenty-year-old head, to instant stardom. I thanked him enthusiastically. I thought it was a good idea not to mention that I didn't have an agent, or, for that matter, that I'd never even met one.

I was ecstatic. I ran out of the studio to a phone booth, looked in the Yellow Pages, and, after several attempts, actually got an agent on the phone. I breathlessly related how I was new in town and didn't know anyone, but Warner Brothers, it seemed, wanted to put me under contract, and would he call and arrange the terms.

After a long silence—that was a pretty common reaction to a lot of what I did and said, I was noticing—he asked me to come over. Within an hour I was over there telling him my story in person. He looked dubious. He told me to go back to where I was staying, and he would call the Talent head at Warners, whom he knew, and get back to me.

I went home and waited for his call. It didn't come. I paced around my room for hours, but the phone never rang. The next morning I was awakened by the loudest siren I've ever heard in my life. It was a test for something, I'm not sure what. An alarm that was supposed to alert a pretty good part of Los Angeles was on the building I was in, right outside my window. I know I was already fairly edgy, but I believe the calmest person in the world would have leaped out of his bed as I did.

After trying to calm down, I decided to call the agent myself. He took my call right away. I was pretty excited. "What do they want to do with me?" I asked him.

"They don't want to do anything with you," he said.

"They don't?" I said.

"No. They thought your quality was too light."

"Too light?" I said. My heart was sinking. "I was doing that light thing for the scene. You see, the character is accused of being homosexual and . . ."

"Yeah. Well, they're not interested."

"Oh. Okay. Thanks, uh, a lot."

"Yeah." And he was gone.

I imagined giving a long explanation of what had happened— the nervousness that had shot me past stuttering into a Scottish accent, the "light" quality that I was really only doing for the part, and I . . . I couldn't think of anyone who would be interested in hearing what I had to say. Absolutely no one. I started to feel strongly that maybe, in spite of *Holiday* and *Boy Meets Girl* and my ability to appear as a memory as Howie, the milkman, I was getting ahead of myself showing up at a movie studio . . . even though my hairline was pretty close to my eyebrows.

Nevertheless, I had arrived with two reference letters, and the next day I went to see the woman who had been sent the second one. Her name was Helen Ferguson, and she was the very successful head of a public-relations firm and a former silent-film star. My only memory of the meeting was her comment that my impact on entering a room was as though someone had just left. I guess what that meant was that she was expecting someone like a young, energetic Tony Curtis to come bursting into her office, and I was just kind of a shy boy. She inquired if I had gained the acting power alluded to in the letter of recommendation by submerging myself in the character. Still reeling from her first observation, I muttered, "I guess so." She nodded skeptically and wished me well. I left her office and was numb—just numb.

I wandered around the streets for a couple of hours thinking the whole thing over. It certainly had been clear to me before Hollywood that I really didn't know what I was doing. I didn't expect to jump into the movies, but I did hope to jump into a training program at the studio. Now it didn't look like I was going to be jumping anywhere.

That night I sat alone in my room and continued to think it over. As I saw it, in the short time I had been bouncing around on the fringes there seemed to have been two things that had gotten through to me: Elizabeth Taylor, and the Actors Studio (the Method) in New York. While I had been rehearsing with my partner on *Tea and Sympathy*, a man named John Harding, who was an actor and director, had watched one of the rehearsals. We were rehearsing in a building that housed a group to which my partner and John belonged. John had said that I looked like I might actually become an actor some day, and what was I doing trying to get into a studio talent program? In his opinion, the real place for young, serious aspiring actors was the Actors Studio, with Lee Strasberg, in New York. It seemed to me, sitting alone in my room that night, that people in New York would be about as interested in me as people in Hollywood were—which, of course, was not at all. But since I had to, I pushed that thought aside and made plans to head to New York. I didn't realize that the Actors Studio auditioned over a thousand people a year—anyone could audition—and something like two of those people got in. It was generally conceded to be the home of the most talented actors in the country.

With youth and ignorance on my side, I rushed to New York and the Actors Studio.

New York, Here I Come!

I had been to New York once before, when I had driven up from Pittsburgh with some other students from the Playhouse to see about summer-stock auditions, and it had led to nothing. I had been so overwhelmed on entering the city that I drove through five red lights. I had been stopped by a policeman but not given a ticket. I think there was an unwritten police-department rule not to give tickets to people who seemed on the verge of a nervous breakdown.

On arriving in New York this time (only a touch less crazed), I got in touch with an old chum from the Pittsburgh Playhouse and we prepared a scene for the audition at the Actors Studio. The Actors Studio is a converted church on West Forty-fourth Street between Ninth and Tenth Avenues, in kind of a run-down section. That building, to a young actor in the fifties, was like the White House to a politician. It seemed a place of magic and mystery. Young actors would stand across the street and gaze at it the way Audrey Hepburn, the daughter of a chauffeur in the movie *Sabrina*, gazed into the main house where the party was.

On the day of our audition, my partner and I, with the other applicants, were told to wait in a small room. There were two other couples waiting their turn. Everyone looked shell-shocked. Success here and acceptance into the Actors Studio was as big an event as could happen to an actor in his whole career. This was only the preliminary audition. If I passed here, it didn't mean I got in; it just meant I got to do it again—next time for Lee Strasberg and two associates. Lee Strasberg, who was certainly known as the foremost authority on acting in the country, would personally have to say you belonged or didn't belong. This waiting room was not a place where you hung out for laughs.

Eventually, our names were called. A man came over, introduced himself, and silently led us up a long, narrow stairway to a large, dark room illuminated only by two spotlights which shone in our faces. He told us to walk in front of them and announce our names and the name of the scene. In the shadowy distance, three judges sat silently on some kind of elevation. No introductions were made. I have no memory of what happened in the next three minutes, but it was something worse than "too light," stuttering, or an inappropriate Scottish accent. I had reached a new height or depth of nervousness. After we finished, the now-familiar silence was there. "Thank you," someone eventually said from the elevation. As we walked out, I caught a glimpse of one of the judges: It was Karl Malden. I had no idea he was nine feet tall—sitting down.

A letter arrived about a week later thanking me for auditioning and regretting that there was no opening for me at this time. At the end of the letter it said I could audition again if I wanted to after a year. I didn't feel ready even to *think* about that. But the whole experience made me more determined to take acting classes and start developing some tools to combat the nervousness and insecurity that were besieging me. At that point the dream of being in the movies went away and was replaced by the dream of becoming a good actor.

After checking some ads in a show-business paper, I got an audition for the classes of Uta Hagen, who was and is one of the most respected actresses and teachers in New York. When I finished, Uta said I could join her beginners' class. I was elated. Even though I was still fairly shy, I threw her a kiss. The classes were given twice a week. They cost three dollars apiece, and each would last until everyone got to do everything they'd prepared, which usually took about five hours. For the next three years, Uta Hagen and her classes became the center of my life. I continued to try to find work as an actor, but I didn't have a lot of opportunities, to put it mildly.

Uta Hagen is married to the fine actor, director, and teacher Herbert Berghof, and together they head the famed HB Studio. Uta has had great success in the theater. She's probably best known for creating the role of Martha, the female lead, in Edward Albee's *Who's Afraid of Virginia Woolf?* I really began to learn about acting from Uta Hagen; it was also the first time I was in an atmosphere where attempting to master the craft of acting was seen as a serious, highly worthy profession. We met on the top floor of a building filled with lofts. It was cold up there in the wintertime, and Uta told us we could either see ourselves as these people—thirty or so—who were sitting in a cold loft on folding chairs, or as artists struggling to learn about an art form in a garret somewhere. I chose the struggling artist/garret concept.

With Uta, I reverted to my old high school ways of asking questions. First, she looked at me warily. Then, when I began to resist some of her teachings, I was regularly yelled at. I couldn't figure out how learning to open an imaginary window or carry an imaginary suitcase was really going to help me, and I'm sure this was evident the few times I ventured up on the stage to open it or carry it. Uta resented that and let me know. At the same time, she made me feel I was talented, but, boy, how much better I'd be if I'd just open some imaginary windows or carry some imaginary suitcases. After a while, she started to call me names like "lazy." And then, eventually, regularly and passionately, she threatened to throw me out of class if I didn't get up there more to do her things. She really disliked me, but at the same time she somehow made me feel she loved me because of all this energy she was putting out in my direction. After all the threats, though, she announced one day that she guessed I only stood behind what I really believed in and kept questioning the rest, and allowed as how "that's the way it should be." By my last year there, I was allowed to sit behind her and give her a back rub. She was really my first teacher. I loved her then, I love her now; but I still think I'm right about the imaginary windows and suitcases.

Even thirty years later, I vividly remember the most important acting lesson I learned from Uta. It wasn't part of her regular teaching precepts ("Ask yourself, 'Who am I as a character? What do I want in the scene?'"). I don't even remember it coming up or ever being mentioned in the couple of dozen or so books on acting I've read, but it was invaluable and Uta gave it to me. I had played Holden Caulfield in a scene from J. D. Salinger's novel *Catcher in the Rye*. It was a scene between the teacher and Holden where they're discussing a terrible essay Holden had written. After the scene was over, Uta said to me there was one "pure acting moment in that scene. Do you know what it was?" Well . . . I was excited by the compliment. I still hadn't heard many in my young career. But I had no idea what Uta was talking about. "Was it the moment where I slowly turned and. . . ?"

"No," Uta interrupted.

"Was it when I lifted my head suddenly and. . . ?"

"No," Uta interrupted again.

I was quickly out of guesses. Evidently, a "pure acting moment" had gone right by and I'd never spotted it. Neither had the class, whom Uta had invited to join in the quiz. Incidentally, that's an aspect of some acting classes I'm avidly against—having students criticize each other. I think the young actor is way too insecure and vulnerable to be subjected to the kind of rampant competitiveness and even hostility that can take place among students. The teachers usually are insensitive enough, let alone the students.

When no one could spot my seemingly invisible "pure acting moment," Uta told me it was when I went to hand my essay back to the teacher, a fine actor named Scott Edmonds. I thought Scott was going to take it, but for a moment he didn't reach out to accept it. Then he did. There was a moment when I wasn't sure what was going to happen next. *That* was the pure acting moment: the moment of not knowing what the next moment was (just as we don't in life). I couldn't immediately repeat it, but when Uta identified it, I understood, and in the future strove to get myself again into a state of not anticipating what was next, of not knowing. Easier said than done, but it was invaluable to have been identified and experienced that once. Thirty years later, it's still about as valuable a lesson as I ever learned about acting, and that alone was worth the three years with Uta.

During that period, I would sometimes go over to the union office, and there would be free tickets to Broadway shows that had opened, not gotten good enough reviews to run, and were just playing out a few days to the end of the week. One of them was a play called *Comes a Day* by a writer named Speed Lampkin. At one point in the play, a character entered to see someone, was told to wait, and while left alone decided to strangle a canary in a cage that was bothering him with its singing. I'm sure the canary wasn't real because you can't kill real birds in plays. Anyway, after strangling the "canary," the actor just stared out at the audience. Even though I was sitting in the balcony, I felt like getting the hell out of there, as it really did appear that this guy might come out and strangle some of *us*. That's the first time I saw the power of the then completely unknown George C. Scott.

Another time, I was walking around the theater district and decided to go in and see a play starring Ralph Richardson called *Waltz of the Toreadors*. I believe seeing Mr. Richardson (later Sir Ralph) in that play deeply affected my acting. It was the first time I fully realized how broadly you could play if you brought inner reality to whatever you were doing. So, while Montgomery Clift was my acting model, as I got into the profession I think the work of Ralph Richardson affected my own playing more than anyone else's did.

I was living in a small single room, Room 410, in the seedy Capitol Hall Hotel in a rough section of Manhattan. Since I never had enough money to pay a month ahead of time, I was forced to stay here, as I only had to come up with the ten-dollars-a-week rent in advance. The room was completely dark day and night. The one window opened on a dark air shaft. People would throw things—mostly beer, vodka, and Scotch bottles—down the shaft and scream obscenities regularly. The crash of these bottles and the obscenities were my daily background music as I'd lie on the bed reading the latest acting book from the library. The bathroom was down the hall and was shared by dozens of people. There were no cooking facilities and I couldn't afford restaurants, so, against hotel rules, I bought an electric frying pan. I had a steady diet of chicken wings. They were nineteen cents a package. So that the hotel maids wouldn't see and report it, I kept the frying pan hidden under my socks in the sock drawer.

I lived in a series of similar places over the next few years. One block I lived on was, unbeknownst to me, one of the most notorious in Manhattan for the drug trade. There always seemed to be a lot of strange, unexplained activity on the street, all kinds of whispered meetings and transactions—but I was so focused on my studies that I barely gave it a glance. Later, when the city decided just to remove the block—tear it down—I learned what all that whispering had been about.

Eventually, when I started to get the lay of the city a little better, I was able to find what they called cold-water flats for twenty-five dollars a month. I don't know why they called them that, since most of the time there was hot water too. These were very small three-room apartments with the bathtub in the kitchen and the toilet, which you shared with three other apartments, down the hall.

As in any profession, the more I learned, the more I realized I didn't know, and I was absolutely compelled to find out. A door had been opened in my mind, and the potential for what a person could do seemed limitless. It was a very exciting feeling, one that most of the time completely overwhelmed any personal deprivations. It must have been that way, because I'd say I'd be the last candidate in the world to be a share-a-toilet-down-the-hall kind of guy.

It's Lonely at the Bottom

Of course, from the beginning I got jobs to support myself. The job I really liked best was driving a cab. I got to go all over Manhattan, and it seemed pretty exotic. My first day on the job I earned about twenty dollars for twelve hours' work. It seemed like a lot at the time, because it was almost one month's rent in a cold-water flat. At the end of that first day, a young woman, my last fare, with whom I'd been chatting during the drive, asked me if I'd like to come upstairs for a cup of coffee. It was about two o'clock in the morning, so she probably meant more than coffee. But I was tired and felt grimy from the twelve hours of driving, so I declined. Going home that night, I thought the job held promise in more ways than one. But in two years on the job, that was my only personal invitation.

I dealt with pimps, prostitutes, and all kinds of night life in every part of the city and every time of the night. The most mysterious place for me in New York was Harlem. I would go up there alone and walk the streets at night. I stood outside the nightclub owned by the great middleweight boxing champion Sugar Ray Robinson. I never went in anywhere, just walked and looked. Twenty-five years later I would be sparring with Sugar Ray on the sidewalk outside a restaurant in Hollywood where I'd had dinner with him. I jabbed him easily in the side. My hand felt like it had hit a steel wall.

Friday and Saturday nights, I would pick up the young couples going out for their weekend dates. There were a lot of young couples around my age; they were going out to do whatever they were going to do, and I was driving a cab. I still hadn't broken out of my shell enough to have a girlfriend. I didn't even have any dates. I wasn't going anywhere. Elizabeth Taylor and the white Cadillac convertible seemed so far away.

I had this little transistor radio that I was very fond of and used to keep on the front seat next to me in the cab. Once, a gregarious couple leaned forward, and the man said to the woman: "Look at that radio! That's a terrible little sound. What a tinny little sound that has." They talked about it as if I were invisible. So the combination of the put-down of my radio and taking the couples on their Friday and Saturday night dates began to put me off cab driving.

I wanted to get a job where I could be away from people so that nobody could criticize me or mine. This was around my early time with Uta and her rough attacks on me. I was already on fairly shaky ground, so I got a job where I could be alone. I became a night watchman for the Pinkerton Detective Agency on the Brooklyn waterfront. My job was to sit in deserted warehouses and call somebody if the buildings caught on fire. I wore a full-dress uniform and looked like a cross between a marine and an usher. I drew a lot of stares and an occasional salute as I rode the subway to Brooklyn, but it was giving me absolute solitude to read and think and not be criticized for asking too many questions or for anything else. At first, the only thing that bothered me was that my wool pants itched.

My hours were from midnight to eight, and usually around four A.M. or so I would get tired of thinking or reading and start to wander around the empty warehouse. It was grim and lonely, but I was insecure and vulnerable enough to do it rather than expose myself to people and the possible upset from their comments. If I sound as though I was fairly edgy, I was. Given that I had no money, no prospects, and no window, it seemed inevitable that there had to be a certain amount of edginess. I was always hearing odd noises as I climbed the stairwells in the darkness of the abandoned buildings, armed only with a flashlight. I would call out loudly as I climbed, warning whoever was there that I was coming. "You'd better watch out because I'm coming up there!" Again, my body didn't know I was acting, so the macho calling out calmed me down as I went up the stairs. Once, when another guard, an older man, which most of the guards were (retired policemen and firemen), came to begin his shift, I didn't see him, and he really startled me. I jumped and yelled, and so did he as I scared him back. Happily, in two years, that was my only surprise encounter. The pay was $1.70 an hour.

When my shift was over, very often I would take the subway and go to a double-feature movie on Forty-second Street. There, I'd be sitting in an almost empty movie house at nine A.M., sometimes watching Humphrey Bogart double features. It was about a 600-seat theater. There would be six or seven people usually, sleeping for various reasons in different parts of the theater, and me sitting there alone in my full-dress uniform with officer's cap.

It was during this time that I started to think a lot about my identity. Was I a guy who was studying acting and working part-time as a Pinkerton guard, or was I a Pinkerton guard who wanted to be an actor? Either way, I found it hard to think of myself as anything.

It's impossible to describe what it felt like coming to New York City at the age of twenty, having nothing, knowing no one. I didn't hang out with my fellow students from class, because I was just too vulnerable to the idle criticism of work that would casually be thrown around. Students would comment on this and that about each other's work until this and that became THIS and THAT and started to be the main definition of the student. I believe I benefited from my effort to keep the criticism at bay until I could stand more steadily on my feet. Still, being in New York City was exciting as well as devastatingly lonely. I would walk the streets of Manhattan, about a hundred blocks a day. I would, with nothing better to do, read every newspaper—seven in all—from front page to back page. I would sit on the steps of the library at Forty-second Street and watch people go by. This wasn't to study acting or people's behavior; I was feeling out of life, and got vicarious pleasure out of watching people in it. I do remember that once, after feeling the real impact of not being wanted and having no one to tell it to, the loneliness got to be kind of an actual physical ache. One day, while I was sitting alone in my room, a small mouse suddenly appeared and looked at me. I don't remember where it went or what happened: I just know I was glad to see it.

Lee Strasberg

The worthiness of the study of acting first felt with Uta Hagen was raised to an even more intense level when I studied with Lee Strasberg. Again, whatever else I was doing, for the next three years Lee Strasberg and his classes became the center of my life.

I was introduced to him by a friend, Eleni Kiamos, a wonderful actress I had met at Uta's who was now with Lee. In 1959, to a young actor, Lee Strasberg had already taken on legendary proportions. When Eleni introduced me as he was coming out of one of his classes, he appeared as a shy, smallish man who ran a candy store. He nodded hello, barely looked at me, and told me to write him a letter saying why I wanted to be an actor. Eleni told me that if he liked what I said in the letter, he would give me an interview; and if I was okay in the interview, I would be eligible for an eventual opening in the class.

I immediately went to work on my letter. I said I thought the study of acting, with the desire to illuminate what life and people are all about, was second in importance only to the clergy—and I meant every word of it. That was the effect of those three years with Uta. Elizabeth Taylor wasn't completely out of my mind—just presently on the back burner behind my effort to better mankind.

After several weeks, I got a letter granting me an interview with Lee Strasberg. I was ushered into the book-filled study of his large, rambling apartment overlooking Central Park, and pretty much repeated what I had said in the letter about acting being second in importance only to the clergy as Mr. Strasberg looked absently out the window and said nothing. He asked me who my favorite actors were. I said, "Montgomery Clift, Marlon Brando, and Paul Muni in his early work." On the "early work" comment, he turned and really looked at me for the first time. The meeting ended shortly after that. He had virtually said nothing, but a couple of months later I got another letter telling me I could come to class.

I think the most important lesson I took away from my years there was one that wouldn't be found in any book on acting. I don't believe it was taught by Stanislavski or practiced at the Moscow Art Theater. Even with Lee's brilliance, I wonder if he could have known the ramifications of one simple point I heard him make over and over again.

We had a singing exercise in which we were asked to pour whatever emotion we were feeling at a given moment into the line of a song. It didn't have to sound good: You only had to let whatever stirrings that were floating or surging inside you out through the song. For some people this might mean a torrent of emotion caused by just standing in front of Lee and the class, among other things. Lee would always encourage us just to let go and let the emotion come out. Many times over the years, students—male and female, but mostly female—would say: "I'm afraid to let myself go." When Lee would ask why, more often than not the student would say nervously: "I'm afraid I'll faint. I'm afraid I'll fall down." Lee would answer offhandedly, "Then we'll pick you up."

I never saw anyone faint or fall down. I'm sure the lesson was meant to be: Don't be afraid to let yourself go. To me it meant that for acting, and something even more important for life. As Lee elaborated, or as I construed it, it meant: Accept yourself, whatever you are. If you did fall down and you were picked up, so you'd be someone who fell down and was picked up. So what? It meant to me that you didn't have to be precious about yourself in acting or life. If you want to define yourself as being a certain way in life, and it turns out you are less than that, then that's who you are. If you don't like it and want to do better, then try as hard as you can to do better; but don't beat yourself up for who you are. Accept your vulnerability and do the best you can. You don't have to turn on yourself, particularly professionally; there will be plenty of people who will do that for you.

I honestly don't know whether Lee was teaching that as a life lesson, but that's what I came away with—and it's about the best lesson I've ever gotten anywhere.

Another aspect of Lee's classes that seemed unique was that in any given class some Hollywood movie star might be sitting there. One day I turned my head to glance at a blonde with no makeup sitting against the wall and thought how much she looked like, and then realized she was, Marilyn Monroe. After class I watched as she walked down the street alone. People's mouths literally dropped open as they recognized her. She had a very powerful, magnetic beauty, even without makeup.

Once, standing alone on the stage to do the singing exercise, I started to sing and Lee started to talk simultaneously. I stopped singing abruptly, and the whole class laughed. I looked out at all those laughing faces, feeling very embarrassed, and only one young woman sitting in the back row wasn't laughing or smiling but only looking at me with compassion for my discomfort. That was the twenty-year-old Jane Fonda.

While Lee didn't have us open imaginary windows or carry imaginary suitcases, he did have us take imaginary showers and become animals, neither of which I chose to do. But Lee, unlike Uta, didn't seem to take it personally that I wasn't being some animal or showering up there.

My understanding of the craft of acting really developed with Lee. Even though he was a man of many words, I hung in there and took some of what he said and applied it to great advantage. It would not be uncommon for an actor to do a scene lasting five minutes that seemed wonderful, and then have Lee criticize it for half an hour. I eventually enjoyed a unique position. Instead of criticizing me for half an hour, he actually pointed out what I was doing as a good example of what he wanted students to do. Once I missed a week, and when I came back he came over to where I was sitting to say hello. He *never* walked over to anyone to say hello; and if you said hello to him, you'd get one back, but you didn't feel singled out if that was it. With the professional world out there being very comfortable with its indifference toward me, Lee's hello meant a lot.

The students in the class started to pick up on Lee's attitude toward me, and I was acknowledged by my peers and sought out as someone to work with. Some of the students even came to me for advice on acting. It wasn't a job, but it counted a lot in the personal-confidence department, which was all-important. My dedication was strengthened by Lee's and my fellow students' acknowledgment of my work. I carried a little notebook with me everywhere I went in case I had an idea or a thought about acting at any time. I was on a job working at the post office once when I noticed three men huddled, talking, watching me furiously write something about acting in my notebook. After watching intently for a couple of minutes, they all walked over and asked politely what all this writing in notebooks was about. I explained it to them, and they looked enormously relieved. They had thought I worked for the Postal Inspectors' Division and was jotting down criticisms of their work.

Between Uta Hagen, Lee Strasberg, reading every book on acting I could find, constantly carrying my little notebook around with me, and sleeping with it by my bedside at night in case I woke up with an idea, I began to be an actor.

Now it became my goal to get someone somewhere in the professional world to think so too.

Stop and See Me Next Week

The confidence gained with Uta Hagen and Lee Strasberg was invaluable. Still, I had to combat the nervousness that was there because of what felt like the powerful determination of the profession to make all of us feel we would do them a big favor if we would just go away.

Whenever I've seen the announcement ACTORS WANTED, and I've seen it many times, it was never an ad for work, but for some acting school looking for students.

In order to explore any idea that might be helpful, I began to think about something most performers consider at some time—changing my name. I had three names I liked: Christopher Fargo, Hutch Saxony, and Rommie Genta. As hard as it may be to believe, even though I was a valedictorian I had never heard the word *genital*. Otherwise, Rommie Genta would never have made that list. One night I was discussing this with a group of people. Later in the evening, one of the fellows driving the car in front of me called out the window: "Follow me, Rommie." I felt like such a fraud, I dropped the whole name-change thing right there and stuck with my own, even though I knew I'd be spelling it for people for the rest of my life.

I also had to think about getting pictures made—eight-by-ten photographs. I asked an agent I had met, "Should I have pictures made?" He said, "Sure, have pictures made. Then the people who don't want to see you will know who it is they don't want to see."

We would all have a single eight-by-ten picture taken, and most everyone would also have an eight-by-ten with four poses on it: The fellas would look like a juvenile delinquent, like a nice straightforward guy, like a serious guy, like he'd just heard a good joke; the girls would pose in a bathing suit, in an evening gown, as a tomboy, and looking sultry. We all would try to look any way we could think of, hoping someone would be looking for one of our looks.

A lot of the talk among us was of pictures: "Who did your picture?" "I love your pictures." "Are you going to get new pictures?" "I have to get my pictures." "Let me see your pictures." Thousands of us would be running all over the city with these pictures and leaving them in casting offices, agents' offices, movie-company offices, theater offices, television offices . . . always outer offices with receptionists. Maybe we worked so hard on the quality and selection of our pictures because it was the only thing we could control, until, of course, we handed them to someone who would put them on huge stacks of other pictures, most often never to be looked at, or, once we were gone, just thrown in the wastebasket.

It was simply an overloaded marketplace. There were way too many actors. There were literally thousands of people with good credits who weren't working, so newcomers would have virtually no chance. A lot of the most sensitive, vulnerable people (which, of course, it helped to be if you wanted to be a good actor) dropped out right there, because there was so much rejection they just couldn't stand it.

A classmate of mine had a big success right away in an Off-Broadway show. One of the large talent agencies saw her, said she was great, invited her over to meet a lot of people, and, at the end of the day of romancing, told her they didn't want to represent her because they didn't think she was a "commercial type." I won't say that single experience turned her away from the profession, but it certainly contributed to her dropping out within the year. And she was as talented as you get.

The rejection seemed unrelenting and endless: Nobody seemed interested in you. You were basically made to feel like you were a pest or worse. You had to be sensitive and you had to be tough; you had to be vulnerable and you had to be persevering. You had to keep going no matter how many times you were rejected, and a lot of people couldn't do it. They just quit. I think the most gifted people I saw at that time quit. It was overwhelming, and ultimately heartbreaking for them.

Somehow, I didn't take the rejection too personally, and pressed ahead. It was as though I expected it. After all, I had heard this was the way it was. Always, since earliest childhood, the message in my house was that to really achieve anything worthwhile takes a long time, and you have to work very hard to be good enough to achieve anything. That always made sense to me. So I didn't really feel there was anything that extraordinary going on with all this rejection. I didn't like it. It just wasn't a surprise. And, besides, as long as I felt I was getting better in class, that was the most important thing. I figured the longer they wouldn't bother looking at me, the better chance I had to be okay when they finally did get around to taking a look. As long as I felt I was learning about acting, that overwhelmed everything else.

Around this time I got to know a lot of young unknown actors who were to become very well known. There was a funny-looking boy in class named Jerry Silberman, and everyone thought: My God, what is a guy who looks like that going to do in this profession?! (This was the fifties, an era dominated by pretty people.) I particularly had taken it upon myself to urge Jerry out of the business. He was talented—there was no question about that—but I saw years of frustration and upset ahead of him. He later changed his name to Gene Wilder, and was one of the first of the group to be recognized. I remember Dustin Hoffman as an unusually intense, serious kid who, out of frustration after years of getting nowhere as an actor, became an assistant stage manager aspiring to be a director. One afternoon I was walking home and saw Dustin standing on a corner near my apartment waiting for me. He said he had tried to reach me on the phone, been unable to, found out where I lived, and just thought he'd wait for me, as he was directing something in the basement of a church somewhere and wanted me to play the leading role. I told him I was sorry, but I couldn't do it because I was working full-time in the post office. He looked sad, and then said he understood. I walked away. About halfway up the block I turned around, and he was still standing there as though he didn't know what to do or where to go next. I thought to myself: Poor guy, I wonder what's going to happen to him.

You could wonder that about almost any of us in the class because most of the group would spend about a decade studying and trying to get work before giving up. In that same decade, we could—and likely would—have prepared ourselves for a career in another profession. But for almost everyone, ten years later they would be unsuccessful and unprepared for anything but the acting profession . . . which didn't want them. It was a scary thought. On the other hand, the kind of resolve and determination it would take to hang in that long would serve a person anywhere. Just the idea that Dustin actually waited on the corner, probably for hours, shows exactly the kind of grit that eventually helped make him a brilliant actor. Orson Welles once responded to a question asking if he had ever considered doing anything other than making movies. He said he hadn't, but if he had he was sure he'd have been successful. He said, "If you can make a movie, you can do anything."

Then there was another actor who was considered talented, except people said he couldn't go very far as he was a little on the short side. He lived on the Upper West Side, which was where I lived. We went up to his apartment one day and he said to me, "You know, when I got this apartment I walked in and it was just a little room and a kitchen, and I took it. Later, I went to hang up my coat and I opened the closet door, and there was a full bedroom and bath back there!" So from way back the sun was shining on Robert Redford.

One day my benefactor, Eleni Kiamos, who had introduced me to Lee Strasberg, recommended me to a director named Joan Horvath who was looking for a young actor to play in an Off-Off-Off-Broadway show. We were paid no money, and hardly anyone came to see it. The biggest audience we ever had was two people. And it was free! Joan, a serious and gifted young director, apologized to me about one cast member whom I hadn't met. He was to play the part of the Cockney neighbor. Joan explained that since no one was paid, sometimes you had to take what you could get. This fellow had been hanging around the theater, and even though he wasn't any good, he was available, Joan said. He turned out to be the future movie star James Coburn, and he was wonderful in the part.

The play was called *Don't Destroy Me*. I played the part of a young man who was very much attached to his phonograph. The playwright wrote that "the boy carries his Victrola around with him wherever he goes." I'm sure he meant a little portable Victrola, but the production didn't have any money and they couldn't go out and buy me a proper one to carry, so they looked around the theater and there was this huge fifty-pound thing in one of the rooms. It wasn't a floor model, but it was big. Joan said: "There, carry that." The play was running three hours and forty-five minutes, and I lugged it around through all my scenes saying: "Bob, you know, I just feel . . ."; "Mother, I just . . ."; "Frank, wait a second!" always lugging this thing. Joan insisted I carry it. It was exhausting; my arms felt like they were going to fall off. And I was never sure why my character refused to put it down. It didn't seem too important to the story.

Joan told me one night that the well-known actor Hume Cronyn had seen the show and said I was going to be very good once I got over my problem. I immediately asked, "What is my problem?" Joan didn't know and, amazingly, hadn't asked, so I never found out what he meant. I thought about it a long time since I was quite willing to go after any problem—the way I talked, the way I walked, the way I looked, the way I stood. Finally, I decided I had so many problems I couldn't possibly figure out which one he was referring to. So I forgot about it.

The strangest experience during the play was when the agent for the playwright, who lived in England, came to see the dress rehearsal prior to opening. The next day, Joan told us that he had committed suicide. We thought it was a bad joke, but she was serious: He had. It shocked all of us. We were assured that it had nothing to do with our performances, and we continued . . . somewhat shaken.

Astonishingly, the show eventually was reviewed by *Show Business*, one of the trade papers in New York, and the reviewer referred to me as "highly sympathetic." He didn't say I was good, but that I was "highly sympathetic." I figured he felt sorry for me lugging around the huge Victrola. You had to feel a little sorry for anyone carrying that thing. I cut the review out of the paper and ran around the city to all the offices where I'd left my picture, and said: "This is the review I got from *Show Business* that said . . ." But nobody wanted to read it, nobody cared.

One day, after running all over the city with this little clipping in my hand for about a month, I entered an office where the agent I wanted to see was leaving. And as he walked up the street, I said, "Could I just walk with you?"

"All right, all right!" he said with annoyance.

"I've been in this play, and they referred to me as 'highly sympathetic.' See, it's right there!"

He grabbed the clipping, looking more irritated. But he read it. "Yes, it does say you're 'highly sympathetic.' Right. Okay, stop and see me next week," he said, just to get rid of me.

"Stop and see me next week!" Well, that's the first time anyone had said that. So the next week I stopped and saw him. And the week after. And the week after. And the week after. And the month after. And the month after. And after about four months of stopping and seeing him, he picked up a phone one day while I was there and was probably thinking, Let me get this kid an audition for something and get him out of here. On the phone, he said, "I've got a young actor here who really hasn't done much, but he seems very much like an actual person. You might want to meet him." He got me an audition for *The Armstrong Circle Theater*, which was a live hour television show in New York. The show was to tell the story of the *Nautilus*, the first nuclear submarine to go under the North Pole. I was to read for the part of a young officer. I knew it was a nice-sized part. I went over to the office of Talent Associates, a company that David Susskind was running. There must have been about thirty-five young actors in the waiting room to read for this part. I sat down and waited for my turn. They gave me a piece of paper with a scene on it. It really didn't reveal anything about the character. I looked over to my left, and sitting next to me studying the speech on his piece of paper was about the best-looking human I'd ever seen in my life. It was the twenty-one-year-old Warren Beatty.

Eventually, my name was called, and I went in for the reading. The director, the producer, and the casting director were sitting in a tiny little room. I was so nervous that I gave an extremely mediocre reading. They said, "Thank you very much," and I got up. Somehow, I couldn't get out the door. They were all staring at me, wondering why I wasn't gone. It wasn't one of those things where you *kind of* can't open the door: I *really* couldn't open the door. I muttered apologies. I worked on the door for some time as they continued to stare at me, transfixed, as though they couldn't believe the various kinds of ineptness I had displayed in such a short time. Finally, after one of the longest fifteen-second periods of my life, apologizing all the way—"I'm terribly sorry, I can't seem to . . ."—I got out.

I went home, and the next day the agent called to say I'd gotten the part. I was amazed. The agent was *really* amazed. I got the script and read it, and saw why I got the role: I was to play the part of Phelps, a guy who can't do anything right.

You'll Make a Fool Out of the United States Navy

My brother later told me that a lot of people who had always thought I was crazy to go into show business sat up and took note when it was announced in the Pittsburgh papers that I was going to be on a live one-hour network television show. I was kind of sitting up myself.

There were ten days of rehearsal, and I seemed to be getting through it okay. It was a big show, with a lot of people in the cast, and not too much attention was being paid to me—which I considered a good sign.

Time passed, and now it was the day of the show. At ten P.M. it was going on the air, and an announcer would say: "Live, from New York, it's *The Armstrong Circle Theater*." It was live! The most experienced people in the world could hyperventilate when they said that. People were about to see it *live*! Millions of people all over the country! And my sole New York experience was *Don't Destroy Me*, where the largest audience had been two people. I was petrified.

A half hour before the show, we were in the studio anxiously standing around the cameras when the director, Bill Corrigan, a slim, tightly wound fellow who had pretty much ignored me until now, came over, took me aside, and said: "If you do what you've been doing you're going to make a complete fool of yourself. Not only of yourself, but of the whole company here. Not only the whole company, but the United States Navy.

"The *Navy*?"

"The Navy."

"Why?"

"You're coming off stupid."

Now, he hadn't said anything before about me coming off stupid, so I figured maybe he was feeling the tension of the moment and striking out at the lowest, or youngest, member of the company—a quality I was to see other directors display later. Or maybe—since I definitely was feeling the tension of the moment—I *had* suddenly started to come off stupid. I was really upset, because I thought I was coming off like myself.

Bill Corrigan walked away without saying anything else, leaving me standing there. It was about fifteen minutes until we were on—live—across the country, where my disgrace of the Navy was going to take place. What tiny little bit of confidence I had was shattered. I felt he hated me. Maybe they all did, and in fifteen minutes everyone across the country would get a chance to see how bad or stupid—or both—I was. Of course, everyone across the country included my family and friends in Pittsburgh, who were anxiously awaiting this event. I really didn't have any idea what to do. At the moment it would have been good to stop shaking . . . which I couldn't.

Suddenly, over the public-address system in the studio, a voice announced that all members of the crew of the ship (which included me) should assemble in a room. They wanted to rehearse a sequence where we were supposed to be laughing heartily at something one of the officers was saying to amuse us. Evidently, they felt that the hearty laughing called for just wasn't hearty enough in rehearsal. I was beginning to learn that genuine laughing was a lot harder to do than crying. Crying, I think I could have come up with. Laughing, after all these years, is still tough. And at that moment, genuine laughing seemed impossible. But there was this assistant director trying to get about fifteen of us to laugh our heads off: "Let's hear it!"

"Ha-ha-ha-ha-ha."

"Again!"

"Ha-ha-ha-ha-ha."

"Again!"

"Ha-ha-ha-ha-ha." All the while thinking, Please, God, get me through this!"

"Again!"

I slapped a big grin on my face and gave a loud, if not real: "Ha-ha-ha-ha-ha."

"Okay," he said, more in resignation than in approval.

That passed, I desperately searched my mind trying to think of a way I might not come off stupid or frightened. I hadn't as yet come up with anything when a voice from the PA system filled the studio: "Live, from New York, it's *The Armstrong Circle Theater*." We were on.

I first appeared in one of the early scenes, where I was sitting down talking to a lieutenant. I heard my heart pounding with excitement and fear, and I thought, God, the microphones are very sensitive, and people all across the country are going to hear my heart, think there's something wrong with their sound, and adjust their television sets.

The camera started to move toward me. Cameras were bigger then, so they had three guys pushing this monster toward me and the lieutenant. I could feel them coming in for a close-up, but a close-up in those days . . . well, they really did come in very close. I thought the thing was going to knock me over. The people at home would see a guy get knocked over by a television camera. It was so close that if I turned my head I would hit my nose against your screen. I got through the show somehow, the pounding of my heart just a tiny bit quieter as the program went on.

After the show, I called the agent to see what he thought. He said, "Very good for a first time."

I said, in my never-ending effort to improve, "Do you have any criticism?"

He said, "Yeah. You had your mouth open all through the show."

Well, I'd asked.

Later, I saw the show on a kinescope, and I did have my mouth open a lot, probably in an effort to breathe. I also felt, mostly because of my open mouth, that I did come off kind of stupid. I hope not too many people noticed.

The appearance on *The Armstrong Circle Theater* was most helpful as a credit on my résumé, but it certainly couldn't in any way be considered a breakthrough. As Walter Matthau once said, "All you need are fifty good breaks." I had one.

A Foot in the Door and Doors Closing on My Foot

I started to get some meetings. I had been on the outside so long that having people actually interested in meeting me felt strange. It was like being invited to a party and wondering if someone had made a mistake. At first, having the meetings was, oddly, more debilitating than not having them.

There was a new Broadway play by William Inge, who wrote *Picnic* and *Bus Stop*, among others, and Warren Beatty was to make his debut as the lead. It was called *A Loss of Roses*, and I met with the casting director to see about being Warren's understudy. I told him everything he wanted to know, and he said he'd get back to me. He called me into another meeting and said, "Well, you're certainly good-looking enough to be Warren's understudy," but nothing happened. Not only did I not get the job, I didn't even get an audition, which would have taken a lot less time than either of the two meetings. I remember wondering at the time, Am I missing something? Why wouldn't they just let me audition? It's only all these years later that I wonder if, when the man I met with said I was good-looking enough to be Warren's understudy, that was a cue. Was I supposed to say, "Well, you're pretty cute yourself"? I have no idea. But there was no audition.

ABC was planning a new television series about an American

Indian detective called *Hawk*. Hawk was a man who wore a knife strapped to his leg under his pants, and if he suspected you were a bad guy, he might suddenly leap into the air and kick you in your face.

I was sent to a meeting to be considered for a part in this new *Hawk* series—what part, I didn't know. The people behind the show wanted to look me over. There was also a network executive there. I walked into the room, was introduced all around, and recognized some important television-executive names. We chatted a while—"What have you been up to lately?" et cetera—as they looked me over. That "What have you been up to lately?" question was always a rough one for young actors, because we'd never been up to anything much. So we had to give these people answers and try not to see their looks of barely concealed boredom. They wanted to hear if we had done anything (which put somebody else's seal of approval on us), and they wanted to see us talk as people (not acting) to make sure we weren't nuts or anything. I always felt executives regarded unknown actors as a kind of dangerous breed, these people who always seemed to want something from them—like a job.

They told me about the American Indian detective, Hawk, and the knife and the kicking. I nodded as though it sounded great to me. (In fact, as a teenager, sometimes while walking through rough areas I did have a knife, never used, strapped under my pants leg—but an American Indian who kicks you in the face?) Then they told me about this woman Hawk has a relationship with. I nodded again, trying to seem suitably impressed. Then they told me about another woman, a nurse, who Hawk also has a kind of relationship with. I nodded again. I'd been there about ten minutes. There was a pause, as though I was expected to do something other than nod and look impressed. I said, "You've now described to me three parts: the Indian, Hawk, and two women—three parts I couldn't possibly, even remotely, be right for. Why are you talking to me?" I said it nicely, maybe even with a little attempt at humor. But there was a long, mildly offended silence in the room. Finally, someone said: "What do you think an American Indian looks like?" My God, I thought, they're talking to me about being Hawk! Me, an American Indian who kicks bad guys in the face!

This was about twenty-five years ago, but I've never ever

looked like an Indian. On the other hand, I thought, This is a lead in an hour-long network series they're talking about here! "What does an American Indian look like?" I asked. "Like me!" I said. "Exactly like me!" But I think I had paused too long before I said I thought I was their Indian, because they looked at me strangely. Everybody thanked me for coming in. I thanked them for having me in. Everyone said how nice it was to meet me. I said how nice it was to meet everyone.

As I walked through the waiting room to the elevators, I saw the next fellow waiting to go in. He had black hair, was dark-complexioned, wiry, tough, intense. That's Hawk, I thought. And it was. Burt Reynolds.

Since I had more than enough free time on my hands, I started to make some modest efforts—I think mostly for my own enjoyment—at comedy writing. I wrote a comedy monologue about Tarzan in truth being Jewish. I wrote that his real name was "Tarzan Mark David Feinberg," probably in unconscious tribute to a boy I knew at Fulton Grammar School named Morton Feinberg.

When we were all about nine, Morton Feinberg showed up one day with a little box in which he said he had a German finger. (This was 1944, while we were at war with Germany.) He opened the box, and there was a finger with some blood around it. Even at that age, I finally figured out that it was Morton Feinberg's finger, which he had inserted into a hole in the box as he held it. The blood, of course, was ketchup.

I was with the William Morris Agency at the time, so I asked who represented people who wrote special material. (Big agencies represent every possible way anyone can make a dime in show business.) They gave me a name, and I made an appointment right away.

Initially, the agent wanted me to send him my Tarzan monologue, but I had performed it myself for a friend and he had laughed so hard I didn't want to take a chance on someone just reading it. I showed up on the day of the appointment, and a dour man with a pasty face, in a little office without a window, half stood up and reached across his desk to shake my hand. He quickly said: "Okay, let's hear it."

I started: "Very few people know this, but Tarzan, King of

the Apes, is Jewish. His real name is Tarzan Mark David Feinberg."

The agent just stared. My heart sank. That opening line was about as good as it got. I had no choice but to press ahead. The whole thing only took about ninety seconds, but it felt like a month. Once, he started to respond, and my spirits soared until I realized he had just cleared his throat. When it was mercifully over, he said: "I don't think it's funny."

I couldn't seem to stop myself from asking: "Not at all?"

"Not at all."

I think that one experience set back any writing aspirations I had for a long time. I was, of course, too inexperienced to even consider the fact that in order for something to get laughs, yes, it helps if it's funny, but it's also necessary for the listener to have a sense of humor. That fact didn't occur to me for years. Many people who flaunt the fact that they didn't enjoy a comedy that made other people laugh are often saying more about themselves than about the comedy. Of course, everyone is entitled to his own opinion, but to state that opinion as though it defines the objective truth about the value of comedy is narcissistic at best. In any case, my Tarzan-was-Jewish monologue went into a drawer and hasn't seen the light of day since.

Eventually, I got a small nonspeaking part in a pilot for a proposed new series called *Man Against Crime*, starring Darren McGavin. I was to appear in a sequence that showed two gangs of young hoodlums playing a game called Chicken. The scene called for two hot-rod cars, each loaded with young kids, to start at opposite ends of a stretch of road, about two hundred yards apart. At the signal, they were supposed to race toward each other at a speed of about sixty miles an hour, and the one who swerved away first was "Chicken." (As though if you waited as long as possible, you were brave. Not dumb—brave.)

When I read the script I wondered how they actually filmed something like that. I assumed it was trick photography of some kind. But when I reported for work that day in a large, open field, I learned it was no trick. The director, Richard Baer, a craggy-looking character whose face I vividly remember, came over and instructed the drivers of the two cars where to go at opposite ends of the stretch of road.

"Tommy, you come racing at Billy at sixty miles an hour, and at the last possible second you turn to your left—that's Billy's right. And Billy, you do the same, turning to your left—that's Tommy's right. Got that?" Billy and Tommy nodded. "Okay, let's do it." And he walked away.

As soon as he was out of earshot, I raced over to Tommy and Billy. "You guys got that?"

"Yeah," they said.

I went right on. "It's your left—that's his right."

"Yeah, yeah, we got it," they said, and walked to their hot rods.

Both cars were open convertibles, and they had me sitting up on top of the backseat of one. The cars took their positions, gunned their motors, and at the signal raced toward each other as fast as they could go. At the last possible second, Tommy and Billy did exactly as ordered and just missed a head-on collision. Not exactly as ordered—I went flying out of the car and landed in a clump of bushes.

The director liked it, but wanted to do it again. Someone vaguely called out from the distance, "Is he okay?" referring to me. When I stood up, they said, "Let's do it again." We did it a few more times, and I decided to make sure I stayed in the car.

I went home that night bruised, and just beginning to realize something else they meant when they said how tough show business can be. If you're not careful, it could literally kill you. I'm sure there are elements of this elsewhere, but in television and, particularly, movies you can't help but be aware that "getting the shot" is everything. Maybe it's because the people making these movies feel so much pressure from above to get it on film that safety considerations are not always what they should be. As the years went by, I became more aware of this as I heard stories of people regularly being injured and sometimes even killed on films.

Many years later, when I made a movie in Acapulco with Farrah Fawcett called *Sunburn*, I had a run-in with the director, Dick Sarafian—a massive, scowling man with a surprisingly warm smile—over the safety issue. In one scene, Farrah and I were to crawl across the floor of our bedroom while, from outside, the bad guys were machine-gunning the whole place. All the explosives were rigged to go off as we crawled. I asked a lot of questions about the safety precautions, as Dick Sarafian's smile decreased while his scowl increased.

Then, because Farrah was bare-legged and it really hurt her knees to crawl quickly across the hard marble floor—mine too, for that matter—I wondered if they could put mats down for us. Dick Sarafian said, "Come on, it's in the nature of the shot. Let's do it." I wasn't exactly sure what "it's in the nature of the shot" meant, but the tension between Dick and me had already approached the unworkable level, so we did the shot, after having been assured by everyone that there was no risk.

After all the explosions, Farrah ended up bleeding in about thirty places on her legs from flying particles of something. Luckily, they were superficial cuts. Everyone looked sheepish as they tended to Farrah. Dick chewed out his explosives experts and then muttered apologies to me and the bleeding but non-complaining Farrah, who, by the way, is one of the nicest people I've ever worked with.

Woodstock

As a result of an audition for a jolly, cherubic man by the name of Arnold Tager, who was directing all the plays for the Woodstock Theater in New York, I became the leading actor at the playhouse for the summer season—meaning I would play the leading role each week, whenever suitable . . . which was often. It was 1960, I was twenty-five, and it was a real turning point for me.

This was my third summer-theater experience. The first two were nonunion theaters, and I had played smaller, supporting roles, rarely leads. Here it was mostly leads, a union theater, and a much larger audience. Where before I had been appearing in front of one or two hundred people, now it was more like five hundred people. The stakes had been raised.

I played all kinds of roles, from serious American drama to English farce. One evening we were all onstage toward the end of our first performance of *Death of a Salesman*, and the audience was actually noisy out front. It seemed they weren't even watching the play or listening to us, but chatting with each other. I couldn't imagine an audience acting that way. It was only at the curtain call that I realized all that "noise" was the whole audience sobbing, opening and shutting purses for tissues, and blowing their noses. I don't even think our production was too good, but that was the power of the play.

Even though it was almost thirty years ago, I still smile when I remember one event from that season that said something about strange career planning. There was an actor at Woodstock named Simm Landres, who had been in the hit musical *The Threepenny Opera* in New York. He left a good part in that show to come to Woodstock to play a couple of supporting roles. After the season at Woodstock ended, he would be back in New York—unemployed. When I pointed all this out to Sim and asked him why he would do that, he looked at me as though the question had never occurred to him. After a long pause, he announced, in a stunning moment of self-revelation, "Because I'm a *shmuuuuck!*"

The tall nice-looking fellow who was working in the parking lot that summer was Chevy Chase.

I was in eight plays in eight weeks. It was invaluable experience. It became evident that I was being received enthusiastically, and my confidence really began to grow.

My agent at the time came up and was full of praise for my performance as Biff, one of the sons in *Death of a Salesman*. Arnold Tager, the director, said to him: "You should see him in a comedy." It was the first time anyone had made that general observation. In time, people would see me only in comedies, and eventually find it impossible to imagine me in *Death of a Salesman* or anything serious.

The praise that season meant everything. Whatever putdowns I'd heard in the past started to fade with the combination of support from Lee Strasberg in the class and appearing week after week in front of a live, paying audience that was happy to see me.

Casting Directors

Around this time I found work on the CBS Sunday morning shows. They would do half-hour dramas with moral overtones. *Camera 3, Look Up and Live,* and *Lamp Unto My Feet* were a few of the programs. A number of actors found work here, because the casts were sometimes large. One of these shows had a standing policy of hiring more people than they ended up needing. It was only after a first reading of the script that the producer and director would decide how to cut it all down. Rather than paying salaries to the dismissed actors, they gave each of them twenty-five dollars for their trouble. Those who were fired were naturally upset. The only explanation was: "You won't be needed."

Although I hadn't been fired, I went to the show's casting director, a heavyset woman who was always sweet to me. She had given me more work than anyone else in New York. I asked her what was going on. She explained to me that this was common practice at the show. I said I thought it was against union regulations, and it certainly made a lot of people feel bad. The casting director countered with: "What's it got to do with you? You're not being let go."

I said I didn't like to see this, and unless they stopped the practice, I was going to notify the union.

Her expression clouded over as she glared at me. She finally said: "If you do that, you'll never work on these shows again."

I said I'd have to live with that.

They rehired the people they had let go. We did the show, and I never worked on the Sunday morning CBS shows again. It was particularly ironic because of the high moral messages most of these shows were delivering.

Twenty-five years later my name came up in a conversation between a mutual friend and that casting director who said she really didn't like me. When our friend inquired why, it was explained that a group of us had once gone to an amusement park, and the casting director's brother had lent me a sweater that I'd never returned. I vaguely remembered an amusement park, but not the casting director's brother or his sweater. Boy, that sweater theft must have been gnawing at her all these years.

Casting directors, to actors on the "outside"—which represents 99.5 percent of the acting population—seem to have the power to open the gates of heaven. All of us labored over how to prepare for meetings with them: how to dress; how to behave. Should you come on strong, or would that be off-putting? Should you just lie back and be yourself? Maybe that wouldn't be interesting enough. Then afterward: What didn't they like? It was all pretty personal—my face, my voice, my clothes? You could believe anything, since you weren't wanted and the reason was hardly ever clear. It was like walking through a minefield for the actors; and, for the most part, for the casting people, meeting new people was a necessary nuisance of the job—and we felt it.

Once I had an appointment to meet one of the biggest casting directors in the city, one who cast movies and everything. I waited in an office full of actors who also had appointments to see her. We were told by the secretary that she was "running late." First, she was running one hour late, then she was running two hours late. Occasionally, an actor would go in, and that would give us all hope. Finally, after running three hours late, everyone had gone in but me. Then the casting woman finally came out of the office, walked right over to me—and past me to the elevator, whose door was opening. She got on and left. The secretary said (without any sense of apology), "She's running late to a dinner."

If the casting director doesn't approve of you, no one else will ever see you. In fairness, they are besieged by everyone for appointments, so they probably get desensitized to the needs of the actor to be employed. The ones who rise above that feeling of disliking actors are special, and even they run the risk of getting heady with their power.

Through quite a removed relationship in my family, I was able to get a meeting with one of the most powerful casting women in New York. It went extraordinarily well. I had still done relatively nothing, but she seemed to be impressed with all the studying I'd done and with what she felt was a serious attitude. She told me that very often she met actors who didn't justify her interest, but I certainly did, and she would be in touch with me shortly with a small role on one of the highly prestigious shows she cast. She had the power to give me a small role on her own (which put her in a very elite group), and asked if a small one would be okay with me, saying if that worked out, larger ones would follow. I said the whole thing sounded just dandy, and floated out of her office. It felt like an enormous breakthrough since it had been months since I'd worked, and nothing was in sight. The interest of a casting director with this kind of power could mean everything.

Walking on my cloud out to the elevator, I ran into a young woman I had known as a fellow student in Uta's classes. It turned out that she was now working as an assistant to the casting direc-tor. I told her of the meeting, and said how pleased I was. She looked at me and said she remembered me from class as someone who took a lot of pauses in my scenes. I had no idea what she was talking about, but instantly worried that she would tell her boss, "You don't want this guy, he takes too many pauses." I quickly said that class and television were two different things as far as I was concerned, and that there certainly would be no "pause" is-sue on TV. She looked at me skeptically, and we said good-bye as my heart sank.

All the way home on the subway, my mind was jumping back and forth between those pauses and whether she would tell her boss that if they hired me they'd never be able to fit their hour show into an hour. A couple of weeks went by, and I didn't hear from the casting director, even though I continued to jump for the phone every time it rang, which was seldom. I decided to call my former classmate and ask her to lunch to see if I could straighten out this "pause" issue, if, in fact, there was one. She took the call and said she was busy now and couldn't go out for lunch. I said, "How about next week?" She said she didn't ever eat lunch. I got the message and said good-bye.

Days and weeks went by. Finally it was clear that I wouldn't ever be hearing from the casting director. I wrote her the most tentative letter, reminding her of our conversation, asking her if there was anything I could do to change her mind. I really believed her assistant had spoken to her about all those pauses I couldn't remember taking in class, and that's what was doing me in. It never entered my mind at the time, because it was all so crucially important—for me, anyway—that maybe, as busy as she was, she just simply forgot about me.

She must have taken offense at my questioning her inaction because a few months later an agent I knew mentioned my name to her, and she said, "If I hear he's even in the building I'm going to have him thrown out." When the agent asked her what I'd done to elicit such a strong reaction, she said, "He just really rubs me the wrong way." (Not mentioning, of course, my terrible sin of calling her attention to a promise not kept.) At least she didn't say I stole her brother's sweater.

Years later, after I became recognized, our paths crossed, and, of course, she couldn't have been friendlier to me. As in any other profession, people find it easier to be nice to people who are successful. Too bad.

Bullies

I began to get little parts here and there, and even played a leading role in a segment of a weekly half-hour television drama that appeared every Saturday afternoon called *My True Story*. I don't think the stories were true; they just thought it was a catchy title. There was a different story every week, and I did mine in about two days. At that time I was also working at the post office five days a week. One day another fellow and I were stacking *TV Guides*, and I showed him my name listed as the lead on *My True Story* that week.

He said, "Hey, that guy has the same name you do."

I said, "No, that's me."

He didn't believe me for a second, and said, "If that's you, what are you doing here?" and walked away.

I thought about it. I was making a little money acting, but not enough to live on and pay for classes. I had moved up in the world. I was now living in a small apartment and no longer shared a bathroom with my neighbors. The place had two rooms that were so tiny, if two people were sitting in one of them and one stood, you felt like you were on trial.

Working full-time, I had very limited opportunity to try to find work as an actor. So after five years of regular jobs—some part-time, some not—I quit the post office. I was going to try to spend less money, if that was possible, and try harder to find acting jobs. Besides, no one had ridiculed my acting for a long while. I didn't know that was soon to change.

I auditioned for the part of a hoodlum in a two-hour play that was being done on the educational channel. It was about the first day of integration in a Southern town. Written by Reginald Rose, the acclaimed creator of *The Defenders* television series, it was called *Black Monday*. After I finished reading for the role, the director, Ralph Nelson, asked me to do it again and to smile as I did it. This was an old villain tradition (smiling through meanness), and by following his direction I got the part. It was such a prestigious production that I would be taken a little more seriously as an actor just by being in it. Robert Redford and James Caan were also playing young troublemakers. Ralph Nelson, who—on that show, anyway—seemed like a real bully (a not uncommon directorial trait, I was to learn), heaped abuse on Jimmy Caan from a booth high above the studio through a PA system for all to hear. If Jimmy had believed all the awful things Ralph Nelson yelled at him, he would have quit right there. Happily, he didn't. While Ralph Nelson went on to have a fine career, Jimmy became far more in demand than Ralph, who, in effect, had been telling him to get out of the business.

In my big scene I was supposed to come in and threaten the owner of a store, played by the great character actor Pat Hingle. Pat Hingle was appearing after a long layoff due to a terrible fall down an elevator shaft. He had lost a finger, and was able to walk only with crutches. And I was supposed to push him around. I did the scene a couple of times, kind of gingerly shoving Pat. Ralph Nelson, again shouting over the PA system for all to hear, yelled: "If you do it like that you're going to come off as a sissy." No reference was made to Pat's injury. I doubt I did anything stronger to Pat on the next try, but there must have been something scary in my eyes because Ralph liked it. He might have liked it less had he known that scary look was coming from the rage I felt toward him. I learned a valuable acting lesson that day: Sometimes what's happening right on the set is what you need to allow yourself to feel to play the scene.

I haven't run into too many bullying directors over the years, but the few that I have, unhappily, stay in the mind. There was one who announced early on, "Don't take me too seriously when I scream and yell; it doesn't really mean anything," and then proceeded to scream regularly—never at me, mostly at little children. He was fired very quickly. He went on to another project, screamed some more, was fired again, and hasn't been directing or screaming much since—professionally anyway.

Then there was the theater director who would begin to shout abuse at us when anyone came into the theater during early rehearsals—when things are not exactly sailing. He wanted to disassociate himself from what was onstage, lest any influential observer think he approved and fire him.

Sometimes a director bullies not by shouting but by his choice of words. One director, when he wanted more energy from me, instead of saying "Give me more energy," said, "You're coming off funereal."

The worst experience I've ever had with a director, oddly enough, came from a man who never screamed, wasn't a bully, and, in fact, was a very sweet guy. The problem was he directed too much. "Turn at the door and smile. Do that thing you do with your eyes, I love that."

"What do you mean, what thing?"

"You know, that thing you do." "Turn your head on this line." "Reach out on this word." "Stress this word." "Say it like this." And what felt like about sixty-seven thousand other directions. This guy was reducing good actors to good puppets. Ironically, he's very successful. But some other actors and I would run into the great beyond if he called. The position of director only came into existence in the twentieth century. This guy is making up for all that lack of direction in past centuries.

There is also the suddenly silent, withdrawn type of director. An eyeline (line of vision) is what an actor sees when he's working. Generally, you want to see the other actors in the scene or the mountain in the distance, et cetera. What you don't want to see, but inevitably have to, are members of the film crew (who must be there) standing very close all around—behind cameras, holding microphones, pulling cable, and so on. Often, someone is directly in the actor's eyeline. You look into the leading lady's eyes, and you see her eyes and sometimes someone else's eyes looking into your eyes. That someone else is usually the director. Once you mention that to a director or anyone else, they just find another position.

Only once in all these years when I mentioned it to a director did I encounter the suddenly silent, withdrawn type. I went over and asked if I had offended him. He said not really, it just reminded him of a time in his past when an actress had asked him to move out of her eyeline. When he responded, "Where would you like me to go?" she said, "Home." Once I explained that I just wanted him out of my eyeline and not home, we were fine.

Another suddenly silent, withdrawn move occurred on a project after an actress asked the director about a move he wanted her to make on a particular line: It seemed awkward. This director walked off the set and pouted in a corner. I went over to him and asked him what was wrong. He said it was the only time in his long career that anyone had ever questioned a direction of his. As I stared at him, he reeled off a list of international stars who had never questioned him. I said, "I find it very hard to believe, in twenty-five years of direction, no one has ever questioned one of your ideas." He peered at me blankly for a moment, I think realizing the ridiculousness of what he was saying. He returned and directed the scene.

The single most withdrawn move I ever saw was when a director called a meeting to discuss a scene with a few of us and fell sound asleep five minutes into his own opening statement. It didn't occur to me at the time, but I think that was my one and only exposure to a director on drugs. I assumed he was just tired—very, very easy to believe. Directors work harder than everyone else: about ninety to a hundred hours a week. So, in my heart, even when they act weird, I forgive them almost anything.

It was 1960. I had now been at it for five years. I was starting to see that all those in charge who had made themselves so unavailable and who were pushing everyone around weren't so perfect. Maybe *they* were the jerks, not us, as they would have liked us to feel. My confidence was helped by that understanding. A lot more seemed possible.

Breakthrough:
I Don't Accept an Apology
from Anthony Quinn

After about six years of living in New York, I got my first audition for a Broadway show. There were so many thousands of actors vying to be seen that most of my fellow students never got that opportunity. All I knew about the part was that they had been looking for someone for a long time.

As I was heading to my audition, I glanced at the address of the theater and the name of the play. I suddenly stopped walking. A very strong sense came over me that said: I'm in this play. It was as though it were already decided. I'd never felt that way before or since.

When I got to the stage door of the theater I was given a piece of paper with a long speech on it. That was it. Again, no description of the character, no indication of what the whole thing was about. I was told to wait my turn in an alleyway behind the theater. There were about twenty young fellows back there pacing around, muttering the lines, trying not to bump into each other as we attempted to figure out how to perform this speech.

When my name was called I entered the stage and decided, Well, I've got nothing to lose, and I really did something bold with the speech. After I'd finished, there was quiet from the dark theater; and then, after a moment, three men literally trotted up to the stage. I later learned they were the playwright, Sidney

Michaels; Neil Hartley, the elegant production supervisor for the famous producer David Merrick; and the acclaimed English director Peter Glenville.

"What have you done?" Peter Glenville asked me.

My answer didn't impress anyone.

"Do you appear in nightclubs?" Sidney Michaels asked.

"No," I said.

They stared at me for a moment. They then said that they felt I had shown a lot of command and ability, and that it was hard to understand where it had all come from. It had come from nine years of study, summer stock, and television, and while it may not have sounded all that impressive, it had gotten me to that moment on that stage. They, almost as a group, then said to me: "Would you like to be in this play?"

"Yes. Yes, I would," I said.

"Well, all right. We'd like you to be in this play. Tell your agent we're going to call right away."

"Okay."

It was so unreal. I've never, before or since, seen a situation where that decision was made in the middle of an audition day. No matter how well someone auditions, the attitude is always, Let's wait and see if someone even better comes along later. But they told me right then and there, and enthusiastically too. I was shocked.

I left the theater and ran next door to a drugstore, where I called the agent at William Morris. I said: "That . . . that . . . that part you sent me up for? They want me."

"Oh," she said casually, "that's nice." It's a very big agency; she barely remembered who I was.

I said, "What can you tell me about it?"

She said, "Well, it's a play called *Tchin Tchin*."

"Uh-huh. Well, who's in it?"

"Well, it will be Anthony Quinn, Margaret Leighton, and you."

I said, "Oh?" my voice rising an octave with excitement. "Anthony Quinn, Margaret Leighton, and me. Oh," I said, my voice rising higher. "Well, that seems like a pretty big thing."

"It is," she said. "I'm very happy for you," her voice betraying no hint of happiness.

But she had gotten me the audition and I did have the part, and at that moment I'd have given her a party.

As I lay in bed that night I remembered the feeling of certainty of being in the play that I had had on the way to the audition. For those who believe in these things, and I do, it was my one and only precognition.

Anthony Quinn was at the peak of his international stardom, and Margaret Leighton was a brilliant English stage and screen star. I was to play her son. I had come from nowhere to a wonderful part in what promised to be one of the biggest Broadway shows of the season. It was originally a French play and had run four years in Paris. I was ecstatic. After basically beating my head against the wall in terms of employment for six years, I had finally gotten my first audition for a Broadway show and got the part, and it turned out to be this. Of course, if the opportunity had come much earlier I might not have been ready for it.

After about three weeks of rehearsal, we went to Boston for the out-of-town tryout prior to the New York opening. All seemed to be going well. One night I was walking home from the theater, which was situated in a pretty rough section of downtown Boston. Living in New York, I had developed a tendency to walk down the street at night with my right hand by my side, held tightly in a fist. Just in case. Nothing had ever happened, and I was determined to break the habit. Coming home from the theater that night, I found myself cupping my hand again, realizing what a rough section I was in. I looked up the street and saw a menacing-looking sailor about fifty feet away coming toward me. I thought, Okay, here's a chance to break this habit. Unclench your fist, and don't even try to watch the guy out of the corner of your eye as he passes. So I relaxed and looked straight ahead, and he knocked me down with a very hard punch to the stomach. Other than that, all went well in Boston.

Just prior to the Broadway opening, I became aware of a show-business phenomenon. We were in the middle of the Cuban missile crisis and Russian ships were about to be intercepted on the high seas by American ships. Television, newspapers, and radio all felt that we might be on the brink of war, certainly closer than we'd been since World War II. The whole nation seemed to be in a state of apprehension. Amazingly, the company and management of the play seemed oblivious to all of this. A Broadway show was about to open, and that seemed to be war enough.

Eventually the Russian ships turned around and went home, and we opened in New York and immediately became a standing-room-only hit. I was received enthusiastically by the critics and the audience. I had broken out of the ranks of the completely unknown.

The day after the opening, Anthony Quinn came to my dressing room, looked at me quizzically for a moment, and said, "I was reading the program, and I see last night was your Broadway debut."

I said, "Yes, it was."

He said very kindly, "I didn't realize that. I would have gotten you something special as an opening-night gift if I had known that."

I said, "Thanks, but it wasn't important."

He looked at me and said, "Let me ask you something. You were cool as a cucumber out there. That's pretty unusual for a Broadway debut. Why do you think that was?"

I hadn't thought about it, but I realized he was right. I said, "Well, everyone's coming to see you and Miss Leighton, and nobody knows who I am or even that I'm in the play. I guess that takes the pressure off."

He thought about what I'd said, nodded, and then said, "Well, you were really relaxed out there and you were real good." He shook my hand, and left.

After he was gone, I wondered about all that relaxation some more. Then I remembered a seemingly little thing that had happened on my way from my dressing room to the stage for my first major scene, which began the second act. Neil Hartley, the production supervisor, stopped me on my way to the stage and said, "The first act really didn't go all that well. It's up to you to get the second act off and running." In other words, he challenged me. He gave me an added incentive to make my big scene as good as possible, and in doing so reduced my nervousness. Of course, the challenge could just as easily have increased my nervousness. Happily, it didn't.

By the time I had auditioned for *Tchin Tchin* I was not an especially nervous actor any longer—relative to how I had been.

Of course, I had benefited tremendously from more experience, but there were certainly thousands of actors with a lot more experience than I had who always had a problem with nerves. I had worked on this. I had made a conscious effort to develop what eventually became a strong point of view. It was simply this: The audience and critics had their jobs to do, and I had mine. Their concentration went to their jobs, my concentration had to go to mine. This really prohibited worrying about what they were thinking. It's easier said than done, but just thinking about that principle helped me. When Neil Hartley threw the responsibility to me to get the second act off and running, he was, without realizing it, giving me added impetus to what was already my feeling that my job was to take care of my performance—period. It was up to someone else to do the judging. It was a long distance from Sir Francis Chesney in *Charley's Aunt*, where I reviewed myself after every line.

A couple of weeks after the play became a hit, and since I'd gotten such good reviews, I thought the producers might consider the possibility of giving me a raise since my take-home pay was $107 a week and I could barely meet my expenses. There were only three speaking roles in the play. Anthony Quinn and Margaret Leighton were each getting several thousand dollars a week, which they certainly deserved; and I was getting $140 a week before taxes. I spoke to Neil Hartley, and he said he would take it up with the general manager. Weeks went by, and when I didn't hear anything further, I assumed the answer was no. When I asked Neil if that was the case, he said the answer wasn't no at all.

"It wasn't?" I asked, surprised.

"No," he said. "Jack [the general manager] didn't answer at all, but just laughed."

Later, that same general manager became a producer and asked me to act in plays he was producing. I probably would have if I had really liked the projects, but I was never inclined to. I have always felt (later, as a producer myself) that the best deal you could make wouldn't be to get people as cheaply as possible, but to have everyone feel they were being treated fairly. It would serve you best for your own soul as well as for the present and future projects. Incidentally, my understudy for a while was the actor/director Richard Benjamin. I can't even imagine what they were paying him.

About a month into the run of the play, Bill Putch, the head of the Pittsburgh Playhouse School, attended a performance and came backstage afterward. He was full of praise, and then, suddenly, as he turned to leave, stared at me in surprise and said: "Well, that just goes to show you you can never be sure."

During the run of the play something extraordinary happened in the middle of the one big scene I had with Anthony Quinn. Quinn, who in rehearsal had thrown a chair from the stage halfway across the theater to punctuate a point he was making in an argument with the first director (whom Peter Glenville later replaced), stopped right in the middle of our big scene together, in front of a sold-out audience of over one thousand people, and suddenly screamed toward the audience: "WILL YOU SHUT UP!"

The audience and I were stunned, not sure what was going on. At the curtain call he stepped forward and apologized, explaining that he was referring to the two men who operated the special "follow" spotlights at the back of the balcony; he had apparently heard them chatting endlessly. I hadn't heard them. The audience reflexively applauded his apology.

Walking back to our dressing rooms after the show, Anthony Quinn turned and apologized to me. I didn't accept his apology. He was dumbfounded. He looked at me as if he wasn't sure if that was allowed. I told him his behavior and his apology were unacceptable. He didn't know what to say to that, and we went our separate ways.

I was outraged at what I thought was astonishing self-indulgence that so baffled the audience and me, it knocked all of us out of the story of the play. I saw him only at the theater, and to me he was a fellow actor who had behaved badly. A couple of days later I saw him walking up the street and thought to myself, My God, that's the international superstar Anthony Quinn, whose apology I didn't accept!

Margaret Leighton was also a striking figure. An unusually gracious, kind person, she resembled an extraordinarily beautiful bird, with her long, elegant neck. Miss Leighton was as reticent as Anthony Quinn, a real-life Zorba, was bold. All through the rehearsal period and the run of the play, Miss Leighton couldn't have been more flattering to me. But one day, about a week before we opened on Broadway, she approached me tentatively backstage. She had a look of real discomfort on her face when she said: "Charles, may I just offer one suggestion to you?" I could tell it was a criticism by Miss Leighton's uneasiness. I thought she was going to advise me to get out of the business. After much hesitation, she suggested I stand up a little straighter: a posture note. I think maybe in the English theater that's a bigger faux pas than it is in ours. She was so apologetic after she said it, it was as though she had called my mother a bad name.

I thanked her for the comment, and reassured her profusely that she hadn't hurt my feelings, but I was never able to improve my posture without concentrating on it while onstage, which is not a good thing to do when you're acting. It wasn't until much later, when I had a pinched nerve in my back and had to do exercises every day for years, that my posture improved dramatically because of strong back muscles. In fact, I went from six feet to six feet one over a two-year period. Unfortunately, I never saw Miss Leighton after that happened. I think she would have appreciated my new posture more than anyone I knew.

After one performance well into the run of the play, I was sitting in my dressing room on the third floor talking to a pretty redheaded girl, Ina Levine, whom I knew from Peabody High School. There was a knock on the door. I opened it, and an older man stood there, out of breath from the long climb to my dressing room.

He said, "I just want to tell you how much I enjoyed your performance."

I said, "Thank you." We nodded good-byes, and I turned back to Ina. After a moment, I stopped talking and said, "Excuse me."

I ran out the door and down two flights of steps until I caught up to the man on the first landing. I said, "I really appreciate your walking up three flights of steps."

He said, "Well, I thought you were very good. I enjoyed your performance."

"Thank you very much," I said.

It was Noël Coward.

After almost a year, the play closed. And despite the wonderful reception I'd gotten, I had no offer to do anything else. I later found that this was quite common, even sometimes for actors who had recently won an Academy Award. I got to thinking about that visit from Noël Coward and decided it might be a good idea to start to explore other possibilities in addition to acting. Like directing. I thought that if I offered myself as an unpaid assistant to Mr. Coward, who was about to direct a musical in New York, maybe it could happen, the price being right. So I called his representative, an attorney. He knew who I was, which really surprised me, and said, "Noël Coward is in Bermuda, but when he comes back I'll have him call you."

"Thank you," I said. I hung up, and my tension level, which was already pretty high from making the phone call, went higher, because from that point on, every time the phone rang I thought it might be Noël Coward.

"Hello? Oh, Bernie, I was expecting a call from Noël Coward."

"Hello? Oh, Stu. I don't want to tie up the line; I'm expecting Noël Coward."

It drove me so crazy that eventually I had to call his attorney and say, "Please tell Mr. Coward that I'm leaving town." I couldn't handle the tension. I just dropped the whole thing.

Now that I had told Noël Coward's office I was out of town, I could relax. But I still didn't have a job.

Things were different, though. While I didn't have work, I was now someone about whom you could say, "He played Margaret Leighton's son in *Tchin Tchin*." And everyone knew *Tchin Tchin*. I assumed it would be just a matter of time before someone wanted me again. I hoped not too much time.

By now, along with everything else, I had learned something invaluable: I had learned how to deal with rejection. After all, that's where I was most experienced.

Since it makes up such a large part of an actor's life, I think rejection is worth considering more specifically. For years on end, when the message is essentially "Go away," you either learn to deal with it or you go away. While there may be many actors who might well take that advice, there are many others who shouldn't. But they also go away, because they are unable to stand the ultimately crushing impact of that message. One of my ways of surviving was not to endow the rejectors with too much wisdom—not invest that much in their bad or good opinions.

I tried to make myself as good as possible, since it seemed to be the only thing in the whole profession over which I had any control, aside from the eight-by-ten glossies. That was my main focus for many years—not making connections, not getting a job, but getting better. I figured that with perseverance the opportunities would come. The question of how good I'd be when they did would determine my future.

I also had an unusual way of approaching an audition. Instead of being intimidated by the success of the people I was going to meet, I thought of all the times they hadn't been successful— which in most people's cases was more than 50 percent. It would help humanize them and defuse the tension. When people showed no interest in meeting me, I remembered Jack Lemmon's wonderful story about when he played Ensign Pulver in the movie *Mister Roberts*, for which he won an Academy Award. Josh Logan, the co-director of the movie (along with John Ford), as well as the director of the Broadway play, said to Lemmon: "Where were you when I was casting the play?"

Jack replied, "I was outside the theater trying to get in to see you."

Also, I fully understood that I could very easily be good but just not someone's cup of tea. There's another story about how the brilliant actor Alan Arkin, then unknown, had done a pilot for a television series. The producer and director looked at the pilot together: The producer saw nothing at all; the director determined that this was one of the finest talents of his generation.

And then, of course, there was the movie scout's famous report on first seeing Fred Astaire. It said: "Can't sing, can't act, can dance a little." Maybe there should be reports on the people writing the reports.

I once had an audition for the famous director Abe Burrows, a heavyset man with a twinkle in his eye, who had directed, among countless others, *Guys and Dolls* and *How to Succeed in Business Without Really Trying*. This audition was for the Broadway production of *Cactus Flower*. As I walked onto the stage, Mr. Burrows called out from the back of the theater: "Your agent tells me you're the funniest young actor on Broadway. Let's see what you can do."

I began my reading, and three lines into the scene Mr. Burrows called out: "That's a laugh line, Charley." I peered into the darkness of the theater. He said, "Try it again." I did, and he again stopped me, saying once more that these lines were intended to get laughs. I said I thought I would with what I was doing. "No way," he said, and the audition came to an abrupt end.

I later got to know Abe Burrows and liked him enormously. But the broad, punchy way he was leading me that day was only one way to do it. Sometimes opposite ways work as well. In the case of *Cactus Flower*, we never got a chance to find out.

Since the overwhelming majority of movies and plays fail, those people rejecting all the actors could very well be making mistakes, since you have to be wrong somewhere to create a failure. I always tried to give myself the benefit of the doubt when I was rejected, particularly if I thought I'd done well. If I didn't like what I'd done, I tried to figure out what was wrong with me, and that was always a rich area to explore. So between figuring out what was wrong with them or figuring out what was wrong with me, I had a lot less energy to be nervous with.

I also was getting help from other people. One was Harry Ufland, who was my agent for more than twenty years. He produces movies now. I followed him through three agencies, the last one his own. I used to tell him, "You should be the actor and I should be the agent," because he had enough emotion for ten actors, and I always missed not having my own office.

Harry rapidly developed a well-earned reputation for being scrappy; others might use another word: *volatile*, or *confrontational*—the emotional currents of a Jimmy Cagney character. He was also the number-one fan of Charles Grodin when there weren't any others. When I first called the William Morris Agency looking for representation, he was the secretary to the man I was calling to watch me on a program that was to be repeated every night through the week. Harry asked what part I'd played, as he'd already seen it. I told him, and he said, "You're fantastic! I'd love to meet you right away." Not exactly what I'd been used to hearing. Because he was a secretary, Harry wasn't in a position to sign me as a client. He got his boss, a high-powered, flamboyant agent named Eddie Bondy, to watch the show, but Eddie's comment was, "He'll probably be another Eli Wallach, but who's got the time?"

Eventually, Harry got a promotion and became my agent. Once, he circulated a six-page memo (he had enclosed a lot of good reviews I'd gotten for something) to about fifty different agents in all departments at the William Morris Agency. He was called on the carpet for wasting paper. Harry angrily replied that if the people there had been paying attention to me, he wouldn't have had to use all the paper. He said it to his boss, who could have fired him. (This same executive years later told me that if I didn't "make it" by the time I was thirty, I should forget it. At the time, I was thirty-two.) Harry told everyone that I was the best thing to come along since . . . well, just that I was the best thing to come along. "You have no idea what you're getting!" he would shout at directors. "Is he a romantic leading man? Are you kid-ding?!" he would rage. It was like having a one-man army on my side. For a lot of that time, he was my lone voice in the wilder-ness calling out: "Look at this man." I wish every actor could be so lucky as to have someone like Harry in his corner.

Trouble Behind the Scenes

Almost a year after *Tchin Tchin* closed, I still hadn't had another offer. With the exception of Harry Ufland, I wasn't having much luck dealing with the William Morris office; most everyone there seemed to be busy looking after the endless list of stars they represented. So, at the suggestion of a friend, I contacted a personal manager by the name of Geoffrey Barr, a man around forty who radiated confidence. Someone had told me he was very good at dealing with large agencies. I figured he wouldn't have to be too good to be better than I was, so I went to see him. He had seen *Tchin Tchin*, liked me, and so I signed on. After about six months with no change, I went to see him again and asked what he would think if I hired a public-relations person. I really had no idea what you did to get your phone to ring—which mine sure wasn't.

He looked at me for a moment and said, "You bore me."

I was stunned. I hadn't been calling him at all. I hardly ever had anything to say, so he couldn't have meant I talked a lot and bored him. There was no doubt in my mind that that one question had done the trick and provoked him to say, "You bore me," which I feel is one of the meanest things one person can say to another. I was devastated. I just sagged.

He went on to say: "If I thought a PR person was a good idea for you, *I* would have told you."

"Oh," I said. I left the meeting knowing it was just a question of when and how I got rid of this guy.

A couple of months later, after more silence from my phone, I went in to see him again, and as he was outlining his plans for my future, I told him politely that I'd be facing my future without him.

"It doesn't seem to be working out," I said. He made a mild, polite attempt to keep me, but I politely persisted, and we said good-bye—politely.

Eventually, the producers of a play, *Absence of a Cello*, called and said they had a part they'd like me for; would I audition? "Yes, I would," I said, and went over the next day. The producers (one of whom, Jeff Britton, would have a big impact on my life later) were there, as were the writer, Ira Wallach, and the director, James Hammerstein. After I had read only a few lines of the part for them, they stopped me and gave me the role. They were very enthusiastic. Things were looking up.

Curiously, in the case of both *Absence of a Cello* and *Tchin Tchin*, I was replacing other actors who had played the roles either out of town or, in the case of *Tchin Tchin*, in earlier rehearsal. Management felt they hadn't made the parts sufficiently amusing. It was flattering and challenging. How challenging, I was soon to find out.

I was playing the part of the young man who is the suitor of the young woman in *Absence of a Cello*. In order to win her, I help prepare her father, who is the lead character for a position in a large corporation. I was a Wharton Business School graduate and he was an eccentric scientist, and I had to show him how to "play the game" to fit in, so to speak. The title of the play comes from a piece of conformist advice I give him about getting rid of his cello: "The absence of a cello makes a good impression." All during rehearsals, Ira Wallach and Jimmy Hammerstein laughed at just about everything I did, and the cast—essentially a group of veteran Broadway players—was very enthusiastic toward me. It looked like I was heading for another success.

When we opened out of town prior to Broadway at the Pocono Playhouse in the Pocono Mountains of Pennsylvania, I didn't get one laugh. I was greeted with total silence by the audience. We were all mystified. I would lie awake at night trying to figure out what was happening. I didn't despair; it was like trying to figure out a puzzle. It was here that I began to appreciate how delicate comedy is. Those of us involved in the production, I realized, can't have the same point of view as a cold, objective audience. Obviously, the audience wasn't seeing what we were seeing. I finally came to the conclusion that the audience mildly resented this tall, nice-looking-enough young man, "a winner," showing this older man the ropes. I decided that if my character weren't such a winner, but actually more of what an audience perceives as a loser, who had this one skill that he reluctantly and apologetically presented, the comedy would work. I decided to wear glasses and play the role more in a "nerdy" fashion. I told Jimmy Hammerstein and the cast that I was going to try something different that night. I made my entrance that evening and, saying exactly the same lines in this new fashion, got a laugh just about every time I spoke, and received five exit hands. It was a very exciting and wonderful lesson about the delicacy of comedy.

On the other hand, the leading actor, Fred Clark, was furious at me. I had told him I was going to try something different, but he wasn't prepared for the extreme difference—and it can be nerve-racking to be hit with that in front of a full house for the first time. I should have shown everyone in a rehearsal first. After many apologies, which Fred didn't accept at first (Anthony Quinn would have enjoyed that), things eventually smoothed over—for the moment. Fred Clark, a famous character actor from Hollywood movies of the fifties and sixties, had a very difficult time with me from the minute all those laughs started to come my way. I liked Fred, and I believe he liked me, but he was never comfortable with me onstage.

Fred was the star and I was the supporting actor. Anyone reading the scenes we had together, and there were a number of them, would say Fred Clark had the funny lines. After I found a different way to play the part, all these laughs seemed to shift. I was getting laughs on looks and pauses as much as on anything else, and these laughs surpassed what was happening for Fred. Eventually, he came into my dressing room and said openly, "I don't understand what's happening. I've got all of the funny lines, and you're getting all of the laughs." He wasn't accusative; he was baffled. He wanted to look me in the eye to convince himself that I was doing nothing improper. Jimmy Hammerstein was appreciative of what was happening, but Fred couldn't understand *why* it was happening. The truth was that when a comedy actor who works from "within" (back to living the part) works with a comedy actor who doesn't but relies on funny line-readings and double takes, slow burns, and a complete extensive repertory of classic comic moves, of which Fred Clark was a master, the actor who's working from "within" will always stand out. In other words, the audience might not realize they're not seeing enough reality until more appears.

The most profound example of this was when Paul Muni started to act in movies, and was terribly different from everyone else. One studio head, who was not a fan of Muni, said to a producer: "If Muni's so good, that would have to mean everyone else is bad—and that's impossible." But it wasn't impossible. I don't think the public's perception would have been "good" and "bad," just that Muni was "better." The same thing happened in the movies when Marlon Brando first appeared, and later, James Dean. That kind of reality took certain performers right to the top, but didn't do a lot for the actors who were around them, unless they worked the same way. I've seen it happen many times over the years when a "technical" actor runs into a "reality" actor. It's not a difference in talent as much as a difference in approach. If Fred had had my background and I his, and I were the lead with the funny lines, I too would have wondered, "What's going on here?"

For the entire run of the play I was received the same way, and throughout Fred was unhappy with me and never hesitated to let me know. "This play is not about you," he would say. The focus had shifted. It did seem to be too much about me, but I didn't know what to do about it. I certainly wasn't going to try to be *less* effective. The director and the writer sure wouldn't have wanted that. So Fred's frustrations grew.

Once, Michael Gordon, a Hollywood director of some of the Rock Hudson/Doris Day movies, came to see the show. Later Fred told me, "Michael Gordon, the Hollywood director, saw the show and loved everyone, but he didn't like you." He just wanted to let me know.

Henny Youngman, who was a friend of Fred's, told him, "Grodin's got weird timing. I don't know what he's doing." Both Fred and Henny were practitioners of rhythm performing: setup/punch line, setup/punch line. Anything that deviated from that convention was comic criminality to them. I understood what everyone meant, but I didn't do it that way, nor would I, particularly since Ira Wallach's play wasn't written in those rhythms. Eventually, Fred came around with some grudging admiration, even though he wasn't ever sure what the hell I was doing. I certainly never enjoyed his discomfort. But in spite of Fred and his friends, I was starting to get a reputation as a good Broadway comedy actor. (Twenty-five years later, when they asked Henny Youngman whom he'd like to see play him in a contemplated movie of his life, he said, "Charles Grodin." I was amazed!)

At some point toward the end of the run of *Absence of a Cello*, I got an offer to go to Hollywood, not to be in the movies but to do a soap opera. Earlier, I had put in a little stint on a soap opera in New York called *Love of Life*—or, as the announcer would say it: "*Love . . . of Life.*" I found it the hardest thing I had ever done. I still feel that. We were sometimes asked to memorize twenty-five pages of dialogue a day and then do it with a minimum amount of rehearsal—live. A lot of people solve this problem by skillfully reading the lines off the TelePrompTers, which are around the set near the cameras. I could never figure out how to do it and be "involved" in the scene, so I didn't do it that way. However, I wasn't able to be involved, no matter what I did. There just wasn't enough rehearsal. Also, they had an organ in the studio, and sometimes when I'd knock on a door and another actor would open it, the organ would give a *da-dum* and really break whatever concentration I had going, which wasn't much anyway. To me, it was always a memory test. I had always chalked up my difficulty with it to inexperience; the job came right after my *Armstrong Circle Theater* "appearance." But one day, as my time on that show was nearing its end, I asked the character woman who had been on the show for years if she enjoyed it. Her answer has stayed with me all this time: "The only thing I enjoy is the last line." So much for getting used to it.

So when the offer came to go out to Hollywood to be the leading man on a soap opera called *The Young Marrieds* for two years, the answer was easy: No thanks. On the other hand, *Absence of a Cello* was getting ready to close. I had once again gotten really good notices, but I remembered that after *Tchin Tchin* I didn't work for a year. Also, I was almost thirty and had absolutely no money. But still—a soap opera? I figured I'd make them an offer they'd refuse: I wouldn't do it for two years, but I would do it for six months. No soap opera likes to have their leading players for that short a time; they must be there more or less indefinitely to establish continuity and audience identification. So there was no way they would sign me for six months. They did.

Shortly after accepting the soap-opera offer, while I was still completing the run of *Absence of a Cello*, Owen Laster, an agent at the William Morris office, somehow got an inspired idea for me to go work on the television show *Candid Camera* and arranged for me to meet Allen Funt, even though I wouldn't be available for six months. It had always been my favorite television show because it was real-life comedy, which you never saw anywhere else. This was the way people *really* reacted in situations—real-life human responses, and they were often very funny. It was a great show for a student of acting to watch.

When I met with Allen Funt, it turned out that he had seen me in *Absence of a Cello* and immediately was prepared to give me my own film unit. I would be responsible for coming up with the ideas and being in those segments. I'd have gone to work there as a guy who got coffee just to be around the place. I was thrilled at such an unexpected welcome. He asked me what I wanted to be paid. Never before had anyone asked me that directly. I said I'd take the minimum amount allowed—which was $350 a week—and if I did well, then we would talk about money. He suddenly looked at me as if I were a fool. I thought I gave him a Humphrey Bogart–type answer—kind of flip, hip, and cool—but I guess he hadn't seen it that way. Anyway, we parted cordially, and I said I'd see him in six months.

I completed my run in *Absence of a Cello*, packed my bags, and, once again, headed for Hollywood.

Ted Knight and the Soap Opera

It was strange going back to Hollywood. In ten years, I had gone from a nervous, frightened, completely raw novice to a Broadway actor coming back with a job. And I didn't even want it. I would have much preferred to stay in New York and go right to work on *Candid Camera*, but I was already committed to *The Young Marrieds*, so there I was.

Ted Knight, who later gained fame as Ted Baxter, the hilarious newscaster on *The Mary Tyler Moore Show*, was starting on the show the same time I was. He was to play Phil Sterling, my boss; I was to play Matt Stevens, a rising young executive. There was one big problem: Ted Knight and I couldn't look at each other without laughing. From the first day we met, it felt as though we were both from the same planet—and it wasn't this one. The problem was even greater because, like many soap operas, we essentially played endless variations on the same theme. Phil Sterling was a leading executive at Forsythe Industries, and Matt Stevens was obsessed with the idea that he had gotten his job with Forsythe Industries because of his relationship with the owner of the company, Irene Forsythe, who happened to be his mother-in-law. Ted and I had one scene that we must have played in different versions dozens of times over a six-month period. As I said, we couldn't stop laughing at each other under normal, everyday-life circumstances, but during this scene it was impossible.

I'll try to re-create what happened as Ted and I attempted the scene, which was taped for airing the next day. Delays were costly, and we all knew it; and yet . . . here's the scene and what happened on an average day in the rehearsal just before taping:

MATT STEVENS [me] walks down the hallway and knocks on the door of his boss, PHIL STERLING [Ted], vice-president of Forsythe Industries.

PHIL
(offstage)
Come in.

MATT
(entering)
Hello, Phil.

PHIL
Oh, Matt. Come in.

Ted's and my eyes meet in terror that we are going to burst into laughter. The people in the booth are watching the monitors intensely. We've all been through this before.

MATT
Phil, there's something I want to talk to you about.

Since I've said that line for months, I can't help it and I "go." The word *about* comes out choked. I'm trying to hold the laughter in. Ted is doubled up. And from the booth, on the loudspeaker, we hear (they were very nice about it): "Fellows!"

Ted and I both say: "Sorry. Sorry."

From the booth: "Take it from your entrance, Chuck."

I go out and knock on the door.

PHIL
Come in.

MATT
(entering)
Hello, Phil.

PHIL
[Ted manages not to look at me, but at my forehead]
Oh, Matt. Come in.

MATT
[I'm looking at the floor]
Phil, there's something I want to talk to you about.

PHIL
Would you like a drink?

Ted is thinking, Here comes all the stuff about whether I got my job at Forsythe Industries because Irene Forsythe is my mother-in-law. Ted goes to the bar, turns and looks at me to see if I do want a drink. Our eyes meet.
We're "gone" again, choking on laughter.
The booth: "Fellows!" A little more insistent.
Ted and I: "Sorry. Sorry."
The booth: "Keep going. Let's get through this, guys."

MATT
No thanks, Phil. There's something I want to ask you.

That's our "killer" line. That's the one we never get past. So we're each looking in opposite directions.

PHIL
(pouring a drink for himself)
What is it, Matt?

MATT
Did Irene Forsythe have anything to do with my getting my job here at Forsythe Industries?

Ted turns slowly and looks at me. Our eyes meet.
Ted and I are gasping with laughter.

The booth: "Fellows, we go to tape in fifteen minutes. We've got to get through this."

Somehow we stumbled our way through the rehearsals and always managed to get through the taping without cracking. Barely. It got so bad that whenever I got the next day's script I quickly looked to see if I had to work with Ted. It became a terror hanging over both our heads. Ultimately, we were able to confine our laughs to times away from the show . . . and we had plenty. The only lapse in the laughs between us was one time when I was driving with Ted down a steep hill in Hollywood at about fifty miles per hour and the brakes failed. I jumped the curb, grazed a tree, and literally went through the brick wall of a garage. No one got hurt, and we even got some laughs out of that one later.

Ted had really been my shining light on *The Young Marrieds.* I made other friends there, including the wonderful actress Peggy McKay, whom I still see. But Ted, in spite of my inability to look at him while we worked, really made the experience for me. I needed all the help I could get because, just as had happened on *Love . . . of Life,* the job was a memory test in which I regularly had to learn endless pages of dialogue. I still was unable or unwilling to use TelePrompTers and I still was unable to master the dialogue to the point where I could be involved in the situation. I was unhappy at not being able to do work that I could be proud of, since I now had the skill to be effective in the right situation, which this clearly wasn't for me. The producer, an elegant, sensitive man named Dick Dunn, who had seen me in *Tchin Tchin* and *Absence of a Cello* and really was responsible for me being there, watched sadly at lunch break as I would eat French fries and mashed potatoes along with several other items in an effort to find happiness. I had gone from being a successful Broadway comedy actor to an unsuccessful, overweight soap-opera actor, and it showed in more than my size. One time Dick Dunn pointed out as gently as he could that I was coming across like a well-known mobster of the time, Frank Costello. (Of course I was supposed to be playing an appealing leading man.) He said management would be satisfied if I could just bring the character up to the Richard Nixon level of appeal.

There was a young man playing my brother on the show whose work everyone loved. He came to me one day and said that the reason everyone appreciated his work and didn't particularly appreciate mine was that they could always tell what he was thinking, and you couldn't with me. He said having a quality you sometimes couldn't "read" might not serve me in soap opera, but it would in movies, where people looked for more complicated work. It turned out, generally speaking, that he was right about movie acting. At the time, however, I didn't fully comprehend what he was saying, but I appreciated his generosity. As a failing soap-opera actor who wasn't even rising to the appeal of Richard Nixon, it was certainly impossible to imagine a career in the movies.

I thought that working with Ted in another situation might cheer me up. I decided that in whatever free moments I could find, and there were few, I would write a comedy album that Ted and I could do together. I wrote it, and the two of us did about twenty-five characters each in around thirty comic pieces. The first place I sent it to, Columbia Records, liked it and optioned it but never released it because around that time comedy albums had come to the end of their popularity.

I played the album for some friends, who laughed a lot, but I was struck by the comment of my boyhood pal from Pittsburgh, Raymond Kaplan, who had moved with his family to Los Angeles at twelve and later became a psychiatrist. He said there was an awful lot of death and destruction in the album, and left me to draw my own conclusions as to what that meant. At the time I had had no therapy, so all it meant to me was that you might find humor anywhere. Today, in listening to it, I can see what Ray meant. Obviously an agitated person wrote it. Of course comedy is often used as an outlet for some upset. I think that twelve years after the fact, I was still reeling from my father's passing but unable to deal with it consciously, and of course I was tremendously frustrated with my work on the soap. I think the producers of *The Young Marrieds* were just as happy as I was when my six-months contract was up. While anyone in career planning might wonder what a method actor with two Broadway successes was doing heading for *Candid Camera*, I always believed that if something interesting to you was offered, do it and forget about the logic of career planning. I was heading for *Candid Camera*, and I couldn't wait.

Candid Camera

On my first day of work at *Candid Camera*, I ran into a new kind of roadblock.

There was an associate producer, a woman named Ann Richardson, who had major influence on what happened around the show, including who was hired and who was not. When I was hired, she was away on vacation. On returning and hearing about me, she came to my office right away. Since I'd known I had the job for over six months, I came to work that first day with more than forty ideas for the show.

As soon as I arrived, Ann Richardson appeared. She was an austere woman who put out strong competitive vibes immediately. In comedy, you don't need competition. In football, yes, it could work for you; but in comedy, you just want support from your co-workers. She said, as though I had slipped in under a crack in the door, that she understood I had been hired in her absence and perhaps I'd like to tell her what my ideas were. I was sure her attitude would change when she heard what I had to say.

After she'd rejected my first ten ideas with either "We've done that"; "We've done something like that"; "I don't think that would work"; "I don't think that's funny"; "I wouldn't want to do that"; et cetera; et cetera; I started to get the drift of the meeting. I rattled off thirty more ideas. "We've done something like that"; "I don't think that's funny"; "I don't like that"; "I don't like that";

"We wouldn't want to do that." Finally, I was finished. She looked at me as though she had just polished off a tasty dinner, and asked what I'd like to do. I'm sure "quit" was the answer she was hoping for. I said I'd like to see Mr. Funt.

The three of us met in his private offices on a separate floor equipped with Jacuzzi and sauna. He, wrapped in a towel and sitting on a table, said: "I understand you two don't see eye to eye."

I nodded.

He asked me what I thought my best idea was. I told him. He liked it and said, "Do it." Ann smiled or something at me, and we went out to do it.

The idea was that I would be a young fella from Pittsburgh who wanted to see if I could have a singing career. We would take over a singing coach's studio. The coach would call about six other coaches, say he had to be somewhere else, and could they come over and hear a singer and give their opinion of his potential. None of the six, of course, knew about the others, and we scheduled them an hour apart. Each coach was paid twenty dollars, I believe, to come over. This was 1966. Joey Faye, a wonderful burlesque comedian with a mischievous look about him, posed as my uncle who had promised my mother—his sister—he would back me financially in a singing career, but he wanted a professional assessment first. Joey had on a suit and tie, and was trying to look very distinguished. The piano player, of course, was also with us, and the whole place was miked, with our cameras well concealed.

Throughout the day the coaches came, and I did the introductions: "Hi, I'm Chuck Johnson. This is my Uncle Frank." I said I wanted my uncle's backing in a professional singing career, and we needed the coach's judgment. I said, "I'll do 'Be My Love.'" "Be My Love" is almost an operatic piece. Mario Lanza had a hit record of it in the fifties. It's a big stretch from "At the Drop of a Hat" to "Be My Love," and, of course, I had been replaced singing "At the Drop of a Hat" eleven years earlier. Now I was a different actor, but pretty much the same singer. I immediately launched into a vigorous, powerful, lousy rendition of "Be My Love."

The coach sat between Joey Faye and the piano player. Joey, the accompanist, and I acted as though it sounded pretty good.

The bigger I tried to sing, the worse it sounded; so, by the end, I managed to be terrible but always sincere.

Throughout all this, each coach would sneak little glances at Joey and the accompanist to see if they were about to be sick too. But, as prearranged, they looked as though they were enjoying it; and I, as the song went on, acted as though I were getting better and better instead of worse and worse. At the merciful end, I would stare at the coach and say: "I really think I could be a good professional singer, and I'd like my uncle to back me. What do you think?" And then I'd look hopeful.

The first coach, a middle-aged man, looked at Joey and the accompanist for help. But they stared at him hopefully too. After about five seconds of silence (Time it: That's long for this situation; usually, the only time you see a five-second pause since Jack Benny—bless him—is when El Exigente is deciding if the coffee is okay in that TV commercial), the coach finally spoke: "It's warm in here. Is it warm in here?" He then went on to say that with proper training, et cetera, et cetera, anything was possible. In other words, he just flat-out lied, or maybe he had terrible judgment. It was downhill on positive responses from that point on, which of course was good for our purposes.

A woman coach, when I'd finished and joyously asked for her approval, angrily responded: "Listen, I manage a baritone *The New York Times* has called 'one of the ten finest singers in this country,' and *this man cannot make a living!*"

I innocently said, "Does he have my range?"

Her mouth dropped open and she just glared at me. She then asked the piano player to hit a key and for me to sing the note he played. After the first note, I hesitated, then asked the piano player if he would play it again, louder. The woman's mouth opened wider in amazement. When I finally deliberately missed the three notes he'd played, she declared triumphantly: "He's tone deaf!!"

Finally, a very distinguished Italian coach with a big chest came in. I could see when I was singing that this guy was really going nuts: He could barely contain himself. He hated me so much (even more than the previous woman), he wanted to kill me. First, he looked like he was going to leap up from his chair and knock me down while I was singing; then, he seemed to get hold of himself and just sat there, looking around violently as I was really getting into it, as if to say: Isn't anybody going to tell him to just shut up! He was probably a rough kind of teacher even if you *could* sing, so with me he was really exploding inside. When I finished, I thought he would vent his true feelings more if I weren't there. So I said, "I'm a little hoarse. I'm going to get a glass of water, and I'll be right back."

I went behind the partition and put on the headphones, and I heard Joey Faye say: "So what do you think? Can the kid have a career?"

The coach was genuinely furious. "I'm numb," he shouted. "I've never seen anything so bad in my life! He's like a chicken with his head cut off! He's like an accident waiting to happen!"

I came running back in and said, "You know, I did 'Be My Love' before a group of Shriners in Pittsburgh, and they gave me a standing ovation. Of course, I didn't do it as well as I just did it here."

He peered at me a moment, then said, "I'd like to hear what the hell *that* sounded like!"

I went back to my office at the end of the day, and I was all excited because the stuff really was funny. The phone rang a minute after I got in there, and it was my agent, who said, "Congratulations."

I thought, My God, good news travels fast! But I soon realized he was being facetious and something was wrong. "What are you saying?" I asked him.

"You're fired," he said.

"I'm fired?"

"You set a record. *Candid Camera* is known for firing people, but nobody ever got fired on the first day."

"Why?" I asked.

The agent said that two of the coaches, in spite of having signed releases, had already called and threatened lawsuits. The furious Italian coach, of course, was one of them.

Allen Funt was very upset. The agent said that Allen had told me in the beginning not to take on professional people. He *had* said something about that, but decided to go on with the idea anyway. According to the agent, *Candid Camera* liked to get messengers and people like that; they didn't like to get professional people "because they really get angry and they'll sue you." In this case, at least, he was right. So Allen Funt fired me.

But I went in to talk to him. I asked him to look at the footage to see how funny it was. He did, and he rehired me, although he cautioned me again about messing with professionals.

I had always wanted to hide a camera behind a receptionist's desk in any large company and have the "new girl" stop everyone for extensive identification; but knowing Allen's attitude, I was afraid he'd try to throw me out the window if I even suggested that one.

One day we took over Le Voìson, one of New York's swankiest supper clubs, during the lunch hour. The idea was to see and hear how people would react to super-super service. The microphone was in the stand that held the salt-and-pepper shakers. If someone took a sip of water, I, as the waiter, would instantly refill their glass from the water pitcher. If someone flicked an ash from a cigarette, I would instantly replace the ashtray with a clean one. If someone took a bite out of a roll and dropped one crumb on the tablecloth, I would instantly appear with a crumb cleaner. Then I would go behind a partition and put on headphones to hear the comments of the various diners.

At first, the comments were: "Boy, this place has *some* service!" But after I had pounced on their bread crumbs a couple of times, the comments were more like: "You know, you can overdo this service thing. This is really starting to get on my nerves!" It was interesting that in the course of the lunch we quietly told six couples that it was a joke, that they were on *Candid Camera,* and not one of the couples would sign a release permitting us to use them on the air. It seemed that every man and woman there was with someone they weren't supposed to be with.

Of course, the segment was never shown.

Another time, when I told a burly man that he was on *Candid Camera,* he looked at me, shocked, and said he couldn't be on *Candid Camera* because he was wanted by the police. As he stared at me menacingly, I quickly assured him that if he didn't sign a release, it wouldn't be shown. He listened a moment and, since he now knew what was going on, he could hear the sound of the camera. He suspiciously asked me why, if it wasn't going to be used, the camera was still rolling. I called out for the cameraman to stop shooting as I continued to try to reassure the criminal. But as both he and I could hear the camera continue to roll, he started to advance on me threateningly. I shouted out again to the cameraman to stop; and when he didn't, I quickly moved back to his camera position to stop him, with the fugitive now clearly coming after me. It was only when I absolutely couldn't get the cameraman to stop filming, as the criminal came even closer, that they both told me *I* was on *Candid Camera*. I was more relieved than anything else.

There was one segment that I particularly liked. We got a large group of tourists to board what they thought was a sightseeing bus to visit the Empire State Building, the U.N., the Statue of Liberty, and other famous landmarks. We then headed for Eleventh and Twelfth Avenues in the Forties, an extremely depressing area almost exclusively filled with garages and warehouses. Ironically, ten years earlier this was the area where I had gone to pick up a cab to drive. Sometimes I would wait for hours and then be told that there was no cab for me. I had spent some of the most depressing times of my life waiting in the Chase Cab Company garage on West Forty-seventh Street, and now here I was back again on the same street, having one of the happiest times of my life.

With Joey Faye acting as the guide, standing with a microphone at the front of the bus, we began to go down one block and up another. I wrote a speech for Joey that pointed out "that trucks come every day to these warehouses to load up with goods that are taken all around the city to supply various stores. Every floor of these warehouses is filled with products that supply all our needs."

The passengers listened to this boring commentary for a while, and then one English fellow suddenly began to shout furiously: "Where's the *U.N.*?! Where's the *Empire State Building*?!"

Joey said, "Those aren't on this tour. This is the Garage and Warehouse Tour, one of our most popular tours. But if you would all turn your heads as we come around the next corner, you might just see the top of the Chrysler Building some twenty blocks away."

The group whipping their heads around to see the top of the Chrysler Building so far away was one of the funniest sights I've ever seen. And then angry pandemonium really broke out on the bus: "What is this?! What kind of a horrible tour is this?!"

When they were let in on the joke, the laughter was as strong as the earlier anger.

One day, after a few weeks, Allen Funt got the idea that we should close down one of the men's rooms at the JFK Airport in New York.

I said, "Gee, you want me to go out and do this?"

"Yeah," he said, "go out there."

I said, "I don't think this . . . I mean, when passengers come off a plane, they really . . ."

He said, "No, it will be really funny footage. Believe me. Go ahead."

"All right."

With dread, I went out there and shut down the bathroom at the airport. I was very surprised that the personnel at JFK cooperated. I guess everyone wants to be in show business in some way.

Arriving male passengers opened a door marked MEN and looked into a blank wall. They were confused, naturally. Eventually, after a few moments, a crowd of men formed.

Finally I told a puzzled passenger: "You're on *Candid Camera.*"

That's when he and everyone else became livid. They really hated the joke. One man said: "I don't care where you're from! I have to go to the bathroom!" That was the gentlest thing that was said. *Candid Camera*, television, and I were all viciously attacked.

After a couple of hours of this I was notified at the airport that a phone call had come in from the *Candid Camera* office saying I was fired again. This time I didn't bother to try to get the job back by reminding Allen I was against the idea. I still thought the show was great, but I wasn't too happy when it caused people real discomfort, which it sometimes did even though you wouldn't necessarily see it on camera. Standing next to people with small beads of sweat on their foreheads caused by the confusion the show would provoke was not pleasant. If we had been allowed to go after some pompous, aggressive professional characters, I'd have fought to stay.

In spite of the firings and the early unpleasantness with the associate producer, Ann Richardson, there was only one time on this job when I got angry. I was walking down the hall when I passed the office of one of the producers, whose name I remember only as Larry. He suddenly screamed something at me. I don't even remember what he said. I only know it was the first time in my professional life that had happened. For a moment I was so startled I couldn't believe he did that. Then a fury consumed me, and I slowly turned and went into his office. I walked up to him and suggested it wasn't a good idea he talk to me that way. His anger was dwarfed by what I was feeling in response, and he must have seen that as he remained quiet. It's interesting to me that while I handled rejection with relative ease, abuse evidently was a whole other ball game.

I never had any bad feelings for Allen Funt, mostly because of a story I'd heard about him before I'd gone to work there. *Candid Camera* first appeared regularly on television as a segment of the old Garry Moore television variety show, which also introduced Carol Burnett. *The Garry Moore Show* was owned by a production company called Bob Banner Associates. For the privilege of being on national television, Allen Funt had to give Bob Banner a piece of the ownership of *Candid Camera* which eventually was worth about twelve thousand dollars a week when *Candid Camera* became its own show. If Allen Funt remained a little upset about that, I don't blame him.

Years later, after I became known, my representative got a call from Allen Funt's office inquiring about my interest in directing a special he was doing. So many people had been fired over the years from *Candid Camera*, I'm sure he had just forgotten that I had been one of them. Since I'd already been fired twice, I declined, saying, "Three times would be way more than enough." But, on balance, what a great comic contribution Allen Funt and *Candid Camera* have made.

Lillian Hellman

So now I had followed an unsuccessful stint on *The Young Marrieds* with a firing from *Candid Camera*. I had no idea what to do. I reverted to my old habit of reading every newspaper in the city from front to back; I also included *Time* and *Newsweek*. I certainly had to be one of the more informed people around, but one piece of information I was still missing was how to get a job in show business. Eventually, from out of the blue, I was offered and accepted a part in a television special of Lillian Hellman's play *Autumn Garden*.

It was an all-star cast except for a sweet, talented young woman named Louise Shaeffer and myself. The company was largely English; the director was English as well, a very nice man named Noel Willman. He gave directions in a way that I have not seen before or since. If he wanted you to play something differently than you were doing it, he would say: "It wants to be a bit quicker," or, "It wants to be a bit more forceful"—as though the lines had their own opinion on how they should be done and they spoke privately to Noel.

Late in the rehearsal period, we were told that Lillian Hellman would be coming by one day to have a look. We all nervously awaited her visit. The day she arrived, those of us she didn't know were taken over and introduced. She was not chatty.

She sat at the head of a long table, and we all sat around and were encouraged to ask her questions. No one spoke.

Finally, Margaret Leighton (whom I was so happy to see after *Tchin Tchin*, even though at this point my posture still hadn't improved), speaking on behalf of the largely English cast and in her very strong British accent, said: "Lillian, some of us are a bit concerned about our speech."

Miss Hellman thought a moment and then said, in what sounded to me like a very thick midwestern twang: "The characters should sound pretty much like I sound, so you'll be fine."

All the English actors shot baffled looks at each other. Finally, Noel Willman announced that we would now do a run-through of the play for Miss Hellman, after which perhaps there would be more questions.

We moved to the rehearsal hall. Most of us were already onstage for the beginning of the play. Miss Hellman and Noel Willman were sitting some ten feet away as Eileen Herlie began. She walked center stage and spoke the first line.

Miss Hellman immediately began to whisper so intensely to Mr. Willman that the run-through stopped. Mr. Willman said, "Excuse us for a moment," and they left the room. We all sat still in our places. Eventually, Miss Hellman and Mr. Willman returned, and we were told to continue. There were no further conferences as we made our way warily through the play, afraid that at any moment something we would do or say would provoke another exit.

At the end of the run-through, Miss Hellman said nothing. Mr. Willman asked again if there were any questions for her.

Autumn Garden is an extremely complex play, and in a different atmosphere this group of players could have questioned or discussed it for hours. That afternoon we heard cautious inquiries, like: "Lillian, do you think I should be wearing my hair up or down?" It went on like this for about ten minutes, until Miss Hellman wished everyone luck and left. I'm sure she meant to be supportive. I admired her dignity and reticence, but I think the whole company could have used at least one collective slap on the back, the absence of which usually has actors imagining a kick in the groin.

I next saw Lillian Hellman almost twenty years later at a small party in her honor. She was seated on a sofa, and different guests would go over, one by one, to visit. She was obviously not well and didn't seem all that much in a visiting mood. After a time, she was sitting there alone for a moment, and I decided to approach her. I told her my name and that I'd been in a production of *Autumn Garden*, and that she had visited us. She didn't comment, but just listened, waiting, I guess, for my point. I recalled for her the incident of Noel Willman and her leaving the room after Eileen Herlie's first line of dialogue, and chuckled that when they'd returned we were reluctant to go on with the second line. She said she thought Eileen Herlie was an excellent actress. I quickly agreed, and once again pointed out how funny it all was, in a way, as we waited for them to return from their meeting, almost afraid to go on. I chuckled again, hoping to induce one in her. I sat there chuckling alone as she stared past me. A familiar voice called out to her, and she turned toward it with interest.

I got up and walked across the room. I considered going back over and asking if she'd heard the one about the two guys who got on a bus and . . . I decided to have a drink instead.

Autumn Garden came and went, with no increase in the demand for my services as an actor, in spite of my having again been well received. Once more, I began to wander around Manhattan feeling out of life, sitting on the library steps and benches everywhere, watching people go by, wondering what to do.

They Stole Our Clothes
When We Were at Dinner

To me one of the most intriguing things about show business is that if you're one of that tiny percentage of people—as I was slowly becoming—who would actually get called and be offered jobs, sometimes those jobs would not only be work, but they could have a huge impact on your life.

I got a call from one of the co-producers of *Absence of a Cello*, Jeff Britton, a sweet man with a shifty look about him. During the run of that play, I had said I was interested in becoming a director. At some point while we were still on the road prior to the Broadway opening, the writer, Ira Wallach, and the director, Jimmy Hammerstein, had included me in one of their conversations about the play. I told them what I thought, and they must have liked what I said because they started to include me in more of their discussions. These two generous, noncompetitive, supportive men were encouraging my interest in being a director in addition to acting. Since it was obvious that no matter how well I was received as an actor, I could still always get home without someone tackling me and offering me a job, it increasingly seemed like a good idea to develop any other ability I might have, and so I made known my interest in directing. This was in spite of the fact that I had been the only student at the Pittsburgh Playhouse who had not been asked to direct a one-act play. "Too weird," was the explanation. "All that 'living-the-part' stuff."

Now here was Jeff Britton calling to tell me he had an Off-Broadway musical he wanted me to direct. The show ended up being called *Hooray, It's a Glorious Day . . . and All That*. It was a satire of the big Broadway musical. I became the co-author with the original writer, a delightful man named Maury Teitelbaum, who also happened to be a practicing dentist in Newark, New Jersey. In fact, during one of our work sessions at his house in Newark, he actually filled one of my teeth. We had a great time working together. I believe *Hooray* was the biggest, most expensive Off-Broadway show up to that time, which was 1966. Not only that, but the show seemed to be terrifically entertaining to the audiences. Previews soon began to sell out. People were saying, "The freshest"; "The most original." Bosley Crowther, then the movie critic for *The New York Times*, came to a preview and was so high on it, he said he'd personally request that the *Times*'s Broadway critic, not the Off-Broadway critic, come and review it. Everyone was very excited. Well, not everyone. . . . In spite of all the enthusiasm and cheering audiences, Jeff Britton, prior to opening, decided we should replace our choreographer, Sandy Devlin, who had contributed mightily to the evening. He felt the musical numbers should be "crisper," or something. I felt they were plenty "crisp," and said that the audience response seemed to confirm my opinion. But Jeff persisted. He even had a current hot Broadway choreographer ready to come in and take over, but I said no. Jeff said he was going to fire Sandy for the good of the show. I said I thought Sandy was brilliant, and I wasn't going to let her be fired. Jeff got increasingly frustrated. One day, between a matinee and an evening performance, it all came to a head between us.

Jeff again said Sandy had to go. I said I wouldn't let that happen.

Jeff said, "I'm the producer, and I have the right to fire who I want."

I said, "I'm the co-writer, and I have approval of who the choreographer is; and if you fire Sandy, I'll get an injunction and close the show." I would have done it, too. I thought firing Sandy was ridiculous; Jeff should have given her a medal for brilliance instead. She was the most experienced musical-comedy person connected to the production. We were standing in the lobby of the theater. Jeff got angrier and angrier. His face turned red, and he began to shout that I was mentally disturbed. His young son was standing there witnessing all this. He shouted louder and louder, really losing control.

"You should see a doctor," I quietly said. "Listen to yourself, Jeff. You're screaming, and your son is standing here, and you say *I* need a doctor."

That slowed him down a little, and he stormed out into the street, I'm sure convinced I was a banana case. Sandy wasn't fired, but, needless to say, my relationship with Jeff cooled a bit after that.

Opening night came. We had a rehearsal in the afternoon, and then a break for an early dinner, and then the show and the critics. This was it. I went out for dinner with Sandy. We came back to the theater about an hour before curtain, and it was instantly clear that something was wrong.

Finally, the stage manager, Fred Reinglass, with a strange look in his eyes that said "trouble," assuring me first that everything was under control, told me that because of some dispute over money between Jeff and the woman who was responsible for all the costumes, she had come to the theater and stolen them. Costumes for twenty-five people in a bright, colorful musical were gone! The opening-night audience had begun to arrive, and the critics would be there any minute. The police were searching for the woman and the costumes. The critics were now in their seats. The place was packed. People were standing in the back. It was already a hot show because of word-of-mouth on the previews. Curtain time came and went. The audience was beginning to stir. We were backstage trying to figure out whether to let the show start with the performers in their street clothes even though the story was set in the twenties, and with a gangster plot at that. Out front, the audience was beginning to clap their hands, their impatience turning to real annoyance. We were twenty minutes late. Critics are never asked to wait, and there must have been one hundred people there from newspapers, TV, and radio. Jeff Britton stepped in front of the curtain and said, "Due to technical difficulties beyond our control, the curtain will be delayed." No one was charmed. A few critics got up and left. The police eventually arrived with the costumes. The show started thirty minutes late. The curtain went up. The opening number, which was always received with enthusiastic laughter and applause, was met with close to dead silence, which was pretty much the reaction to the rest of the first act. At intermission, a dozen more press left. The second act went better, but, basically, a show that had been playing to sellout audiences in previews and been received joyously was lying there on that night like a flat mistake. It was a disaster.

In spite of that, there were still a handful of great notices—not including the crucial *Times* critic, the Broadway one. One critic, Martin Gottfried, who shortly thereafter was selected as the outstanding theater critic in the country, picked it as one of the top-ten shows of the year. But it wasn't enough. There was very little business.

I tried to help the show run by going on some radio and TV shows. First, I went on an FM-radio show called *Broadway after Dark,* hosted by a sweet, heavyset, pasty-looking man with a pencil-thin moustache named Bobby Maurice. The "station" (microphone) was in Bobby's living room in an apartment on the Upper West Side. Three other guests and I sat around a table with Bobby. After the broadcast, I asked him how far the station carried. He seriously asked me, "What street do you live on?" It didn't get to my street. As I was leaving Bobby's apartment, the three other guests gave me their pictures and résumés in hopes that I might employ them.

After that, I went on the *Joe Franklin* TV show. Joe Franklin has, for years, been for me one of those people who "help me make it through the night." I think he is the most comforting TV personality I have ever seen. He's had his own show on radio and television probably longer than anyone in the world. Joe turns up at weird times: six A.M., four P.M. He usually turns up for me in New York or Los Angeles around two A.M. with a group of unknown people he treats as superstars. Most of the guests probably wouldn't be booked on *The Tonight Show,* or, actually, on any show, and Joe treats them as legendary figures. Somehow, this ends up being funny and strangely touching—struggling unknowns hearing praise they've never heard before and probably won't hear again, at least until they once more get booked with Joe.

When I went on, he introduced me as "the hottest young

director in town." What was amazing was that, for a second, I believed him: He appears to be incredibly sincere. I've only been on *Joe Franklin* that one time, but I watch him plenty. Joe had actually seen *Hooray* and called it "the freshest, most brilliant, exciting, wonderful, delightful new show in town"—or something close to that. I like the guy, what can I tell you?

There was a late-night radio talk show at that time called *The Long John Nebel Show*. I went on to continue what I knew was a fruitless effort to publicize and somehow save *Hooray*. I talked about the show, and then I suddenly stopped and said, to Long John's surprise (and even my own), "You know, it really doesn't make any difference what I say about this show. It's not going to run."

In three weeks, we were closed. Seven months of hard work went down the drain. I must have been in some kind of shock. I didn't even talk to Jeff Britton or the costume lady to find out why that had happened. It had, and it didn't seem to matter why. We had worked for seven months on the show, and it really was good enough to have been a success. People had loved it before that nightmare opening night. The composer, Art Gordon; the lyricist, Ethel Bieber; the co-author, Maury Teitelbaum; the choreographer, Sandy Devlin—all of us were dazed.

After *Hooray* closed, I spent the next six months in my room, pretty much staring into space, missing a beautiful New York spring, summer, and early fall. As I've said, I managed to detach my feelings often from these blows of rejection, and sometimes only the fact that I had holed up in a room for months would be evidence of the depression I was obviously experiencing. That, a numbed look, and a low voice.

I had no job, and nothing in sight; the *Hooray* experience had put my directing and writing aspirations on the back burner, if they were on any burner at all. No one was offering me an acting job. I had now been at this for about fourteen years, showed a lot of promise, and even had a number of successes. But I had no money at all.

I once again thought of Hollywood. Most of the work in television had moved out there, and so for the third time I headed west. The original idea of Elizabeth Taylor and Montgomery Clift and the movies was the furthest thing from my mind: I simply needed to make a living.

I had no idea when I left New York that Hollywood television now was pretty much dominated by westerns. I was about to become a cowboy.

The Cowboy

Marv Minoff, one of my agents at William Morris in Hollywood in the sixties, told me a story of something he witnessed at this time. He was walking by an office where they were casting a western TV show. He looked in and saw me sitting there in a room full of tough-looking cowboy types waiting to audition. I've always looked more like an Irish kid from an Ivy League school, so Marv said he just shook his head sadly when he saw me so obviously out of my element. A few days later there was a booking slip saying I had been cast in the western. He was startled and had no idea how that could happen.

I vividly remember sitting in that group as well. I looked more like an agent for a cowboy than a cowboy. Since the stars of the series were, of course, the heroes, the guest parts were always villains. There were guest killers, guest blackmailers, guest rustlers; and often these villains were crazed, enraged characters. It was evident that I had to do something unusual to break into that unlikely field, and I did.

When my name was called I went into the office, where there were four people. I kept my head down, discouraging any chatting. Quickly they asked if it was ready and I nodded. I then looked up and let out the rage. (Rage: something most actors with years of rejection can do very well.) I tried to create an actual sense of danger in the office—looking around at everyone with something in my eyes that clearly made them uncomfortable. As the audition went on, they looked at me in terror with a real question of whether all this rage would be confined to the audition. When it was over they gave me the part, I think because they were so relieved that I didn't attack them.

To help the overall situation I let my hair grow very long and grew huge red sideburns—muttonchops. My hair was brown but my beard was red. My dad's nickname as a boy had been "Red."

Shortly after that first show I phoned a director whom I'd worked with in New York, a very nice man named Charley Dubin, and asked him if he was involved with anything I might do. He was directing a segment of another western series and said, "I'll give you a part on the show. But can you ride?"

"Oh, sure," I said. I hung up the phone and immediately headed out to a riding stable since I'd never been on a horse in my life. (On the first show, riding hadn't come up.) I climbed onto the horse, and was shocked at how high it was just sitting there. It never occurred to me that it was quite a drop to the ground without even moving.

The instructor, a grizzly, hard-bitten character of about sixty who probably had been a cowboy in better times for him, sensed my insecurity and said: "You've got to show him who's boss." I think the horse thought he was talking to him, because he turned around and gave me a mean look. I don't know if horses can laugh, but suddenly this horse seemed to be laughing, and he wiped his lips on my leg just in case I missed the point.

I spent a few days out at the stables achieving virtually nothing. The instructor never seemed to tire of his put-down lines: "Hell, no horse is going to listen to you if you hold the reins like that!" I've always thought it is one of the worst facets of human nature that people who are very good at one thing tend to lord it over anyone entering their area.

The first day of shooting, when no one was looking, I managed awkwardly to board the horse, and it immediately began to do anything it wanted to do: a lot of trotting back and forth in different directions. Some handlers held him in place and eyed me suspiciously.

Charley Dubin came over to a few of us sitting on horses and said: "Okay, the first shot is you guys come galloping down that hill, ride through that creek, and disappear around that bend."

My heart was in my mouth. The other fellows rode off to get into their starting positions at the top of the hill. I sat there. The director looked at me quizzically. "Charley," I said, "that's a heck of a first shot! I don't know if I'm that kind of a rider," leaving out what kind I was.

He said, "Come on, Chuck. You said you could ride."

"Yeah, that's true," I said, my heart sinking.

He looked at me sympathetically, and had someone take my horse to the starting position. He said it was a very wide shot, so I should do whatever was necessary to stay on the horse.

When they called "Action!" I wrapped my arms around the horse's neck and shut at least one eye as he took off like a bullet down the hill, through the creek, and around the bend. I somehow got through the shot and the rest of the show, but not without a fair amount of snickering from the crew and my fellow bad guys in the cast.

After the show, I took myself back to the abusive riding instructor, and after a few weeks was at least able to get on a horse without reducing onlookers to helpless laughter.

I was in another western TV show as the right-hand man of Charles Bronson. I had a theory in those days that the cowboy with the deepest voice—the macho sound—would be the cowboy who would go the furthest in this field. I think Charles Bronson might have had the same idea, because in my first scene with him, when I entered and said in a deep voice: "The Jackson gang is coming over the ridge," he looked at me as if to say, What's this guy doing with that low voice?

He said, in a deeper voice: "How many of them are there?"

I said, in yet a deeper voice than his: "Looks like about eight."

He said, deeper yet: "You sure?"

I went a little deeper still: "I'm sure."

He gave me a long, hard look and said, deeper than anyone could go: "Okay."

(As the years went by, the deep-voice ploy was surpassed for toughness by the Clint Eastwood Whisper, as it's known in the trade.)

We had lunch that day at the Universal Studios commissary, where there are huge color portraits of all the major actors and actresses working with or under contract to the studio. I've heard that, for reasons not completely clear, sometimes a portrait is moved, causing the star at lunch almost to lose his soup until he spots himself elsewhere on the wall.

The day of the deep-voice encounter, Bronson and three or four other villains and I were sitting at a table waiting for our orders. Bronson's came first, and he began to wolf it down. When he was about halfway through, and our lunches still hadn't come, I joked to him: "Why don't you start?"

He finished chewing whatever he had in there, slowly turned, looked at me, and said: "You know, if I ever have trouble with anybody, I don't push them or shove them or anything like that . . . I just bite their jugular vein." He then gave me a long, meaningful look.

After lunch, I let *him* have the deeper voice.

Years later, while getting into makeup for a movie, I heard another Bronson story. The makeup-room time is about six or seven o'clock in the morning. Actors drag themselves in, coming to life slowly, nothing really rolling yet. There's a lot of mundane chitchat: "What time did you go to sleep last night?" "I feel a cold coming on." "I like the cinnamon danish better than the other danish." The actors slowly try to rejoin the world, because shortly they're going to be out there in front of the cameras in full burst of life—hopefully.

The story goes that Bronson came into one of these mundane morning chitchat sessions and sat silently for about five minutes, listening. Finally, he spoke. Loudly. "Chit . . . chat. Chit . . . chat." He had a certain way of saying it. All chitchat stopped immediately.

I was building a reputation as a villain in westerns with my ability to appear frighteningly menacing. I got so good at it that once, when I was a guest villain on *The Virginian*, a western television series, the star, James Drury, took me aside and asked me if he had unintentionally offended me in some way.

I said, "Of course not. Why?"

He explained, "I really get a chill playing these scenes with you. I honestly get the feeling you'd like to kill me."

I assured him that what he was getting might be real, but it had nothing to do with him. I don't know if he knew what I meant, but he seemed reassured. Eventually my ability to convey menace became so strong that other actors referred to me as the "super heavy."

I had heard that James Drury, after several years of doing it, just hated being the Virginian. It was only the money that kept him there. The series filmed at Universal Studios, and the Universal tour tram went right through the places where the shooting was done. Drury felt like a monkey on display, and threatened to quit unless they kept the sightseeing tours away from him. He also refused to work past a certain point in the afternoon. He just hated being there. In fairness to Jim, I should add that this happens to a lot of series stars after a certain amount of time.

(Over the years I worked with only one star of a series who seemed genuinely happy to be there. When I commented on how unusual I found his happiness, he whispered into my ear, "I'm drunk.")

One oven-hot day, I was watching Jim Drury sitting on a rock in a dirty, dusty street, with flies buzzing around his head. He was waiting for the next shot. Even if I hadn't known how unhappy he was, I could see it written all over his face. In my best *Candid Camera* attitude of innocence, I walked over to him and said, "Boy, I really admire you. Here it is, hot as hell, a miserable place to be, the flies buzzing all around . . . and you don't mind it at all. What a pro!"

All the time I was talking, he was staring at me. At some point, when he realized I was kidding, he laughed so hard he fell off his rock.

One day I was at Paramount Pictures doing a guest appearance on a television western called *The Guns of Will Sonnett*, starring Walter Brennan. I was playing a vicious hired gunslinger called "Bells" Pickering. Bells always hung a little bell on his holster after he killed someone. At this point in his career, there was quite a jingling when Bells approached.

A Paramount casting director named Joyce Selznick came over to see me while I was waiting for my next scene as Bells. Ironically, Joyce was the same casting director who had, years before, kept me waiting for hours and then left because she was "running late." She later became a booster of mine in New York. After learning that I had about half an hour till my next scene as Bells, Joyce took me by the hand and brought me in to meet a director on the lot named Roman Polanski, who was about to do a movie called *Rosemary's Baby*.

I'm in the Movies with Roman Polanski

I walked into the room in my cowboy outfit to meet Roman Polanski. He was there with a lot of others involved in the picture and everyone looked a bit startled as this jingling cowboy entered. Roman had drawings done to fit his specifications of what each character in the movie should look like, and they were all over the walls of the office. It turned out that if you could look past my muttonchops, I resembled the drawing of Rosemary's (Mia Farrow) young obstetrician.

When Roman saw me come into the room, he looked at the wall and looked at me, and looked at the wall and looked at me. Roman, who is somewhere around five feet four, was very young-looking. He was born in Poland and has a thick accent. He suddenly got excited and started to jump up and down like a boy. "Yes, yes, you be doctor! Good, good! You shave your face, you be in movie. Good!"

Now, I'd been around long enough by then to know that it wasn't really because I looked like some drawing on a wall that I would be cast in a movie. Somebody's going to say, Have him audition for the part; and then of course I may or may not be in the movie—no matter what I look like. But Roman didn't seem to be doing it that way. He shook my hand, and before anybody could say anything I got out of there. The minute I was out of the office I heard another casting director say: "Roman, don't you want to audition him?" I ran down the hall and out of the building, all the while jingling loudly. The next day I heard I got the part . . . thanks to Joyce Selznick, and to Roman Polanski's ability to look past muttonchops and to some artist somewhere.

Incidentally, the other casting director who asked if Roman didn't want to audition me was Hoyt Bowers, whom I had met twelve years earlier at Warner Brothers—the one who had said my quality was too light. I'm sure he didn't remember me—especially since I was now standing there as a ruthless killer.

In *Rosemary's Baby*, Mia Farrow as Rosemary becomes convinced at some point that her husband and a number of other people are either witches or practicing witchcraft and are, in one way or another, trying to do her and her baby harm. And she's right.

The scene we were to film on my first day was Mia coming back to me, her original obstetrician, whom she had left months earlier on the advice of these witches to go to a (unbeknownst to her) witchcraft obstetrician. She relates the story of all these witchy goings-on and desperately asks for my help. Well, I, as a young doctor, naturally don't believe the witch stuff and think she's hysterical. But I want her to think I believe her so that I can give her a sedative, have her lie down, and then call her husband to take her home. Mia finished her hysterical story about the witches. I looked at her, took a pause as though considering the possibility of what she'd told me, and then said, "Well, you may be right." Mia is thrilled. She believes me: Finally, she's going to get some help.

Roman Polanski leaped up and said: "Take out pause before you speak."

I said, "Well, it's a pretty farfetched story she's telling, and if I say right away, 'You may be right,' without thinking it over for a moment, I think it's less likely that Mia or the audience will believe me."

Roman stared at me. Since it was my first day, I didn't know you didn't talk back to Roman Polanski. Roman, in the tradition of many European directors, wasn't really so hot in the give-and-take department. Their version is: They give, you take. He told me he was paid quite a lot of money to know about these things, and he didn't want the pause, didn't think it made it *more* believable, thought it made it *less* believable, and asked me to do it again, without the pause.

I resented his attitude and the crack about him being paid all this money to know about things. I told him I knew a couple of things myself, but I would do it as he asked. I did it with less of a pause. But I wasn't through. After the filming was completed that day, I went up to him and said I had thought about everything he'd said—and here I took not a short but a long pause and said: "I think you're right."

"Good!" he said. "Of course!" he said.

I said, "Did you believe what I just said?"

He said, "Yes."

I said, "Well, I don't mean it. I just wanted to show you how much more convincing it was with the pause."

He glared at me. I'd obviously made my point. He continued to glare, trying to figure out if he hated my guts or admired me. He decided he admired me, threw his arm around my shoulder, and invited me to come with him to watch the previous day's film.

The next day, after sleeping on it, Roman reconsidered the situation and decided he hated my guts after all. The first time I asked him about something, he said loudly: "I don't care what you do!" And it was like ice after that.

Some of the other actors, notably John Cassavetes, were also having trouble with Roman's autocratic attitude. Roman is a very gifted director, and I believe he did a beautiful job on *Rosemary's Baby*, but I could never accept that actors should be treated as pawns or puppets. The director ultimately is in charge and will decide just about everything, but doing that without first seeing what the actor might have to offer robs the actor, the director, and the picture.

Roman's activity off the set was also new to me. He would regularly practice drawing a toy pistol from a holster he sometimes wore, delighted as he increased the speed of his draw. Roman was a good friend of Tony Curtis and would talk to him regularly on the phone from the set. I got the feeling that at least part of the time they hung out together they practiced their quick draws, and probably had a hell of a good time doing it too.

At the end of my last day on the picture, I went to say good-bye to Mia Farrow, whom I liked enormously. She has the same genuine sweetness off-screen as she has on. Mia had recently married Frank Sinatra. For weeks, everything they did when not front-page news (which it mostly was) was close to it. There probably were very few people in the country who didn't know that Mia Farrow and Frank Sinatra had just been married. Certainly there wasn't a soul in show business who didn't know.

I went up to Mia before I left and said that if she wasn't married or dating anyone, I'd really love to take her out. The look on her face before she realized it was a gag was just what we were always looking for on *Candid Camera*—kind of like, I can't believe this is happening! Of course, her smile after she realized it was a joke wasn't bad either.

The Graduate

I was working in westerns for about a year and had played my part in *Rosemary's Baby,* but I still was just able to pay the rent, and that was it. However, I couldn't help but notice that I was being referred to more and more as someone on the verge of real success. Somebody told me that Aaron Spelling, a big television producer who had produced *The Guns of Will Sonnett,* had said that he thought I was the best young dramatic actor in Hollywood. (Never comedic, only dramatic. My comedic reputation was confined to Broadway.) It was all real nice to hear, but I still had about forty-five bucks in the bank after almost fifteen years in the profession.

Then, one day, a director I knew told me he had read a book and tried to option it to make a movie starring me. When he tried to acquire the option, he learned that Paramount Pictures had already bought the book and intended to make a movie out of it. He strongly advised me to read it. I did, and loved it. It was called *The Graduate.*

I went about trying to get an audition. The movie was to be directed by Mike Nichols. This was his second picture; the first had been *Who's Afraid of Virginia Woolf?* Prior to that, he'd had an almost unprecedented string of successes directing on Broadway, including *The Odd Couple* and *Barefoot in the Park.* The picture was already touted by many to be the big upcoming comedy. I tried to get an audition. The casting director told my agent that he knew me and liked me, but this was about a recent college graduate and I was almost ten years older than that. I called Joe Schoenfeld, who was the co-head of the William Morris Agency's movie department and a real supporter of mine, and asked if he could call someone and have me meet Mike Nichols anyway. He did, and within a day or two I arrived for the meeting.

I walked into the outer offices. Mike was escorting a boy, who looked to me to be about twelve, to the door. I looked like the kid's uncle. After the boy had left, I said to Mike, "Isn't he a little young?"

Mike, never one to miss a beat, joked: "He's playing the part."

Seated now with Mike, the casting director, and the producer, I said that I realized I was a little old for the part of an about-to-be college graduate, but I thought I could make up for it in other ways—implying acting. Mike asked how old I was. "Forty-seven," I quickly joked, and Mike, without batting an eye, said, "That's the right age."

He agreed to let me come in and audition. About a week later I went in and read twenty-eight pages of the script for him. I had never in my life been received so enthusiastically.

That night Mike called me at home. He said he hadn't imagined he would ever hear the part read like that. He asked me to stop eating immediately and try to get down to looking so skinny I would pass for a new college graduate, and then ended the conversation with: "You are our number-one choice for the part. We have no second choice." He said they wanted to see how I would look on-screen, and so a screen test was necessary . . . but only for photographic purposes: They had already seen me act it.

I hung up the phone. Mike's words reverberated in my head: "You are our number-one choice. . . . We have no second choice. . . . I never imagined I'd hear the part read like that." I walked around the small house I was renting in the Hollywood Hills in a daze. This was it! After fifteen years, here was the opportunity of a lifetime: a great part, a great script, a great comedy director! All I had to do was lose the weight and get down to boyhood size, and that was that. Or was it?

The next day the agent called to tell me, yes, they wanted to do the screen test, but since screen tests cost a lot of money, they wanted to have the deal set with me before the test. "That's how these things are done," it was explained. They didn't want to spend the money on the test, want me, and then my agent might ask for—who knew? "Okay," I said. "Great." I wasn't uneasy about them wanting to make the deal first: It just made it all seem more real. I couldn't imagine not being able to make a deal. That seemed out of the realm of possibility.

The next day the agent called me with their proposal. The deal, conditioned on them wanting me, was this: They would have a seven-year contract with me. "Uh-huh," I said. And they wanted to pay me five hundred dollars a week to star in *The Graduate*.

Now, to put this in context, I was being paid one thousand dollars a week to be a guest star on a western TV show. I did that about six times a year for my total income, which put me not that far above the poverty level. But five hundred dollars a week to star in *The Graduate* seemed way too low to me. I wasn't thinking about the money, but about the fairness. And the agent agreed with me that it just wasn't right. Unfortunately, at that moment, no genie appeared to say to the agent and me: Fairness-schmairness, take the deal. Pay them, wash their cars if necessary—take it!

I didn't. We said no. I said no without any hesitation. First of all, I believed they would come back with a better offer; but mostly it just seemed wrong. Consciously doing something wrong or unfair seemed impossible to me. It was as though a sense of fairness were a very real thing—not an idea, but as real as kicking someone, which I felt they were doing to me, as well as to anyone else who would be exploited.

The producer, Larry Turman, a man experienced in the ways of Hollywood, called me at home to ask me if I was out of my mind. He pointed out that this was the chance of a lifetime for a young actor. I knew that, I said, but I added that even though they had just become aware of me two days ago, I had already been very well received in two Broadway shows, and I felt—

He interrupted to say that he knew the price wasn't right, but everybody got exploited in their first starring role, and the opportunities it could open up would more than make up for this. He swore to me that I was making a big mistake. I said I didn't know how to do something I thought wasn't fair. We said good-bye.

I still wasn't disheartened—I was absolutely certain they would make a fairer offer. I was right, but there was something else happening that I didn't see coming at all.

After two weeks of phone calls between the producer and my agent, the price was a thousand dollars a week. Within the hour after it was agreed to, there was a messenger at my front door handing me an envelope. In the envelope was a ten-page scene and a note from Mike Nichols saying that if I had any questions to call him at home. It also said I would be expected at Paramount Pictures the next morning at seven A.M. to do the screen test.

I called Mike. I said I couldn't really learn all this and be good enough by the next morning. Mike reassured me, saying it was only a photographic test; and he was very nice. But something had happened in the two weeks' negotiating period: They were resentful of me—they thought I was going to be a difficult person to work with—and, without fully realizing it, I was resentful of them as well. I felt that the whole craft of acting was being given short shrift by expecting me to prepare this much material and excel at it in such a short period of time.

From the minute I had gotten that first phone call from Mike I had stopped eating, as he had suggested. I hadn't been that much overweight—maybe a little—but I also didn't look like I had just graduated from college. In the two weeks while the negotiations were going on, I had become a Metrecal liquid-diet freak. When I showed up at the studio that next morning, I said hello to Mike, and he didn't even recognize me. However, I'm sure that in his mind all it meant was that he just had a thinner guy who was going to be difficult.

Eventually Mike began to talk to me and Katharine Ross, who did end up as the girl in the picture, about the scene we would be filming for the test. He then asked both of us if we agreed with how he saw it. Katharine easily said yes, and I said I didn't know if I agreed or not because I hadn't really had time to study it. This was not an answer Mike was looking for. My answer not only surprised Mike, it surprised me. It was only at that moment that I started to be consciously aware of how much I resented my position. I felt like a fighter with one arm tied behind his back.

Mike and I have since become friends, but at that moment I think each of us wanted to turn around and go home. I was uncomfortable throughout the whole day, not really knowing the lines, not really feeling I could do my best; and Mike seemed to be just as uncomfortable with me. At one point he asked me if I would jump up and down on the bed.

I said, "Why would I be jumping up and down on the bed?" Mike said, "I just want to see you do it."

I said, "Of course I could jump up and down on the bed, but what am I doing there jumping?" (I thought I was back in my imaginary-suitcase days.) I'm sure now that Mike just wanted to see how loose I could get. I knew I could get as loose as anyone would ever want, and even looser if I had enough time to learn the words they were asking me to speak—sometimes very rapidly.

Eventually, rather than deal with my requests for an explanation for the desired jumping, Mike let it all drop. It was not a good day. I got through it somehow, but I felt I was operating at about 40 percent.

I drove home after the test feeling I had just blown the opportunity of a lifetime. It hurt me that when the major chance had finally come after fifteen years, circumstances didn't allow me to give my best, which I felt would have gotten me the role.

A couple of days passed, and Mike called. "How would you like to do *Catch-22* with me?" he asked. That was to be his next picture, based on Joseph Heller's best-selling novel. I said, "On any other day, that would be a very welcome invitation." We both said we were sorry this hadn't worked out. I think I was a little sorrier than Mike; I'm sure he felt he was getting rid of a handful of trouble.

Later, when we did work together on *Catch-22*, it was clear that there was no trouble at all. By the way, Dustin Hoffman, who, of course, played the part, stopped arguing at seven hundred fifty.

But that day, *Catch-22* was still two years away—and, once again, I had no job, still no money, and no real prospects. I was down. It felt like the absolute low point of my career. I knew I could do the part, and yet I wasn't going to do it. It hurt. Instead of playing the leading role in a big comedy, I wouldn't be doing anything at all. Not only that, but my money had now entirely run out. I was thirty-two years old and broke. I borrowed eight hundred dollars from the Actors' Credit Union. At a certain point, when despair had reduced my voice to a low monotone, my protective armor took over and I felt nothing. I was, once again, numb.

And then a telegram arrived . . .

Lovers and Other Strangers

The telegram read: AM ARRIVING IN LOS ANGELES MONDAY. WOULD LIKE DISCUSS GENE WILDER PROJECT WITH YOU. It was signed RENEE TAYLOR. I don't put this in the category of what I consider to be the precognition of knowing I was going to be in my first Broadway show, *Tchin Tchin*, but here again I felt certain that this telegram was going to mean something very significant to me. After my experience with *The Graduate*, I sure hoped so anyway.

It's ironic to me that Renée Taylor, who was to play such an important part in my professional life, had been a classmate of mine with Lee Strasberg for at least a year and we had never even spoken. She had great success as a so-called "dumb blonde" who said unintentionally witty things as a regular guest on *The Jack Paar Show*, which preceded *The Tonight Show with Johnny Carson*. Renée, however, was not dumb, and the unintentionally witty things she said were not so unintentional. She is an unusually gifted actress and writer.

She and her new husband, a young comedy writer and television-commercial director named Joe Bologna, had written about twelve short pieces that they wanted to turn into a play for Broadway. They'd gone to Gene Wilder to involve him—to star, direct, anything. Gene was considered smart, and was more established than Renée, Joe, or I. Earlier I had been asked to play a part in a

Broadway production of *One Flew Over the Cuckoo's Nest,* thought the part was wrong for me and perfect for Gene, and suggested to the director, Alex Segal, that he get Gene Wilder.

Alex said, "Who's Gene Wilder?"

I said, "Meet him and you'll see."

Alex met him and cast him.

Gene and I had been friends for several years. He had told Renée, in his inimitable fashion: "There's a man named Charles Grodin in Los Angeles. Take your work to him, and he will know what to do."

Renée said, "Who's Charles Grodin?"

Gene, again in his unique style: "You asked my advice. Go find this man."

I'm sure that when I arrived for the meeting with Renée, she was expecting someone with long, flowing white robes and a beard. I talked for about thirty minutes about Renée and Joe's work, which she had sent me. I told her what I thought was funny and what I thought should be developed or cut; but whatever I said, I said with considerable respect for their enormous talent. Renée never spoke. Finally, after I couldn't think of anything else to say, I just stopped talking. Renée still didn't speak, but just peered at me.

At last, she stood, pronounced me a genius, walked to the phone, and called New York to tell the female producer of the show, Stephanie Sills, that she had just met the man who was going to direct the play and also the man that Stephanie was going to marry. For a guy with no money and no job and no prospects, it didn't feel bad to hear this. Renée ended up batting .500 on her predictions.

I never gave a lot of thought to the extent of my directing skills, until I started to meet and work with more and more directors. As a breed, they're too autocratic, too self-important, and not open enough to hear what others have to say. Of course, this has always been an accepted concept of what a director is—always in control, always knowing exactly what he or she is doing. Not to appear this way is taken as a sign of weakness. I've always felt exactly the opposite on the subject. The directors who can say "I don't know" or "I'm not sure" have been the best I've worked with. Of course, it's little egos that are easily threatened by the contributions of others. Too many directors are always keeping score, playing power games. However, there's a whole significant group of directors who are not like this and who are extremely talented and helpful.

I flew to Chicago to meet Joe Bologna shortly after that. In 1967, he was a warm, jumpy, volatile fellow. He had met Renée when someone had put them together with the idea of Joe writing for Renée, who was appearing in outlying night spots in New Jersey with names like Club Excelsior. I don't know how much nightclub material came out of their meetings, but these short plays that I had read did, as well as their recent marriage.

Joe and Renée were in Chicago to fix a comedy called *How to Be a Jewish Mother* that was heading to Broadway but was in trouble out of town. It starred the legendary Yiddish theater actress Molly Picon. A lot of the discussion of the problems of the play, Joe said, centered on what Molly should be talking to or where she should be looking as she addressed her deceased husband.

When I saw the play, they had a cloth dummy in a chair that she talked and sang to. As I said, it was a show in trouble. Joe told me about a meeting he had just come from where someone said: "Maybe we should go from two intermissions to one," and someone else jumped up and said: "Don't change the intermissions. They're the only thing that's working!" I laughed, and then we spent an hour trying to figure each other out, circling warily, until the name Milos Forman came up.

In 1967, Milos Forman was an acclaimed Czech director, but pretty much unknown in this country. Today, of course, he's the Academy Award–winning director of the films *One Flew Over the Cuckoo's Nest* and *Amadeus*. It turned out that Joe and I had seen his early Czech pictures and were both bowled over by the reality of them. We decided to proceed, based on that.

A few months later, Renée, Joe, and I were living in their house in the woods in Woodstock, New York, in the freezing dead of winter—twenty degrees below zero—working to turn those twelve short pieces into a Broadway show. Even though my entire experience in this field consisted of a failed Off-Broadway musical, Renée and Joe were listening to my advice as though I were Noël Coward. They seemed very comfortable with me. I, on the other hand, had never met anyone like them.

They would read me something new they had written. I

would give them my notes. They would disappear into another room for about three hours, and I would hear all kinds of screaming and yelling come blasting through the door—not cursing, just yelling. Then they would emerge from the room. I kept expecting them to announce they were getting a divorce. But they always seemed in perfectly good spirits, as though nothing had happened. They would read me what they had done. I would suggest a few more changes. They'd go back and scream and yell for another hour, and then come out, easygoing again. At first, I was confused and uncomfortable with all this screaming followed by sweetness, but then I got used to it and started to look on it as kind of a performance piece—real, but still a hell of a show in itself. After several weeks of this, we came back from Woodstock with five short comic plays.

The plays were sent around to various investors for financing, and were unanimously rejected. "Minor league," "Amateur night," "Not funny," were some of the kinder remarks. Renée and Joe looked at me not skeptically but What-do-we-do-now? I suggested we rent a small hall and read the plays aloud to a group of a hundred or so potential investors. They agreed. Stephanie Sills, the producer, sent out the invitations. The evening came. Renée, Joe, a few other actors, and I were the performers. Sitting on chairs, we read from the script. We'd now see if it was "amateur night" and "not funny." I had told Renée and Joe that what they had was some of the funniest comic material anyone had ever seen. Some of the same people who had said it was unfunny were in the audience, which numbered around sixty. Here was the moment of truth.

We began to read from the first play—and the laughs began immediately. They never stopped. At the end of two hours, the applause was overwhelming, and from the very same people who had earlier been so dismissive of the script. Renée and Joe embraced me. All those laughs I had said would be there were there. At the reception afterward, Renée walked around introducing me to everyone, saying, "Here's our genius. Here's our genius." I had never felt so appreciated in my life. It seemed a long way from *The Graduate*.

And it was good news for everyone. For me, it was a chance for a major stepping out. It was one thing to be a successful supporting actor in two Broadway shows, but to be a director, at thirty-two, of a big Broadway comedy that was to open first out of town at a fifteen-hundred-seat theater, and then come to one of Broadway's best theaters . . . that was stepping out and into a spotlight that could only compare in opportunity to that Actors Studio spotlight. But I was determined, and certainly a lot more confident, that there would be a positive result this time.

An extraordinary thing happened just as the play was starting to gear up. Again through the intervention of Gene Wilder, I was suddenly offered my first starring role in a big-budget major-studio movie. It was called *Start the Revolution Without Me*. Gene was the star, and he persuaded Bud Yorkin and Norman Lear, the powers behind the movie, that I would be perfect for the other starring role, that of his brother. I was already too committed to Renée and Joe even to consider dropping out of the play for the movie, so that was that. It didn't bother me too much (even though I thought the movie script was very funny) because I was completely consumed with the work on the play.

First, Renée and Joe and I, along with Stephanie Sills, were deeply involved in raising money through a string of backers' auditions at which we performed. A bizarre incident happened at one of them after I got the offer to be in *Start the Revolution Without Me*. One of the people connected with the production became convinced that I was going to "throw" a big backers' audition we had coming up. The word *throw* is used here as in "throw the fight"—meaning deliberately lose for some secret gain (usually money). Here, the accusations meant I would "throw the reading" (not perform as well as I could) so the play wouldn't raise its money, and I'd be free to star in the movie. I found the whole thing funny. Joe Bologna, on the other hand, was deeply insulted on my behalf. He pinned the production person against a wall in a room off where we were about to begin the backers' audition when the person wouldn't stop hysterically claiming, "The fix is in! The fix is in!"

Once we raised the money, we began casting. That went on for months. It was a large cast, and I was determined to see as many people as possible and give them the chance I had always found so hard to get. I even went to the required open auditions where any member of the union can come to be seen by someone connected to the production, usually a stage manager. I conducted those myself and met thousands of people, most of whom hadn't ever worked on Broadway and many of whom hadn't worked anywhere in years. I looked so young I believe they thought I was an assistant stage manager. I found one of our understudies there. In the regular auditions, I again saw literally thousands of people (I think setting some kind of record). In wanting to be certain I was making the right choices, I asked some of the actors to audition as many as four times. One good actor got fed up at his fourth audition and slammed the script to the floor. He said to me: "You're worrying the part to death. I could do this with my hands tied behind my back!" I understood his anger and frustration, but I still hadn't found a cast that was strong enough for those parts. In everything I've ever directed, there are always a couple of people—usually actors, not actresses—who come in unable to conceal their rage at being in an auditioning situation. They will inevitably say things like, "Aren't you familiar with my work?" "Didn't you see me in [such-and-such]?" "I'm not a very good reader." "I'm going to have to move the furniture around a bit to have this work for me." Having been through so much of this myself as an actor, I have only empathy for the person auditioning, no matter how crazy he or she gets. And yet, on this play, even I was once put to the test.

One young actor came in and started attacking right off the bat: "Why do I have to audition for the young parts? Why can't I audition for the old parts? That's what's wrong with the theater: all this typecasting!" This was all said right after "Hello."

I said, "I think I can get older people who would be better for the older parts."

He belligerently said, "How do you know that if you haven't heard me read them?!"

I said, "Go ahead and read them."

He did. He finished and said, again challengingly: "So!"

I said, again: "I think I can get older people who would be better for the older parts."

He stared at me a moment, nodded grimly, and left.

Happily, he later became well known (playing parts his own age).

As much as I feel for the actors' discomfort in auditioning, the people putting on the project have so much time and effort invested in it that these auditions become necessary to try to avoid making mistakes. The exception to this, of course, is if you're hiring someone to do something that everyone involved has seen him do before. I say "everyone" because in most plays *everyone* has cast approval—writer, director, producer, and, sometimes, the star. It's not that easy to get everyone to agree on anyone. I believe that casting is everything, and if you don't have the right actors, all the writing and directing in the world won't do it for a play. Fine comedy actors, in my opinion, must be as good at serious acting (reality) as they are at comedy. Because of those demands, this is a relatively small group of people.

Lily Tomlin (who has won a Best Actress award on Broadway) likes to tell the story of her audition for me. When she finished, I asked her if she'd ever acted before. She was crushed, she said, and ran to a phone booth to tell a friend how terrible she must have been. I always remind her that the reason I asked her that was because she had been recommended to me by the director of a musical review (Sandy Devlin, the musical stager from *Hooray*) she was in, and I thought she was a musical performer, even though I thought she gave a good acting audition. But, whatever my rationale, I inadvertently was as insensitive to Lily as others had been to me.

In any event, we ended up with a magnificent cast.

Eventually, the first day of rehearsal finally came for the play, which was called *Lovers and Other Strangers*. There were a lot of people gathered on the stage that day: ten members of the cast, many of whom had distinguished themselves in other Broadway shows; four or five understudies covering all the parts—also excellent people, any of whom could play the parts they understudied unusually well; of course, the writers, Renée and Joe; Renée's mother, Mrs. Frieda Wechsler; the producer, Stephanie Sills; top scenic costume and lighting designers; highly experienced stage managers; a number of assistants—a lot of people. I started to welcome everyone, and suddenly was acutely aware that all eyes were on me. I wanted to tell them how excited we were to have them all, and how I saw the play and all that, but I realized I was very, very nervous. I had learned how to deal with rejection but now I had to learn to deal with having authority—which also, unexpectedly, was nerve-racking. I had auditioned and approved every single member of the cast, but now, sitting there in front of all of them, I realized that many in the company were older and more experienced than I was. My directing experience consisted of one show that had run three weeks. (I couldn't go around telling that costumes-were-stolen story to everyone I met.) As soon as I realized my voice was shaking, I shifted gears and switched my speech to a short introduction of Renée's mother, Mrs. Frieda Wechsler, a short, extraordinarily warm woman with a lisp and a lot of guts, who always enjoyed making a statement. Mrs. Wechsler basically said how happy we were to have everyone there and how we all felt that, with hard work, we could have a success—pretty much what I would have said if I could have spoken.

Lovers and Other Strangers dealt with love, romance, and marriage. I don't know if it was life imitating art, or what, but as soon as this company got together, all kinds of romances broke out. I gave notes after each rehearsal. Sometimes one of the performers would be able to leave early because I had said all I had to say to him. His lover would sit there fidgeting, looking furiously at me to give *her* notes and let her get the hell out of there and into the arms of love. All the romances were topped by Renée and Joe calling me to a private meeting one day to tell me they were expecting.

We opened in the fifteen-hundred-seat Fisher Theater in Detroit to rave reviews and sellout business. It was a complete triumph. The papers were raving about Renée and Joe, and even me. Renée's mother told some of the movie people from Hollywood who had descended on us in Detroit that we wanted five hundred thousand dollars for the movie rights. When they looked faint, she whipped out a rave review from *Variety* and read the entire thing to them as they stood and nodded and looked increasingly nervous.

The road to Broadway was not entirely smooth. It was concluded at some point prior to the Broadway opening that one of the young women in the cast should be replaced. I was the only one against it, yet it was considered my job, as director, to tell the young woman. It seems unfair now; I should have said to the others: "You want to fire her? You tell her." I didn't want the job. But some kind of tradition was being followed, I guess. When I did walk over to the actress, it took me so long to get to the point that she thought we were just having an idle chat. As I got closer to saying what I had to say, I started to develop chest pains, which turned out to be tension. I had to lie down. She got me a

Boy on a pony: no thoughts of being a villain in Westerns

A guest appearance on *The Big Valley* television series—1967. I think they gave me the part because they were relieved I didn't bite them at the audition.

The Guns of Will Sonnett—1967. Bells Pickering added a bell to his holster every time he gunned someone down. This is how I looked when I met Roman Polanski for *Rosemary's Baby*.

Our grammar school basketball team

THE CIVITA

PEABODY HIGH SCHOOL

Pittsburgh, Pa., Friday, September 26, 1952

GRODIN, THOMPSON WIN 12A ELECTION; SWAILE, MORTON TO LEAD 12B CLASS

Charles Grodin of 8-230 was chosen president of the 12A class in the election of class officers Friday, September 12. At the same time Dave Swaile of 7-219 was elected president of the 12B class in balloting which was conducted in the 12B homerooms. The 12A's met in the auditorium to vote.

Election headlines: still my favorite notice

Grammar school graduation. This was the time of my first appearance in a play—*Getting Gracie Graduated*.

CHARLES GRODIN

High school graduation and college entry. My father passes away in between.

Sir Francis Chesney—Pittsburgh Playhouse, 1954. The lady is Elsie Ford, who later married the filmmaker Robert Downey and appeared in his movies.

The Little Hut—Rabbit Run Theater. Madison, Ohio, 1954.

Dick Scanga. He gave me my first job, was the first to fire me, and was my first and last mentor.

August 30, 1955

Helen Ferguson - Publicity,
~~8619 Sunset Boulevard,~~ 321 Beverley Drive
Hollywood, California Los Angeles, California

My dear Helen,

After all these years, I don't suppose you remember me.
I am Don Hall, the friend of Bob Stack's, who was a thorn
in your side.....and for that matter I guess Bob's side,
too.

But that was long, long ago and many years have passed.
I have gotten away from the theatrical side of my life
almost completely except for my intense interest in new,
young talent.

I suppose that I have a hellava lot of crust writing to
you, but my association with you via the mail made me
realize that you, too, are one who has an intense interest in new, young talent and that your standing, background and integrity are such that I can write to you
(in behalf of someone else) for advice if nothing else.

Here is the story: I have a slight interest in a local
summer theater...you might say that I dabble at it.....
This season we secured a young man (20 years old) as a
juvenile type. You can believe me, Helen, when I tell
you that this kid is not only talented but that he is
the most talented young man that I have run across in
my 25 years in theatrical work. I would hesitate going
any further except that my opinion is back by almost
everyone who has seen him. He never once played a "leading" part this season but people came back week after
week to see him. He is tall (6'1"), very nice looking
and has a tremennous personality. That is usual for
a juvenile, of course. But his talent is most unusual.
He can really act. Each portrayal is entirely different
and a living, breathing, believable character. And his
characterization are 100%.

There is no doubt that this young man will make the grade.
It is only a question of where, when and how soon. For
natural talent, such as his, will out one way or the other.

Don Hall's letter. Hollywood in the fifties didn't agree. Don Hall sadly
passed away from complications after gallbladder surgery long before
I was recognized.

He has decided to come to Hollywood immediately after the
season. No words, warnings or talk will delay him. I
have tried to point out that it is very rough and that
to go out there cold is a mistake. But, in a few weeks,
he will be on his way...and that is that.

I told him about you and advised that if he ever needed publicity
representation that you are the one to seek. I told him that
you were the type that he could go to in the very beginning
that you would go along on the basis of reasonable fees with
the future as a gamble. And I believe that I am right in
telling him this - am I not?

I am wondering if it would be too much for you to meet
with him, talk with him and advise him when he first comes
out there. He is not of the opinion that he will crash
the movies right away but hopes to work in some sort of
a theatrical group....or do something.....where he can
eventually develop and be seen.

I hope that I have made it clear that although he is a
young, good looking, personable type that he is equipped
with a tremendous talent. He is not just a leading man
type......but rather a young man with "leading man"
physical attributes but with more talent than these old
eyes have seen over these many, many years.

Finally, I want to make one thing more very clear.....I do
not and never will have any interest (commercially or
financially) in him. My only interest is to help him
get a start. It would be a shame if such a talent was
to go to waste. Therefore, I am appealing to you......
one who I know thinks along the same lines....to see if
there is anything that you can do to help his start.....
for if the start is made, and properly, nothing will
stop his progress.

I would appreciate your reaction to this request. If you
wish to meet with him, then I will see that you are put
into contact with him after his arrival. His name is
Charles Grodin. He has relatives and friends in L.A.
so he is not coming exactly cold-turkey.

I hope that you don't think I am being too bold in writing
to you about this but I would be remiss to my ideals if I
didn't do what I could to help.

                                        Cordially yours,

dmh-fg   Don Hall

POLICE DEPARTMENT
CITY OF NEW YORK

EXPIRES MAY 31, 1959

CHARLES S. GRODI

Driver 62018

PASSENGERS—For your protection keep a record of abov
name and number. Refer complaints to a Policeman or t
Hack License Bureau, 156 Greenwich Street, New York City

Police Commissione

L. D. 9.

Hack license. I drove for two years. For a while it was my favorite job.

The obligatory 8 x 10 glossy, 1959

The obligatory composite photo, 1959

THE ACTORS' STUDIO, INC.
432 West 44th St., New York 36, N. Y., PL 7-0870
LEE STRASBERG CHERYL CRAWFORD ELIA KAZAN

May 12, 1961

Mr. Charles Groddin
263 West 90 Street
New York City

Dear Mr. Groddin:

Thank you very much for the work and thought shown in your audition at the Actors' Studio last night.

Although you did not pass your audition the Directors felt that you should be encouraged to study, or to continue studying, and hope very much that you will come and apply for another preliminary audition when you feel ready.

Sincerely,

Gill Crowe
Secretary

Actors Studio. This was after my second try. I tried once more and was rejected. They invited me to join them in 1975.

MIKE NICHOLS

July 6,1967

Dear Chuck,

I enjoyed your letter. I am still planning for you in "CATCH 22", which unfortunately, is very far away.

Best of luck,

Mike

Mike's note. I think it felt further away for me than it did for Mike.

807A PST NOV 12 67 LA025

L-LLE054 (SY NA149) NL PD NEW YORK NY NOV 11

CHUCK-GROWDIN

8460 HOLLYWOOD BLVD LOSA

PLEASE CALL ME SUNDAY NOVEMBER 12 AROUND 11PM AT THE BEVERLY
HILLCREST IN REGARDS TO A GENE WILDER PROJECT SINCERELY
RENEE TAYLOR.

Telegram. This turned out to be directing *Lovers and Other Strangers*
on Broadway, and was a real turning point.

Courtesy of Joseph Abeles

Absence of a Cello, on Broadway in 1964. Left to right: Ruth White,
Charles Grodin, Ruth McDevitt, and Fred Clark.

With Alan Arkin in *Catch-22*

On location with Elaine May in Miami in 1972 for *The Heartbreak Kid*

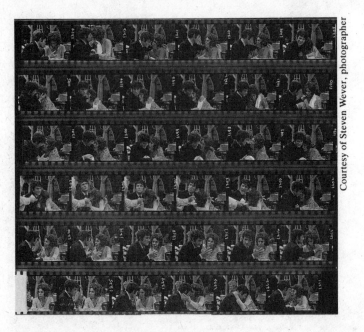

This is the painful sequence in *The Hearbreak Kid* where I leave my wife on our honeymoon. I still feel the backlash.

SIB293 957P EST DEC 18 72 NYI287(2036)(2-083374E353)PD 12/18/72 2036
 ICS IPMRNCZ CSP
ZCZC 2132747451 TDRN BEVERLY HILLS CA 14 12-18 0836P EST
PMS MR CHARLES GRODIN
HOTEL WINDERMERE 92 ST WEST END AVE
NEW YORK NY
THE BEST KEPT SECRET IN SHOW BUSINESS IS NOW OUT IM THRILLED
 FOR YOU
    HARRY

Harry Ufland's telegram after *The Heartbreak Kid* opened successfully

11 Harrowhouse, 1973

11 Harrowhouse review ad: Even with these reviews this movie stopped my career in Hollywood for a couple of years. It's a jungle out there.

Herb Gardner and me in Boston in 1974, burning the closing notice for *Thieves*.

King Kong, 1976. As the breakdowns of the mechanical ape became longer and more frequent, so did John Guillerman's bouts of staring off into space

Courtesy of Martha Swope

Same Time, Next Year, 1975

Charley's Aunt—La Mirada Civic Theatre, Santa Ana, California, 1984

Movers and Shakers, 1985

FRED de CORDOVA
Executive Producer

October 3, 1985

Mrs. Ruth Pearson
362 Plymouth Street
Cambria, California 93428

Dear Mrs. Pearson:

I'm terribly sorry that you didn't enjoy
the Johnny Carson-Charles Grodin "spoof".
Both of them did!

Over the years, they have played the same
"game", and we look forward to each appearance.

On the other hand, I'm delighted to set the
record straight.

Best wishes,

Fred de Cordova

Fred de Cordova

FdeC/bjf

Fred de Cordova's letter—there have been many letters of complaint.

Midnight Run, 1988. The rapids in New Zealand—the end of four months of filming.

glass of water, and as she was trying to calm me, I told her she was fired. It was doubly difficult for me because I couldn't tell her how much I disagreed with the decision and how good I thought she was. I thought that would be disloyal to the others. I know she felt like lying down herself, but she kept applying cold compresses. Two days later, the whole section that the young, talented actress had been in was cut from the show, and two additional actors had to be let go. But it was certainly easier to be dropped from the show because the scenes you were in were cut. Personally, I don't believe in firings unless it significantly affects the show. And I'd venture to say that more than the overwhelming majority of the time it doesn't. This time it didn't.

We finished our highly successful run in Detroit and prepared to move to Broadway. The stage of the Brooks Atkinson Theater in New York was considerably smaller than the stage of the Fisher Theater in Detroit. When we moved the scenery to the Brooks Atkinson, it seemed that our four large sets would come rolling in and out on tracks that were awfully close together. I went to the head stagehand and said, "Are you sure there's no chance at all that these sets could sway a bit, and one coming in quickly could hit one going out quickly?" He stared at me as though that was the dumbest question he'd ever heard. When I persisted, saying, "Forgive me, it's my first Broadway show, and I just don't know about this," he said: "Kid, I've been in this business thirty-five years. Trust me." Always being an optimist, I did. When we started to preview, the sets regularly crashed into each other. Starting right there, until the present, I became kind of an optimistic skeptic.

When we opened on Broadway, we got the biggest laughs I'd ever heard in the theater; they were like thunderclaps. In spite of that, the play received mixed notices. *The New York Times* loved it, which is supposed to be enough; but there was a certain amount of vitriol on the other side. The phrase "Neanderthal theater" sticks in my mind. The play was bold and maybe a little ahead of its time in the sexual-humor department. So, alongside the people screaming with laughter, there was a certain group heading up the aisles in the middle of the evening. The questionable sexual dialogue—and that's all it was: dialogue—represented far less than 1 percent of the play. The biggest laugh of the evening came when a woman turned to her husband in bed and asked demandingly: "Are you gonna make love to me or not?!" The man thinks a second and says, "I owe you one." It was the biggest laugh, and also a line that offended a lot of people. It neither made me laugh nor offended me. I was a much bigger fan of Renée and Joe's nonsexual humor, which was 99 percent of the play.

Business was in trouble from the start. We'd had the theater on what's called an interim booking, meaning another play was booked into the theater six weeks after us (my old friend Dustin Hoffman in a play called *Jimmy Shine*); and since we had the money to move (it would have cost twenty-five thousand dollars), we felt we should. The movie rights had been sold for two hundred and fifty thousand dollars. Today, that would be equal to a million dollars. The writers got 60 percent of that, and the production 40 percent, which meant that the production had a hundred thousand dollars from the movie sale. Business increased from the first week to the sixth week by 150 percent. We had tried everything to keep going. The actors went around to the various ticket brokers and asked them to do what they could to steer people to the show since the brokers had liked it. I spoke to other producers who had loved the show in an effort to get them to take it over. Joe Bologna and I would stand in front of the theater where our *Times* review was blown up and comment, as though we were passersby: "I hear it's very good." A few people overheard us and bought tickets. Renée and Joe rounded up about fifty relatives and gave them money to buy tickets. They formed a line. We said to our general manager: "Look, we've got a line!" But Renée and Joe ran out of relatives before that plan could work. None of our plans worked. Heartbreakingly to all of us, the play was allowed to close when our six-week booking was up.

I felt very strongly that the producers should have spent the twenty-five thousand dollars and moved *Lovers and Other Strangers* to another theater. We had more than doubled our business from the first to the sixth week, we had a rave review from *The New York Times*, and, most significantly, the show, overall, was loved by the audience and had great word of mouth. A lot of people felt that if it had moved it could have run for two years. Its longevity possibilities, I believe, were proved in that it still is being performed regularly, some twenty years later, all over the country in amateur and stock companies.

Those people responsible for the money always feel they have total control and owe no explanation to anyone, even though in this case most of the money was raised, of course, by a series of backers' auditions performed by Renée, Joe, and me. I've always resented this autocratic attitude of "money people." I think that when people work very hard for the better part of a year for little money, they are owed every chance and consideration. While, conceivably, by trying to go on running, money may be lost, work and effort going down the drain to me is worth more than money. The producers had actually wanted to close the play sooner, but I did some figuring, and got Renée and Joe to join with me (against the advice of their business manager) to indemnify the producers against any losses they might incur to finish out the six weeks. We would be responsible for any losses, and also share any profits. We ended up making eleven thousand dollars in profits for the remaining weeks. Recently, I was at a gathering, and one of the producers (a nonvisible one at the time of the play who had raised less than half the money and been influential in persuading Stephanie Sills to close the show) came up to me, introduced himself, and said: "I put up the money for *Lovers and Other Strangers*." I controlled myself for a moment, and the politest response I could come up with was, "Well, not *all* of it." He seemed taken aback. I wonder what he would have felt if I'd told him what I really thought of him.

I've always been proud of the successful movie that was made out of the play and of how the play continues to be done regularly all over the country to this day, and probably will for the rest of our lives.

When I said the telegram from Renée changed my life, I meant that with *Lovers and Other Strangers* a lot more people in the profession became aware of me. At that time I met my professional benefactor—Elaine May, of the legendary comedy team of Mike Nichols and Elaine May. Elaine was Renée's mentor. I met her for the first time at Renée and Joe's apartment. I was there when she came in. When we were introduced, she graciously said, "Gene Wilder says wonderful things about you." Here, I made a misjudgment that I'm sorry to say I've made several times. I'll say something meant to be a joke, with absolute certainty that the person I'm speaking to will know it's a joke (especially if it's a comedic expert like Elaine May). If the person doesn't realize I'm joking, I'm stuck with the serious content of the line. Elaine, and many others since—when I first met them, anyway—haven't known I was joking, and there turned out to be some uncomfortable situations. On that afternoon, after Elaine spoke, I replied: "Boy, you're really coming on, aren't you?" She looked at me startled, because, of course, all she had done was to pay me a nice compliment. I, in return, in an effort to make her laugh, had only made her uncomfortable. It was very awkward. I muttered that I was joking, but I could see she didn't know what to make of me.

The truth is, I loved her even before I met her, but at that moment it was all uneasiness. Years later, when I met Art Carney, whose skin looked like a baby's, the first thing I said was: "Do you ever shave?" I was sure he would laugh. He didn't. He acted as though I had attacked his skin in some way. He didn't know in what way, just that his skin had been attacked. I've stopped making the assumption that because someone is a comedic person he or she will "read" me right away. Of course, there will always be some who, no matter what I do, won't know what I'm talking about; but I've concluded that it's a risk you take when humor is as important to you as any pleasure in life. You tend to keep your eyes open, hoping to spot some at any time. Nevertheless, I always feel worse than those people who are uncomfortable when they don't know I'm kidding.

My first professional encounter with Elaine May came while we were previewing *Lovers and Other Strangers* in New York. She had seen the play, and Renée asked me how I would feel about meeting with her. I said I would be delighted. Renée, Joe, and I went to Elaine's apartment. She had a number of thoughts and suggestions about the evening. She prefaced every comment with: "I'm sure Chuck has considered this," or, "I know Chuck has probably tried this." I was mightily impressed with her sensitivity. She is a pure artist, consumed by and dedicated to the work as much or more than anyone I've ever met. Years later, in my apartment, I read her a long screenplay I had written. She sat in a chair for four hours, barely moving, her hands folded on her lap, never wanting any food or drink—just concentrating. When I finished reading to her, she proceeded to talk about the screenplay for hours. Clearly, she hadn't missed a word. She has worked for months on end to help friends whose work was in trouble, and for no salary, either.

Shortly after the play's closing, I was directing Renée and Joe in a short piece they had written for public television. In the middle of the first day of rehearsal, I said to Joe, "You know, I should be playing that part and you should be directing this."

He said, "Well, we did base the part on you."

I said, "I thought there was something familiar about it."

So Joe took my position as director and I climbed into bed next to Renée, and we proceeded with this comic love scene. One of the people who saw me act for the first time in that short ten-minute piece was Elaine May, and an idea was born in her mind that was later to change my career drastically, more than anything before or since.

Catch-22 and Mike Nichols

About six months after *Lovers and Other Strangers* closed, a casting director for Mike Nichols called and asked me to audition for *Catch-22*. I read for the role Mike suggested, and he seemed very happy. Then he said, "Out of curiosity, let me hear you read a few other parts." Eventually, I read about six. Mike then announced to everyone that, as far as he was concerned, I was capable of playing any part in the movie. I went home feeling good and thinking that maybe Mike would now believe *The Graduate* reading and not *The Graduate* test. Of course, whatever he believed, he had nothing to regret with the success they'd had with Dustin.

I can't even now say for sure why, when I was offered a good part in *Catch-22*, I turned it down. Nobody was turning down Mike Nichols in those days, or in these days either—especially not an unemployed actor/director/writer. But I turned it down. I was working on writing something, and I guess I just felt like writing at home in New York rather than being one of a large company of actors somewhere in Mexico, where much of the picture was going to be shot. It was a totally unpragmatic move, as I still wasn't exactly what you'd call solvent. But, in spite of the abbreviated run of *Lovers and Other Strangers*, I felt there was increasing evidence that when I was given authority good things could happen. So it really wasn't difficult for me to turn down the movie until Mike Nichols called me at my apartment.

First of all, to an unemployed actor, it was like the head of a studio calling. "How are you?" he almost sang. He makes you feel he means it, and I believe he does.

"I'm fine," I said, quickly trying to figure out what was going on. Is he mad at being turned down?—what?

He quickly moved to: "I think you'd be *won-der-ful* in the part." He was getting his money's worth out of the three syllables of *wonderful*.

I said, "It may be the only part I can play." (It's the role of a crazy person.)

I was mostly joking, but Mike seemed to understand exactly what I meant, and laughed.

I said, "I have this script I'd like to write that I'm working on."

He said, "You'll have plenty of free time to write while acting in the movie."

I said, "Okay, I'll do it."

That was that. I was completely charmed by Mike. I hear he has the same effect on almost everyone who meets him.

So there I was, about a year now after the close of *Lovers and Other Strangers,* in Guaymas, Mexico.

After the tremendous success of *The Graduate,* for which he won an Academy Award as Best Director, Mike Nichols commanded even more respect than ever before. He was able to attract an all-star cast led by Alan Arkin, which also included Tony Perkins, Orson Welles, Bob Newhart, Jon Voight, and Martin Sheen, among many, many others. It was such a coup to be in the picture that everyone felt as though they were being knighted to be part of it. Mike, although very pleasant, was now so powerful that there was an added tension: The fear of being fired was in the air.

I was struck at the first reading of the screenplay, as we all sat around a huge table, by how much most of the cast sounded like Mike. I figured that most everyone thought if they read the part like Mike, he would, at least subconsciously, like something about their performances, and they'd be safe. It was a peculiar reading, with at least ten people in the cast sounding pretty much the same: Mike-like. Instead of being pleased, Mike looked a little nonplussed; he didn't say much, but suggested we break for lunch, come back, and do it again. It was a little better the second time, but not much.

We were all given the rest of the day off. I went back to my room and did my usual staring into space—thinking about what had just transpired. After a couple of hours of this, the phone rang. It was John Calley, the producer (and later head of Warner Brothers Studios), calling to say that he and Mike would like to see me and that he would send a car to pick me up. I had no idea what was going on. My first thought, being an actor, was that they were going to fire me. Since I couldn't come up with a second thought, I was stuck with that first one.

The car arrived quickly, and a Mexican driver drove me out of our hotel, onto the main road, and then, eventually, up into some winding mountain roads. After about a twenty-minute drive we came to a house sitting on the side of a hill. I got out of the car, walked to the door, and knocked. John answered and seemed cheerful, a good sign, I thought, as I tried to figure out what was happening. I went inside with John and was greeted by Mike, who was sitting on a sofa. After all the How-are-you's were exchanged, John took a seat next to Mike on the sofa. I sat on a chair facing them. It certainly didn't feel like an about-to-be-fired atmosphere.

Mike and John said they felt that the first reading by the cast wasn't all that impressive. I nodded. They said they felt that the script sounded better the second time, but they both felt that the situation could be improved if they replaced the actor playing the role of Colonel Cathcart. As soon as I realized they weren't talking about firing me, I started to breathe normally. I defended the actor they wanted to fire, saying it was only a reading, and with direction, I felt . . . John interrupted to say that they wanted me to play this raving maniac who sends everyone out to their deaths. It was one of the parts I had originally read for Mike. It called for a man of fifty-five; I was thirty-four and looked twenty-four. It could be done with makeup, they said. So I was being elevated from about the tenth role to the third. I was pleased and sad at the same time. I thought the actor who was about to be sent home was good, and told them I thought the problem wasn't the actor but the "Mike" imitations and the script. It seemed too episodic to me, I said; there was no single strong story to follow. Mike said he hadn't noticed the imitations, but agreed about the episodic problem. I have no idea if Mike and John felt it was inappropriate for me to give them my opinions of the script as I was a supporting player way down the rung, but I wasn't really concerned. In creative matters, I feel anyone can speak if it's done respectfully, and I was respectful.

I asked Mike: "What do you do about the episodic problem?"

He said you had to make each sequence exquisite in its own right.

I said, "Isn't that pretty hard?"

He said, "It certainly is."

We stared at each other a moment in silence and goodwill, each hoping for the best.

They asked me not to speak about the impending cast change until they had told the unsuspecting current Colonel. Absolutely by chance, I witnessed their notifying him from my room. The actor was on the hotel grounds admiring some Mexican flora or fauna as Mike and John walked over to him and began to chat. I looked away and lay down on the bed.

That night the news of the firing was all over the hotel. I was sitting with a few of the older cast members, and they were speculating about who would be moved up into the Colonel's role. "You could do it," each said to the other. No one looked at me or even imagined that it would be the unknown younger actor sitting quietly at the table, not participating in the speculation.

The next day, as rehearsal continued, there I was, to everyone's shock, screaming at all these older cast members as the Colonel. And I was tough. I hadn't scared The Virginian for no reason. The makeup work hadn't begun yet, and while I was scaring everyone with intimidating yelling, I was a boy Colonel. They started, over the next several days, to apply all kinds of rubber makeup to my lineless, creaseless face, until, after several hard looks at me, the cinematographer advised Mike that all that makeup just might end up looking like makeup.

Martin Balsam, a wonderful character actor, was flown in from Hollywood to play the Colonel, and I was returned to my original role. The actor who had moved up from a smaller role to my role was moved back down to his smaller role, and became openly hostile to me, feeling I had somehow done him in, even though he admitted it made no sense.

Mike and John called me to another meeting to tell me they were sorry they had put me through all that rubber makeup, hoped I was okay, didn't really expect me to go back to my original role at the same salary, and would a ten-thousand-dollar raise make it easier? In fact, I didn't mind all the experimentation at all, but kept quiet through their speech, and by doing so picked up the equivalent of my entire income for three years' work not that much earlier.

It was odd spending several months in Guaymas, Mexico, which is known primarily for its shrimp. After a while, even a large group of comedy actors housed in one hotel, the Playa De Cortes, run out of funny things to say to each other, and eventually *anything* to say to each other. It reminds me of an evening, while working on another picture, *Sunburn,* when I had dinner with Art Carney and his wife. My date was delayed two hours because of work. When she arrived, Art said, "Boy, am I glad to see you. We'd just gotten to the point where Chuck asked me where I went to high school . . . and I was about to tell him."

Even with all the good funny actors down in Guaymas, I could never really find a way to pass that much waiting time—and there was plenty, even when you were called to work. The first day of shooting, we were all called at seven A.M. Ten hours later, at five P.M., we were sent home, as the cinematographer was still preparing his lights for the first shot. (The lighting in the picture was wonderful.) Then, of course, there'd be weeks when I wouldn't be called to work at all. I did a certain amount of writing and reading, but soon I reverted to my old ways of just wandering around. There was a group that enjoyed playing charades and other party games; there was a group that kept the bar in business; and I'm sure there were other groups doing other things. Again, just as always in those days, I felt like the perennial outsider. I patrolled the grounds so regularly that it would have been appropriate to be wearing my old Pinkerton uniform.

Eventually, the movie company started to ship down old films from Hollywood for us to see to help pass the time. But by then, all the waiting had nerves a little raw. At dinner one evening, when I casually commented I had recently seen an old film that was on its way to us and hadn't liked it as much as I remembered, an older actor sitting next to me suddenly exploded. "What right do you have to say that?! We're going to see this movie, and now you've ruined it. You've just ruined it!" He was beside himself with fury, as though my comment were a crime against humanity. With my *Candid Camera* background and general frame of mind when confronted with weird behavior, I always first assume a joke. But then I saw he was genuinely distraught. He was so furious I had a moment when I wondered if I actually *did* commit a sin of some kind. After all, everybody down there was deprived of the entertainment and diversion offered in our own country. Maybe I had underestimated how crucially important these old Hollywood films were to this company of actors— or at least to that deprived actor. I considered all that within about five seconds, and then thought: *Naaaah!* I'm really not sure where all his upset came from, but I doubt it had much to do with me or that poor old movie. I just let his explosion run its course and said I was sorry I had upset him. The next day he apologized as passionately as he'd exploded. He said, "I'm terribly sorry. I simply don't know what got into me."

One night I got tired of patrolling and joined the group in the bar for a couple myself. Along around midnight, with no reason to get up early the next day except for more Pinkerton rounds, I decided to climb an almost perpendicular mountain stretching up into the sky in the distance. I asked if anyone wanted to join me. Everyone promptly looked at me as if I were nuts, except Suzanne Benton, a curvy blonde who was one of the few women in the picture. We climbed up this steep mountain lit only by moonlight. It took us about four hours to get up and down. The next day we heard all kinds of stories of snakes and worse that were up there. In the years that followed, I heard other versions of what had happened up on that dark mountaintop, growing more and more romantic with the passage of time. But Suzanne and I know we climbed up, we climbed down; there were no encounters with other animals or each other. Oh, okay, once, to help her down from a steep rock, I took her hand.

Soon, everyone began to focus on the impending arrival of Orson Welles, who was to play the small part of the General. Orson of course was considered by everyone to be an old film master, and Mike a young one, and we were curious to see how that would work out.

Orson arrived, dazzled everyone with his show-business an-ecdotes, and pretty much attempted to take over the filming of his sequence. "You're not going to use *that* lens on *this* shot, are you, Mike?"

Mike nodded, smiled, was respectful, and, well . . . oh, just great. Whatever he felt as Orson openly moved into his territory, he acted benign as hell about it.

Tony Perkins had been an old friend of Orson's and was a new friend of mine. He introduced me to Orson as "someone you would enjoy knowing." Orson looked at me as if I were an end table and continued to talk about whatever was fascinating him. I like to believe I've always handled these rare slights with a writer's detached eye, but I must admit that I felt my spirits mo-mentarily sink—no matter what I'd like to believe.

The picture took an awfully long time to make, cost a tre-mendous amount of money, had much brilliance in it, but suf-fered from not having a strong story line. Some of the sequences were exquisite—but not all. As Mike had said, that would be really hard.

I met Mike Nichols in 1967. I've seen him many times since then, and every time I do I can't help but feel that a party has just begun. He's a pleasure. Even during my regrettable encounter with him during *The Graduate*, it just seemed like an unfortunate off day. He has the courtly manners of an Old World gentleman, and the one true oddity in his personality is for me, strangely, his most charming attribute: He is unashamedly given to hyperbole. "This is the most moving theatrical event I've ever witnessed." Or even, "This is the best casserole I've ever tasted." Recently, after a social gathering, he actually kissed my hand, bowed, and announced: "You are the funniest person I've ever met in my life." Well . . . I know the theatrical event, the casserole, and I probably weren't, but he sure makes me feel good.

The most significant relationship to come out of the whole *Catch-22* experience was the friendship I formed with Art Gar-funkel, who was making his acting debut in the picture. Several months after the picture was finished, back in Los Angeles, he introduced me to his partner, Paul Simon, and that, in turn, led to a most remarkable experience.

CBS, AT&T, and
Simon & Garfunkel

It's difficult to overestimate the fame and impact of Simon and Garfunkel in the sixties and seventies. The television networks had been pursuing them for years to make a special. They were being called the spokesmen of their generation, and the power of their performances and careers was enormous. They had received—and rejected—endless offers to do television specials. I think their reticence was due to what they felt were the uninteresting ideas being offered and maybe some built-in resistance to all the "establishment" people who were approaching them.

After we became friends, they asked me if I might want to get involved with them in some way on this nonexistent special. As they saw it, my attributes were that I seemed to have a lot of ideas and feelings about things, and, maybe more important, that I had never done this before, so my input probably wouldn't have any "conventional" influence. I reminded them that I had only co-authored and directed a failed Off-Broadway musical (they were sympathetic to the disastrous opening-night aspect) and directed a Broadway comedy. But television? Oh yeah, there was *Candid Camera*, but I hardly seemed to be the guy for this job, I said. I told them I would try to find some people who would be more appropriate for them.

After several meetings with people who worked in television

in some way but not too much, I met a television commercial director of rising reputation named Michael Cimino, who later brought a whole movie studio to its knees with *Heaven's Gate*. His ideas for the special were interesting, but as he spoke there was a look in his eyes that made me feel that for him to be happy, in a very short time not only I but Simon and Garfunkel would be working for *him*. After several weeks of interviewing people, I started to feel more a veteran of the medium, but of course I'd still done nothing. I asked myself what I would like to see as a Simon and Garfunkel special, what I would like to see from these "spokesmen of their generation," a designation that filled them with self-ridicule.

The basic network idea for Simon and Garfunkel was a musical show where "the boys" (as they were widely referred to within the television industry) would sing their hits, have some big-name television guest stars, and call it a "special." For this, because of their wide popularity, the network, CBS, was going to spend eight hundred thousand dollars, the largest budget for an entertainment special up to that point, which was 1969.

After much consideration, the special I suggested to them simply would show how the music of Simon and Garfunkel was shaped by their times. A harmless enough sentence at first look. Here's a second look: For example, we would intercut "the boys" singing "Mrs. Robinson" with white women jeering and screaming at little black children on the first day of integration at a public school. "Here's to you, Mrs. Robinson. Jesus loves you more than you will know—wo, wo, wo." "The boys" stared at me.

This special would introduce the song "Bridge Over Troubled Water." On the screen, we would see footage of our three recently assassinated leaders: John Kennedy, Martin Luther King, and Robert Kennedy. That sequence would conclude with people across the country looking stunned at the Robert Kennedy funeral train. This was all existing footage. "The boys" continued to stare.

Shots of soldiers being carried away on stretchers in Vietnam would be the picture as we would hear the music of "Scarborough Fair."

In short, it would be a special that essentially said: "Let's get out of Vietnam, let's stop persecuting blacks, let's show what's wrong with America, and raise a banner for the more tolerant, compassionate side of the American character." I continued on, giving several variations on this theme. The proposal pretty much represented what Paul Simon, Art Garfunkel, and I felt about our country in 1969. I said, "A lot of people would hardly call this an entertainment special." I thought, from the little I knew about it, that it wouldn't get high ratings, and that they could do a lot better with a special-guest-star-Glen-Campbell type of show. But here was an opportunity to put down for the record just who they were, what they stood for—and besides, what the hell were "spokesmen for a generation" supposed to do with a special anyway?

I said it was just an idea, and if they wanted to do a straight-ahead musical special with your current guest stars, I would help them with that too. They decided to go with the social and political idea. None of us had any idea at the time what we were headed for in America in 1969, with Richard Nixon and Spiro Agnew in Washington and the country still at war in Vietnam.

In 1969, the Smothers Brothers had just been removed from the air because of what was considered to be "too liberal" comedy. There had never been an "entertainment" special such as what we were planning. This was closer to a CBS documentary special—"War on Hunger," for example. But this was nine o'clock Sunday night, Bob Hope time. The network, the ad agency, and the sponsor—AT&T—requested that I present an outline of what the show was going to be. I did. I held nothing back. I told Art and Paul that I thought, in spite of AT&T's commercial sentiment to reach out through the telephone to someone, they would reach out to us and say: "Knock it off, sing some hits, do some skits, and forget about Vietnam and equal rights." We waited. Nothing happened. There was no comment from any of the interested parties, basically CBS and AT&T.

We went out and hired a man by the name of Robert Drew, who was considered to be the king and originator of video verité. He had done many award-winning documentaries. Bob was to be the executive producer and provide all his production facilities. When I outlined the show to him, he sat impassively at his desk under a photograph of Nelson Rockefeller and suggested we do a special about the making of a song instead. I explained that we wanted to make more of a statement. He casually announced that he thought we would be heading into some—if you'll pardon the expression—"troubled waters," but agreed to proceed with providing his facilities and expertise.

I waited a while longer to hear any objections from CBS, AT&T, or their ad agency. Still, no one responded to the outline. I could only assume that all parties were so excited about having the long-coveted Simon and Garfunkel special that no one bothered to read the outline. I went ahead with the show.

While the Southern white ladies screaming at the little black children integrating weren't in it, there was The Poor People's March on Washington; parts of Martin Luther King's "I Have a Dream" speech; the assassinated leaders; the soldiers in Vietnam; Coretta King saying, "Poverty's a child without an education"; footage of a young Jesse Jackson; César Chavez; and interviews with Simon and Garfunkel, pitting them squarely against the war in Vietnam, Art saying, "It seems to me we'd better have a very clear, very strong reason before we kill people," implying that with all that was being said he still hadn't heard that reason. It was a powerful collection of material interspersed with Simon and Garfunkel on tour.

There was a film crew following Simon and Garfunkel around the country, and I would go back and forth from wherever the shows were (where I'd be interviewing Simon and Garfunkel) to Bob Drew's production facilities in New York (where I was putting all this together with two master editors, Ellen Gifford and Luke Bennett). It seemed bizarre to all of us, but Bob Drew was off in a room on his own assembling footage for his making-of-a-song idea. I guess he was waiting for the boom to drop from CBS or AT&T. But still there was no word at all from them.

Finally, after months of work, the editors and I put together the first rough version of the show—"an assemblage of the material." It ran almost twice as long as it had to, but it was our first chance to get a look at something put together. I showed it to Art and Paul and Bob Drew. At the end of the screening, Bob, Paul, Art, and I went to Bob's office for a meeting. Bob sat under the photograph of Rockefeller, an old friend, and announced that the show was not "airworthy," a phrase I had never heard but rightly assumed meant "not good enough to be on the air." Not only that, he intended to have his name removed from it.

Paul and Art looked uneasy. It was hard for them to be objective about what they had just seen. After all, they were recording artists, not television people, and whether something was worthy of being on the air was not really their area of expertise. I'm sure they felt that for eight hundred thousand dollars it should at least be "airworthy."

Bob, who, by the way, is a large, imposing man who could have easily been cast as a president or an ambassador, paused to let the weight of his words sink in. He then continued. "The only way this show can be saved," he said, "is if Chuck removes himself from control and turns the reins over to me."

Now Bob, Paul, and Art turned and looked at me for my response. Here was Robert Drew, of Robert Drew Associates, the king of the field we were now in, the father of video verité, and he was saying: Get rid of this guy! I was now the object of everyone's scrutiny, with my having been fired twice from *Candid Camera* TV credit. It was a very tense moment. It was a heavy rejection. But while Bob may have been the king of video verité, I had become one of the kings of dealing with rejection. My personality has always been what you might call easygoing. I have almost never shown irritation, annoyance, or anything relating to a contentious personality at work unless actually screamed at, as happened on *Candid Camera*. Inwardly, I was furious. Outwardly, I casually responded: "Well, I think the show is going to be very good, very powerful. It is exactly what it's supposed to be. The only thing really wrong with it is it's too long—but then that's right for an assemblage. I have a couple of suggestions myself." And then I looked Bob in the eye. "Bob, you have never been a supporter of this show. I think, for your own political reasons, it makes you uncomfortable. You've been off in a room on your own with your making-of-a-song idea, an idea in which none of us has any interest. If you really would like to help the show, I suggest you could best do it by going home and not being around, as your negative presence only depresses all of us here." I was trying to control my anger, but I think I only partially succeeded. This wasn't saving face. The editors and I thought the show was great, and I really resented his "not airworthy" crack. Later, when I'd hear movie-studio people say something is "unreleasable," I'd always think, Compared to what (considering what's been released in the movies)? So, "not airworthy," considering what's been on television, really offended me, given how much good and hard work had been done by everyone on the show. I was very angry.

Paul and Art looked at me for a long moment. This was a side of me they hadn't seen. Their eyes shifted back to Bob, who acted as though I hadn't spoken at all. There was more silence.

I went on: "I will work with the editors through the night cutting the show down, and I suggest we look at it tomorrow at a closer length to what it will be and see what everyone feels then." The meeting broke up in uneasy silence.

I worked through the night with the editors, cutting the show down closer to size. During the night, at a break around four A.M., I went off by myself to get a sandwich at an all-night delicatessen. As I sat in a corner booth alone, I lifted the sandwich and noticed my hand was shaking. I wasn't sure if I was nervous or exhausted. But shaking or not, I went back and continued to work with the editors.

The next day, Bob, Paul, and Art came back to the editing room to look at the new, improved version, which would now be called a "rough cut." At the end of the running, Bob announced: "That's the finest rough cut of a special I've ever seen in my life." I believe Bob was sincere in all of his opinions. I think he panicked after seeing the first cut and, because he didn't know me at all, had no faith that I could fix it up until he saw it done. Then he expressed his support.

As we all once more filed back to his office for another meeting—Bob leading the way down the hall, Art following, Paul behind Art, and me bringing up the rear of the procession—Paul suddenly, without missing a step, did a full somersault like a professional gymnast, a move I've never seen him do before or since. We were all showing new sides.

The meeting was cordial this time. Without announcing it, Bob stopped working on his making-of-a-song special and, as I had suggested, made himself a rarely seen presence on the premises. The first hurdle had been passed, though I still had no inkling of what was to come.

We completed the show. Still, we'd never heard from CBS, AT&T, or their ad agency. The show was delivered. A few days went by, and more silence. And then the phones didn't stop! Meetings were called. First, representatives from AT&T and their ad agency: "The show is outrageous! AT&T can never sponsor it in its present form," they said. "It will offend millions of Americans who are for the Vietnam War," they said. "Telephone rates are controlled locally, and in Alabama the man in charge is Bull Connor [the police chief who was responsible for turning the dogs and hoses on all those blacks]—and he sure isn't going to like all that poor-people-marching stuff," they said. "There are seven affectionate references to the Kennedys. There is a nice touch on Adlai Stevenson. Where is Ike?" they wanted to know.

I said that this show reflected the thoughts and feelings of Simon and Garfunkel, and they had been for Stevenson.

An ad man said: "Ike playing golf—that's a nice shot."

I said again, "This show represents the feelings of Simon and Garfunkel."

A number of people in the room—there were about ten—glared at me. Finally, a representative of AT&T said angrily, looking me straight in the eye: "You're using our money to sell your ideology."

"What's my ideology?" I asked.

"The humanistic approach," he bitterly answered.

I smiled, thinking he was joking. When I realized he was serious, I asked, in all innocence, "You mean there are people who are against the humanistic approach?"

"You're goddamn right there are," he answered.

I was thirty-four years old, and the thought had never occurred to me. Well, not in America. Not as a corporate position. Isolated bigots, but as a matter of major policy? No.

An ugly silence filled the room. Paul told me later that when the guy had said there were all these people against the humanistic approach, I had risen half out of my chair for a moment. I had controlled the impulse to slug him, thinking he was one of these nonhumanistic characters.

"Not me," the representative from AT&T quickly said. He was referring to all those other people out there who were against humanism. But if it were a choice between business and humanism, well, humanism definitely had to go.

They made several requests for deletions. Where Coretta King said, "Poverty's a child without an education," they asked that the sound be taken down.

I said, "To what level?"

They said, "Inaudible."

They gave us their lengthy list of further deletions and suggestions for references to be included, announced that there was no way AT&T's name would be on this show in its present form, and left.

Paul, Art, and I sat there alone. I said, "Can you see these guys going home to dinner tonight and telling their wives and children that they knocked Coretta King talking about poverty off the air? What kind of a life is that?" I asked them what they wanted to do. They quickly said they liked the show a lot, were proud of it, and didn't intend to change one thing.

I said, "That's what I thought. Let's just see what happens next."

That night I went out for dinner with some friends and had a bizarre experience. From an adjoining table in the restaurant, we heard a man say, "Yes, Simon and Garfunkel are under the spell of this Svengali character, Charles Grodin." Somebody in my group turned to him and said, "Charles Grodin's sitting right here. Why don't you tell him what's on your mind?"

I looked over and recognized a man from the ad agency that represented AT&T. There was a moment of severe tension, and then I said, "Forget it," and both tables uneasily resumed eating. It was obvious that the ad agency was under tremendous strain and could lose the AT&T account. I only wondered why they hadn't done their job, read the outline, and spared themselves what they were going through now.

The next day CBS called. They wanted to see me to discuss their problems with airing the show. Paul came with me. In spite of—or maybe because of—all the tension, the whole situation was taking on a comic aspect. Paul asked to wear my overcoat (which came down to his ankles) to the meeting.

In a two-hour conversation with the head of Program Practices (censor), William Tankersly, a tall, thin gentleman in his late fifties with goodness in his eyes, I argued that the show was a sincere presentation of the point of view of two of the world's most celebrated musical artists, and while many people might not agree, it was what it was. Even though such a show had never been on the air before as an entertainment special, maybe it was time for one. Amazingly, the CBS man agreed. He judged us to be sincere and neither snide nor ridiculing, but as having an honest difference of opinion with our government on many fronts.

AT&T removed its name from the show, and Alberto Culver became the sponsor at a considerably reduced cost. CBS had the movie actor Robert Ryan film a prologue explaining that "what you are about to see might offend some people and be dealing with subjects that are controversial, but this is a show representing the points of view of two artists who have earned the right to be heard in this way."

The show began with beautiful shots of America, and Paul and Art singing the song "America" on the track. The pictures were of wheat fields and mountaintops and other beautiful vistas of this country. They gradually, slowly, turned to riots in the streets and people bleeding. Robert Kennedy's funeral train sped on as the show came to its first commercial break. At that point, one million people turned off the show. It was one of the lowest-rated "entertainment" specials ever. While it got rave reviews all around the country, it also got almost as many reviews disputing its right to exist at all as an entertainment special. One of these came from *TV Guide*, who three weeks later reported that they had received their largest volume of mail disputing their position. The special elicited great anger toward Simon and Garfunkel from many of their fans, or possibly the parents of their fans who held opposing positions. The White House requested a copy of the show. *The Washington Post* wrote an editorial expressing amazement that "in the present political climate" such a show even reached the air.

I think the special certainly did hurt Simon and Garfunkel's future television career. I'm pleased to say that almost twenty years later Paul and Art remain among my closest friends. I feel that show is the finest achievement of my professional career. It put Simon and Garfunkel and me squarely on the record for all to see . . . at a time when a lot of people didn't want to be on the record. The William Morris Agency, which represented me, told me bluntly that because of all the trouble I'd caused, I could forget about working in television for a long while.

The show was never rerun.

The Year Before

By now I was no longer even thinking about acting. My attention had almost completely turned to writing and directing. While I was always interested in that work, I'm sure that turning my full focus toward it had more than a little to do with the stunningly sporadic nature of my acting career. In the previous eight years, as I've said, I'd been successful in two Broadway shows, played good supporting roles in two big movies, and again been praised highly. I had risen to guest-star status on a number of network television shows, in both New York and Los Angeles, but I would still wait several months or longer between jobs. It was just the nature of the profession. My income for almost all this time averaged about five thousand dollars a year. So my attention started to turn toward other things I might do.

At the time Mike Nichols asked me to be in *Catch-22*, I was writing a screenplay based on a novel called *Balloons Are Available*, by a brilliantly witty author named Jordan Crittenden. Someone at a small movie company in New York had sent me the book, thinking I would like it. I loved it! It made me laugh more than anything I had read since *Catcher in the Rye*. The book was free to be optioned, so I sent it to Norman Lear, who seemed interested in working with me. Together we optioned it, and I went about writing a screenplay, which I finished during the nine months' shooting and waiting of *Catch-22*. When Norman read what I had written, he was disappointed, because he felt I had more or less just transposed the novel into screenplay form. To a significant degree I had, because I thought it worked best that way. So I now owned the script, but without a producer. The people representing me said there was a producer in Hollywood named Michael Laughlin who was married to the movie star Leslie Caron, and was currently one of the few producers in Hollywood who seemed to be able to get anything he liked done. I sent the script to him, and he wanted to produce it. We made a deal, and I flew to Hollywood to meet this "get-it-done" producer. He was very cordial on the phone and invited me to his house for dinner the next night. Michael struck me as extraordinarily low-key, which was the opposite of what I had expected. At one point he left the table, leaving me alone with Leslie. I commented, as delicately as I could, "Michael seems surprisingly laid-back for a Hollywood producer."

Leslie, sensing my concern, said, "Wait till you see him in a meeting."

I said, politely, I hoped, "I really look forward to it."

The next day I spoke to my agent, and said that since I had given up 50 percent ownership of the project in order to be in business with this dynamo, was he sure Michael Laughlin was as dynamic as everyone had reported. "Wait till you see him in action at a meeting," the agent also reassured me.

Michael arranged a number of meetings with various heads of studios. When the day of the first meeting came, I was almost bursting with curiosity to see his dramatic transformation, as Michael continued with me to be intelligent, very nice, but stunningly low-key—definitely not a sweep-you-off-your-feet type of guy.

We walked into the meeting at MGM. Their five top executives were there. I was impressed with that. Leslie and the agents know what they're talking about, I thought. Hellos were exchanged, everyone was very nice. Then there was a silence as the executives looked at us to begin. I watched Michael with great anticipation.

"We have a very funny comedy," he began, still in his laid-back fashion. He's going to build in force, I thought. He went on in the same vein. "Chuck here has written it and he will direct it.

I don't know how many of you are aware that Chuck is a director" (all this still low-key). There was a long silence as everyone, including me, continued to look at Michael, who then turned to me and said, "Chuck, anything you want to add?" That was it! That's all he was going to say!

I was taken aback a moment, and then added a few unmemorable comments of my own. And that was that. Everyone said how happy they were that we'd come in . . . and we were gone.

Variations of this scene went on at three or four other studios, always with top executives. Nobody made the picture. In fairness to Michael, he had recognized how witty Jordan Crittenden was and he did want to make the movie. So I do think of him as a nice man with good taste. But when you're looking for Lee Iacocca . . .

Once again at a juncture when nothing seemed to be happening, Renée Taylor and Joe Bologna reentered my life. They asked me to join them in writing the movie version of Woody Allen's hit Broadway play, *Play It Again, Sam*. Why the studio hadn't asked Woody to write, star in, and direct the movie I'm sure is a long story—and I don't know it—but they didn't.

Renée and Joe had become very much in demand as a result of the success of the movie version of *Lovers and Other Strangers*, for which they wrote the screenplay. They were so busy that eventually they withdrew from *Play It Again, Sam* and I became the sole screenwriter. I was surprised the studio proceeded with me alone, as it was a major project and I'd written only one unproduced screenplay. When I asked why, the producer, Arthur Jacobs, who made all the *Planet of the Apes* movies, said he liked the way I had handled myself in the one meeting we had. Much later I realized how many people made big deals on their ability to "meet well." The profession, including both movies and theater, is filled with people who are great talkers; they can dazzle you with their intellect in discussing what a movie or play could or should be or what's wrong or what's needed. But as far as actually writing a good script or actually directing something—well . . . for a lot of them, they'd be better at giving seminars.

I wrote a script that Arthur Jacobs and the director, Herb Ross, seemed to like a lot. I had retained about 50 percent of Woody's play and had written about 50 percent original material.

Negotiations had begun with a comedy star to play Woody's part, until Woody opened in a movie he had co-written, directed, and starred in called *Bananas*. It was hilarious and it was a success—and the studio decided they wanted Woody after all. Woody was sent my script, and expressed admiration, but felt it would require more of an actor than he thought he was. I thought he was a wonderful actor, and believe the future proved me right. In any case, Woody wrote a screenplay pretty much retaining the material of his original play, and the movie was a success.

I had worked about six months on a screenplay that wasn't filmed, but it was sent to a movie producer named Martin Ransahoff. He had originally owned the rights to the movie version of *Catch-22*. When Mike Nichols agreed to direct *Catch-22*, one of his contractual conditions was that he wouldn't have to speak to Martin Ransahoff. Most directors—or producers, for that matter—would prefer controlling those they spoke to (make that "had to listen to"). When I met Marty Ransahoff, he told me that agreeing to that condition of Mike's was the most humiliating thing he'd ever done. He could barely talk about it. Sidney Pollack, who directed *Tootsie* and *Out of Africa*, among many others, told me recently that he'd become his own producer to save the energy of daily having to persuade another person that what he was doing was okay.

This is a field loaded with people who want to be in charge, and when there are about three of them on the same project—well, you wouldn't want to be there.

Marty Ransahoff read my screenplay of *Play It Again, Sam* and hired me to do a screenplay of a short story of Philip Roth's called "An Actor's Life for Me"—which, incidentally, has little to do with actors. Again I wrote a screenplay everyone seemed to like. They were negotiating with Alan Arkin to star, and I was going to direct my first picture. But Alan and his representative decided—possibly correctly—that it was too loaded with sex. People who knew me couldn't even believe I had written it, but I explained that it was an adaptation of a Philip Roth story, and I had just gone where his story led me. I had now spent another six months on an unproduced screenplay, as the project just seemed to evaporate. ("Unproduced," by the way, is the overwhelming status of most screenplays.) Careerwise, I was kind of treading water at best.

If I was experiencing any depression over this, I sure wasn't aware of it. I had enough money to live on, I had a lot of good friends, I had a lot of laughs, and I enjoyed writing the scripts, even if they weren't being made. I was fine.

Around that time a friend of mine was involved in the Off-Broadway production of Bruce Jay Friedman's play *Steambath*. The play was experiencing "difficulties" in previews. (Translated meaning: People didn't like it—or not well enough.) I read the play and thought it was wonderful. My friend asked me to come down, see it, and tell him what I thought. By the time I got there, they had fired the leading man and a new one was going in. About a week later, my friend called and said they were going to fire the leading man again, and asked if I'd like to take over the role. I said it sounded dangerous. I had the feeling I would be fired too. The other two actors who had been let go were well known, and I was still what you'd have to call an unknown. But I loved the play, and said okay.

I was thrown into the part so fast I didn't even know the lines. I managed to get through a few performances and was just beginning to get the feel of it when I was fired too. My friend argued: "Don't you notice how the applause goes up when he comes out for his curtain call?" But I was fired.

Eventually, a fourth actor, very well known, played the part. The play opened, the critics said the leading man was miscast, and it soon closed. I still thought it was a wonderful play—and that was later proved in successful revivals. But I had been fired.

The first time I had been fired, singing "At the Drop of a Hat" in summer stock, hadn't really bothered me because I wasn't a singer. The *Candid Camera* firings didn't bother me much either. But this did. I was still a little shaky on the lines in places, but I was also heading toward doing the finest work of my life. And I was dismissed. Rejected. Not after an audition or singing, but after actually acting—supposedly my strongest talent. This was really tough. This was really rejection. To be dismissed. Fired. I wasn't ready for it. No matter how I tried to look at it, I was rejected doing what I did best. I was either really good or I wasn't. The people in charge of *Steambath* were saying I wasn't. I felt they had made a mistake. But I had nightmares about not being wanted every night for weeks. I decided that I'd better take my life back into my own hands and start to write again.

I walked around for days trying to think of what to write about, but I couldn't come up with anything because all I could think about was being fired. One day I realized I should write about getting fired. So I did. I wrote a play. I made it a comedy, as I didn't want to depress everybody. I sent it around to just about every producer in New York—and everyone rejected it. No one liked it at all. So I had now written three unproduced screenplays, been fired from an Off-Broadway show, and written a play that absolutely no one liked . . . when I got a phone call from Elaine May.

The Heartbreak Kid

Since I had met Elaine May during *Lovers and Other Strangers* I had seen her from time to time, usually to participate in readings of scripts she had written. There were no more embarrassing moments where I'd make an oblique joke she wouldn't get. In fact, after our first meeting she seemed to "get" just about everything about me. (In case you're wondering, we never dated.) I don't follow horoscopes at all, but I was surprised and impressed when I learned that, while we had been born in different years, we had the same birthday.

At some point in the last couple of years, Elaine had begun to tell me and anyone else when the subject of actors came up that as far as she was concerned, I was *it*. In fairness to other actors, I don't think Elaine was getting out and around that much, since she was spending a lot of time alone writing, and Elaine has never been one to stay on top of the latest show-business news (or, for that matter, anywhere near it). When anyone said to her, "If he's so great, how come we haven't heard of him?" she confidently responded, "You will as soon as he gets the part where he'll have the real chance."

She told me she was being asked to direct movies, and as soon as she found a good one I could star in, that's when everyone would see what she saw. It had always been nice to hear . . . especially since I had mostly been hearing it during the recent unproduced/fired period. Now Elaine was actually calling with the script and the starring part.

The movie was written by Neil Simon, and it was called *The Heartbreak Kid*. Elaine sent me the script, and of course I wanted to do it. But now I had to be approved by Neil Simon and the producer, Edgar Scherick. I found out much later that every young movie star in Hollywood who knew of the project wanted to do it, but Elaine persuaded everyone that the picture really required an unknown. I'm not sure how she did that.

Elaine had me come into their offices and read the whole script aloud for Neil Simon, Edgar Scherick, and her. Elaine was my supporter, but Neil became the greatest audience I ever had. Still, Edgar and Neil wanted me to do a screen test. After my experience with *The Graduate*, I was determined to get the script well in advance—which I did. I made the test in a loft (not a studio). It was the home of the assistant director, Michael Hausman. Mike, who later produced *Amadeus*, is a warm, supportive man, and that really helped the atmosphere. After I finished I went home and waited for the phone to ring. A couple of days later, it did. The associate producer, Eric Preminger, Otto's son, called me and said, "Well, it looks like you're the Heartbreak Kid." They offered me a modest amount of money, and this time I said, "Yes, thank you," before they could finish offering. While Elaine was just one vote in their decision to ask me, I know she was prepared not to do it without me. With friends like that, you don't need any more friends.

I first got to know Neil Simon at this time. I've always liked him, and over the years have spent more time with him, having appeared in two more movies that he wrote, *Seems Like Old Times* and *The Lonely Guy*, which he co-authored.

I found him extremely likable, obviously brilliant, but, more than anything else, complicated. As I said, when I first read the entire script aloud, no one laughed louder than Neil. After I was signed for the picture and we assembled for a full-cast reading, I foolishly decided to begin to "work" on the part right there. Actors can approach a reading of a script in two ways. Usually, I will try to read as effectively as I can so that the writer, director, and everyone else can really "hear" it. The other approach is to use a reading to feel your way around the deeper realities of the story without worrying about performing. Since I had already performed the entire script at the audition, and then performed it again at the screen test, I felt I'd use this reading to begin to "explore" the story, which I did. When the reading was over, and I wasn't particularly effective (you never are when you are just exploring), Neil wanted to fire me. Elaine reassured him, saying, "You already saw him perform it." She understood what I was doing and persuaded him to be patient.

It was tougher to persuade him about Jeannie Berlin, who was playing my wife. He just didn't think she was attractive enough. He wanted Diane Keaton, who was then still a relative unknown. I thought Jeannie was plenty attractive and Diane wouldn't be enough of a contrast in a story that has a Jewish groom leave his Jewish wife for a gentile princess, so to speak. I thought, and Elaine agreed, that Diane was more like a gentile princess than a Jewish wife. Neil tells the story himself of how he persisted even into the filming to try to get rid of Jeannie because she wasn't attractive enough. He kept telling Elaine to get someone better-looking, and Elaine said, "Okay, if you bring me someone who looks more attractive who can act the part, I'll do it."

All during this time, Neil didn't know that Jeannie Berlin, whom he kept calling unattractive, was Elaine May's daughter. Incidentally, not only is she plenty attractive, she was nominated for an Academy Award in the role.

Neil also had never worked with Elaine before and wasn't used to the way she worked. His major successes came with an unprecedented string of hits in the theater: *Barefoot in the Park*, *The Odd Couple*, *The Sunshine Boys*, to name a few of a very, very long list. He was used to people saying his lines exactly as written—period. In the theater that is a condition of the Dramatists Guild: You don't change one word without the author's consent. In the movies that's not the case. The director makes a determination on any changes, with very rare exceptions when the screenwriter has a special clause. There is a group of writers you could count on one hand who have the power to get that not-change-a-word clause for a movie script. Neil is one of them.

So when he attended our early rehearsals, and Elaine had Jeannie and me singing different songs that we might be singing as we drove to Florida on our honeymoon, Neil asked: "Where does it say they sing?" At the same time as he was understandably objecting to the improvising with which Elaine, Jeannie, and I were so comfortable, he also regarded Elaine so highly that a compromise was struck. We would film every word of the script exactly as written, and Elaine would be free to do whatever else she chose by way of improvisation, and then Elaine would put the movie together. While Neil agreed to this, I assume he found the whole situation extremely trying and, after the first couple of days of rehearsal, he was never again seen around the movie set.

I think it was very difficult for Neil to "go" with all of Elaine's decisions on this movie, and I'm grateful to him that he did.

After two weeks of rehearsal, we began filming in Miami Beach. Things seemed to be going very well, but no one was saying much. It's the occupational paranoia for actors that when anyone shows up around where you're working, and you don't know who he is but he looks like he could play your role, part of you thinks: I'm out—he's in. It's a fantasy, fueled by the actual firing of actors that does go on. I've been fired as an actor, as a car jockey, and once as a shoe salesman. None of it feels good, but, as I've implied earlier, you *really* don't want to be fired as an actor. When someone does show up who looks like he could play your part, it's usually a fellow delivering coffee or something; but until you *know* that, there can be some bad moments.

Three weeks into the filming of the picture, I was sitting around with some people during the lunch break when someone casually said: "I saw Dustin Hoffman out there walking along the beach." I chuckled, thinking it was a let's-scare-the-hell-out-of-Chuck joke, but no one else laughed. A number of people had seen Dustin out there walking. I couldn't finish my lunch. I felt the movie was going well, but Elaine wasn't the kind of director who slaps you on the back or anything, so you could never be 100 percent positive what she or anyone else felt. I asked myself, Would they actually reshoot the three weeks and start over with Dustin? He had had enormous success with *The Graduate*, and anything seemed possible.

The more I thought about it, staring at my food, I was convinced I was out. The whole thing was so upsetting, I had no choice but to go right to Elaine and confront her on it. I went to her suite, where she was having lunch. I edgily took her aside in a small room and said, "Dustin Hoffman's down here."

She looked at me and waited. Finally, when I didn't say anything else, she said: "So?"

I said, "You didn't know that?"

She said, "No, should I?"

I said, "I wondered if he was down here to replace me."

She looked at me in disbelief. "Are you crazy?!" she asked.

"A little, I guess," I answered, and slunk out of the room.

It turned out he was down there visiting his manager. Why he couldn't have seen him in New York, where they both lived, I have no idea.

Elaine is a brilliant director. She never adjusted the situation to make it easier for the actors, but forced the actors to deal with the reality as it was. For example, in the scene where I married Jeannie Berlin in the living room of a West Side apartment in New York, it was discovered that the aisle was way too narrow, and when some of the heavier people walked down it in the wedding procession there'd be a certain amount of squeezing to get through. Elaine didn't widen the aisle, and as a result the procession looks very true and very funny.

In another sequence, when I'm trying to make a good impression at dinner on Cybill Shepherd's parents (played by Audra Lindley and Eddie Albert), she directed Eddie Albert to never, ever look at me, but just to continue eating as I talked. The direction was simple; the result was devastating.

Eddie Albert was another fascinating person. His reaction to me was similar to Neil Simon's after the reading where I was "exploring," not performing. He wondered if I was actually the person who was playing the lead in the picture. But when we began to film, he was extremely supportive and complimentary to me. He was an enigmatic figure—not the most outgoing of men. Once when we were in an elevator together in Miami Beach, it stopped at a floor and about five middle-aged or older people got on, instantly recognized him, and began to compliment him without seeming end. "Eddie! Eddie! Eddie Albert, you're my favorite!"

"Eddie, we love you! We watch you all the time on *Green Acres* [a TV situation comedy that he'd been doing with Eva Gabor]! Eddie, how's Eva? We love the two of you together!"

"We loved you on the stage, on television, and in movies! Eddie, we love you!"

Throughout all this, Eddie was just staring straight ahead.

Soon, even his adoring fans began to notice that Eddie hadn't spoken. One of them finally said: "So, Eddie, how's it going?"

He looked at the ceiling and said only, "No problem."

The elevator mercifully got to our floor and we got out, without Eddie ever having looked at anyone.

Eddie also had a lot of very strong ideas about what we should or shouldn't be eating, and since he's a magnificent specimen his ideas always got an ear from me, even when I knew he was just having fun. "You're not going to eat *that*, are you?!" he might say about anything just as I was going to take a bite. "A lot of the ingredients in that are made up from the paint they scrape off of battleships!"

He sure wasn't used to the way Elaine worked either, with me pulling sudden improvisations on him and Elaine shooting more film than he was used to. (Film, by the way, is about the least expensive element of a movie.) The reception scene, which Elaine and I knew would probably be our ending, took a day to shoot. Eddie privately commented to me that he had no idea why the hell we were spending so much time on it since he thought it was only going to be a few seconds in the film. He commented on this and that wryly to me under his breath, but never questioned Elaine and did absolutely everything she asked with good spirit. He was nominated for an Academy Award as well.

Sometimes Elaine helped reality along a little. One scene called for me to drive up to a boating area, get out of my car, and run to a yacht, where Cybill had invited me for a day at sea, against her father's wishes. In a short period of time (Elaine asked me to count to myself and showed me the rate of counting) I was to drive up, take off my clothes, change to boat clothes, and run as fast as I could to get on the yacht before Eddie Albert (also doing a fast inner count) could get the boat away from the dock and out to sea, away from me. Somehow it was timed so that with a big jump from the dock onto the boat, I always made it—just. Elaine gave new meaning to the concept of "stretching the actor."

The movie was not without its more-than-average number of pitfalls. I was to play a young man who meets a beautiful blonde on his honeymoon and leaves his wife for her, and it was supposed to be funny. Well, it could be funny to a lot of people, but I felt that to many others—mostly young women—it could be something other than funny. How about scary or hateful?

Ironically, in real life I had a wonderful relationship with Jeannie Berlin, who played my wife, whom I left and no relationship at all with the girl I left her for, Cybill Shepherd. It wasn't until years later that Cybill and I got to know and like each other a lot, but at that time we had no personal relationship at all, which probably helped the tension between us.

We completed the filming in the spring, and all seemed to go well. The picture was to be released at Christmas. I went back to New York feeling optimistic and looking forward to seeing what would happen when it opened.

Everybody Can Be Wrong

Maybe I was buoyed by the experience of doing *The Heartbreak Kid*, but, once again, I was going to try to get my play on about the man who was fired. It was as though I were saying, Okay, maybe I was fired and had all those nightmares, but at least I would get a play out of it. I still had never paid a price for perseverance. There was only reward. I had done some readings of the play, and the audiences were very responsive. And even though it had been turned down by so many producers, I had faith in it.

I sent the script to Alan Arkin, who had become a friend during *Catch-22*. The good news came quickly this time. He liked it even more than I did and agreed to star in it. With Alan in it, we were easily able to get the play booked for a week in upstate New York. My producer was my good friend Dick Scanga, who, ironically, was the director who fired me years ago from singing "At the Drop of a Hat." His delicacy ("Let's have Jimmy Reilly do it") was typical of Dick. He was an all-around theater person: a producer, a director, a writer, a stage manager, a lighting designer—anything. Over the years he had become the closest thing to a mentor I'd had. We would go to movies, and Dick would always ask what I thought and why, and how I felt I could make it better, whether it was about writing or directing or anything. Over a twenty-year period, he was always helpful to me. It was a blessing to have an older, more experienced, gifted professional as a friend. Dick even helped me enormously on a personal level. As a young man I felt considerable guilt. I mentioned earlier that once I refused to look at a beautiful view because I didn't think I deserved to. That had to do with my father's passing. But there were other feelings that said deprivation was an okay and proper idea. I identified a lot with Ralph Nader, who had a single room with a phone in the hall even after he was famous. Also, César Chavez, whom I later visited in his modest little house in Delano, California. Dick pointed out that, overall, I had a too scrupulous conscience. I'd never heard that phrase, nor have I since; he may have made it up. But what he was saying was that no one was perfect and to give myself a break if I wasn't either. Amazingly, once he suggested the idea to me, I did it, and instantly felt better. Still do. This was reinforced with Lee Strasberg's "Accept yourself." I got great early help from Dick in work and in life. Of course, this give-yourself-a-break advice doesn't apply to everyone; certainly not to people who regularly give others a bad time, or career criminals, for example.

Now Dick was producing my play. I directed it, and we had a wonderful cast, headed by Alan Arkin, Renée Taylor, and Louise Lasser. And it was a smash. We sold out every performance. This play that no producer was interested in suddenly had three offers to go right to Broadway. Unfortunately, on the financial side, they all pretty much wanted to ease Dick out of the picture. True to his fashion, Dick tried to persuade me to take the deals and forget about him, or he would even stay for the pittance (my word) they were offering him. He said the low percentage for him wasn't even unusual, given the new guys would be putting up the money. But I always count talent, quality, intelligence, and working every minute of the day on something at least as important as money, so I decided not to do it.

And, ironically, by now I felt it needed more work. At this writing, about eighteen years later, a New York production of the play *One of the All-Time Greats* will be done at the Roundabout Theatre.

There were some curious sidelights to having the play produced. In a one-week run it's not unusual for the cast to supply their own clothes, when the budget is limited and the play's action takes place in the present. One of the women in the play was unhappy because she felt she would have a bigger impact than her role possibly could have given her. She showed up for dress rehearsal in a dress that seemed to be made up of a hundred little mirrors which shot out reflected light in all directions. This outfit couldn't have worked for the star of a musical, let alone a supporting character in a straight play. When I asked her if she would please wear another dress, she said that was her only one. (The others didn't fit, she claimed.) When I said I would give her the money to buy a new dress, she said there wasn't time for alterations. I was in the midst of a neurotic game with her, so I stopped playing. Once I stopped with my questions and suggestions, she sought me out and asked, "What should I do about the dress?" I told her I'd said everything I could. I suppose she couldn't think of anything else to do or say that would make me and everyone else unhappy any longer, so the next day she managed to show up with another dress.

Then there was the actor playing the Chinese waiter. A message was sent to me in the audience in the middle of the first act on opening night saying the actor wouldn't be making his next entrance unless I came backstage right away and got the stage manager to apologize to him. I don't know what I was asking the stage manager to apologize for, but I hurried backstage and an apology was made. Normally, of course, I would have tried to figure out what was going on, but I was kind of interested in getting back to my seat to see the rest of the opening-night performance.

So, aside from the lady with the mirrors and the actor who wasn't going to go on in the middle of the play, it was an enjoyable experience. I'm not mentioning these people's names, as they still are active in the profession and I'm not interested in damaging their careers as they damaged the experience for me and the others. We are all neurotic one way or another at times, but these were two events where nets would have been in order.

Incidentally, the fact that the play was a tremendous success after being rejected by everyone who read it wasn't that unusual. I was later to realize that comedy scripts submitted to potential backers are almost always rejected. The exception, of course, is when they're written by someone very successful. They are the most difficult types of scripts to read and "get"—even though, astonishingly to me, virtually no one seems to acknowledge this. They're usually most appreciated by other people who work in comedy, but when submitted to business people the comments are almost always, "I don't think it's funny," or dozens of variations on that sentence. The certainty with which that opinion is expressed has irked me more than just about anything over the years; and later, when many of these scripts turn out to be funny and successful, these same people say: "They must have done a lot to it." Often virtually nothing was done except that it was acted. Scripts are written to be performed, not read and judged by people who aren't qualified. Years later, I gave a copy of this play script to someone in the Shubert Organization, which owns most of the Broadway theaters. He read me a reader's report that, among other things, said about the play: "It cries out for a laugh line." This play, in which cast members kept coming to me and saying, "What do we do when the audience's laughter keeps stopping the show?" which it often did. Ah, reports! I have heard only one person in my life ever admit, "I have no idea how to read a comedy"—which is the fact for almost all these people. That one person, by the way, is a longtime successful head of a movie studio.

When you begin to realize that some of the biggest successes of all time—comedies and drama in the theater and movies— have initially been rejected by people who supposedly should know better, you can't take all these rejections too seriously. The scripts include: *Star Wars; E.T.; Same Time Next Year; One Flew Over the Cuckoo's Nest; I'm Not Rappaport; American Graffiti; On the Waterfront; The Graduate; Terms of Endearment*—to name just a few of a long list of hundreds of wonderful pieces of work. Then, of course, there are endless stories about movie companies that actually *saw* the finished pictures and were unhappy, until the public proved them wrong. *American Graffiti* was initially intensely disliked by the head of the studio that made it. *One Flew Over the Cuckoo's Nest* was rejected by Columbia Pictures when they saw the movie and had a chance to buy it. This happens all the time. The point is that no one really knows until the public sees the picture—not some executive viewing a picture alone in a screening room, and certainly not some businessman reading a script. For me it is a pragmatic issue. When rejected, I have to keep trying to find a way to get a piece of work on, but my opinion of an audience's interest in a project can really only be changed by the audience.

Comedy and
Emergency Rooms

As Elaine May prepared *The Heartbreak Kid* for its Christmas release, Renée Taylor, whom I had just directed in my play, called and once again asked me to direct something she and her husband, Joe Bologna, had written. I was delighted. It was like working with family.

The show was a television special to be produced by and star Marlo Thomas. I had known Marlo socially in New York, and she was a friend. The special was called "Acts of Love, and Other Comedies." It was a highly ambitious show that was to take Marlo through stages of life ranging from teenager to motherhood, saying humorous things about dating and romance and infidelity and . . . well, life. The guest stars were Jean Stapleton and my friends Gene Wilder, Art Garfunkel, and Joe Bologna, who was now having a successful career as an actor as well as a writer. The script and cast were wonderful. Gary Smith and Dwight Hemion, considered tops in their field, were responsible for the look. Everything but the schedule pointed to a great show. The budget demanded that I deliver a show of extraordinary quality in a short time. I felt that Renée and Joe and Marlo expected this of me.

I entered the four-day rehearsal period, and by day three was feeling tension and pain in every part of my body; I didn't see how I could get the show to the level of excellence the script deserved in such a short period of time. (This reminds me of the famous last line of the dying actor when someone at his bedside said, "It must be so hard to die." The actor replied, "No, dying is easy; comedy is hard.") I joked about the pain, but one day my friend Herb Gardner, the playwright, came by and suggested we take a little trip down to Bellevue Hospital's emergency room. I had symptoms for a lot of things you don't want, but was only diagnosed as under too much stress, and suffering from lack of rest. I went back and continued rehearsal. We then began the taping. In a very, very short time—again, four days—I was trying to do something wonderful. Again my body started to say: Hold it! What's happening here? How 'bout some sleep? I was getting four hours a night, but I pressed on. One day, I, who am not a drinker, had someone go out and get me a flask and fill it with gin. I kept it in my back pocket, and when the pain got really bad, I whipped out the flask and took a swig.

Marlo sidled up to me and said, "What are you doing? People are going to think you're an alcoholic."

I said, "I don't care. I don't even drink. But right now, I've got a lot of pain and a show to do," and took another swig.

I got through the rest of the taping feeling less pain, and made a mental note to stay away from future shows with tremendous aspirations and short schedules.

When the special was completed, I learned that ABC felt it was absolutely essential that it have a laugh track. They argued that audiences are used to hearing laughter when they watch comedy on television, and it would be extremely detrimental to the show not to have laughter at the appropriate places. I argued that people watch comedy movies on television without a laugh track guiding them where to laugh. I thought it was patronizing to the audience, and, besides, the idea of having all this fake laughter after all the comedy moments would compromise the integrity of the show. If that weren't enough, I also realized that most of the people laughing on these recorded tracks weren't living anymore, and that, for me, will take some of the fun out of any comedy.

Marlo was our spokesperson, and finally she said the network felt very strongly and they *had* put up the money, so I reluctantly went along on the condition that I supervise the placing of the laughs.

There's a man in Hollywood named Charley Douglas who

has a laugh machine, and Marlo and Charley and I met to put laughs in our show. Charley wheeled his machine in and started to place his laughs as the show began. I watched him silently for a while, and then as he put his laugh in at a particularly funny moment in the first scene, I found myself suddenly leaping up and surprising everyone, mostly myself, by crying out: "You call that a laugh! That's one of the funniest moments in the show: Let's hear it!" I really got into it after that. I had him showing me every facet of his machine. He could give you titters, chuckles, guffaws, screams, more women than men laughing, more men than women . . . endless varieties and combinations. And I took advantage of every nuance he could offer, as Marlo sat behind me laughing at my turnabout. In this case, I figured: If you can't lick 'em, join 'em.

We won an Emmy, and maybe that's what made me forget that mental note about avoiding such shows in the future, for when the chance came to do another special two years later, I agreed again. I couldn't possibly have foreseen the bizarre circumstances that would precede the decision.

Welcome to Hollywood

$\mathbf{F}$inally, Christmas rolled around and *The Heartbreak Kid* opened. The movie was an instant critical and commercial success, and all at once—suddenly, after seventeen years—I was considered a movie star.

Every closed door in Hollywood—which was *every* door—was suddenly open. "We'd love to do something with Chuck. What would Chuck like to do? We'll find it for him" replaced "He's not right for the role. There really isn't anything in it for him." It seemed to me, and I've seen it proved endlessly over the years, that Hollywood respects quality but worships success. And if they think you're giving both, well . . .

It was ironic. From being fired from an Off-Broadway show, *Steambath*, to *The Heartbreak Kid*, I was going from the depths to the heights of my acting career within one year in one move, and I, of course, had the same ability. (There was a further irony here. Both *Steambath* and *The Heartbreak Kid* came from the original work of the same writer—Bruce Jay Friedman. Neil Simon's screenplay of *The Heartbreak Kid* was based on a short story by Bruce Jay Friedman called "Change of Plan.")

It is an awful frustration for some actors to know that if they got the right part, they could go from being an unknown to being a star. See Sylvester Stallone in *Rocky* or Dustin Hoffman in *The*

Graduate. Sadly, for all the talented people out there, they are rare exceptions to the rule of aching unemployment.

Everywhere I'd go there'd be movie scripts waiting for me. There were literally stacks of them. They were offering me virtually every possible movie to star in because I was the new guy and I'd been up at bat once and had a hit. I went on *The Tonight Show*, and after my second appearance Bob Dolce from the show called and said Johnny Carson wanted to put me under an exclusive contract. Bob said he had only done it twice before, with Joan Rivers and David Steinberg. I wouldn't be paid any differently, but I would be on once every three weeks and in the early part of the show, not at the end, as I had been the first two times. For my part, I was only not to appear on any other talk shows. I asked why Johnny Carson wanted to do that, and Bob told me Johnny had said, "That kid really knows how to tell a story!" Over the years, I was no longer under contract but continued to appear regularly. It's now been eighteen years, and there's nothing in show business I've enjoyed more than going out there without a net with Johnny, whom I like very much—mostly for his generosity to other performers and his continued capacity to enjoy what others do. That appreciation is something very few top comedians have for other humorists, and it means everything when you are appearing with him. Many people have asked me what my relationship with Johnny Carson is, since we often seem to be "going after each other." We often *are* going after each other, but no matter how it sometimes may appear, our purpose is always just entertainment. And for the last eight years or so neither one of us ever has any idea what will happen when we are out there together. It's my longest ongoing professional relationship.

I went to about ten cities around the country to publicize *The Heartbreak Kid*. When I got to Miami, I decided to call Professor Fred Koch, who had been my acting teacher for my six months at the university there almost twenty years earlier. He was now retired. I got him on the phone and explained who I was and what his encouragement for my "Friends, Romans, countrymen" had meant to me. There was just silence from his end until I finished. Then he said: "These are the kinds of calls that keep a teacher going." I said that was exactly what he had done for me.

Since I was doing all this traveling around the country for the movie, I thought it was fitting that I meet Gordon Stuhlberg, the head of the studio (20th Century-Fox) releasing the picture. I told some friends I was going to call him. They said that was an odd thing to do because he was so busy and this was just one of many pictures they had. I called him. He invited me to lunch, and brought every major executive from the studio along to meet me. Discussion began for me to star in pictures for the studio for years to come.

One evening I went to a big dinner the studio gave and was introduced to Groucho Marx: "This is Chuck Grodin, from *The Heartbreak Kid*. You saw the movie, Groucho."

He looked at me and said: "Hated the movie, loved my seat."

I think he was kidding. But with all the success and acceptance, I sensed there was also a portion of the audience and the industry that found this character—this guy who leaves his wife on his honeymoon—an unsettling figure, to put it nicely. More like: Watch your purse when he's around.

In fact, the first review I saw of the movie, in the *New York Daily News*, actually had this headline: YOU'LL HATE HIM, LOVE THE MOVIE. Well, they meant the character, but I knew some of that character identification was rubbing off on me. I could tell this particularly during interviews with some young women reporters who were surprised I wasn't some kind of a devious character. I had a particularly unusual experience with a newspaperwoman who was interviewing me in the first city on the tour. After a long lunch, the woman asked what city I'd be heading to next. I told her, and she said, "I wouldn't mind going there with you."

I wasn't sure what she meant, so I said, "Don't you feel you have your story?"

She said, "Oh, I have my story. I just wouldn't mind going out with you . . . or staying in with you—whatever."

I knew the interview had gone well, but I didn't know it had gone that well. I had a girlfriend at the time, so I wasn't about to take up the offer. She added that she would just need to tell her boyfriend, who was waiting across the street in a doorway at that moment. I explained that, for so many reasons, it didn't seem like a good idea.

On the other hand, there was the newspaperwoman who, in the middle of an interview, asked if I had possibly seen the review from some film quarterly I'd never heard of that she was digging out of her purse. To put this in context, it was hard to find a bad review of *The Heartbreak Kid*, but what was even harder than that was to find a rave review of *The Heartbreak Kid* that panned me. That would be pretty tough, since I was in just about every minute of the picture. This woman had found one. She handed it to me and seemed to enjoy watching me read it. She asked for my comment. I just shrugged and said, "Everyone's entitled to his opinion." That seemed to disappoint her.

I found that, happily, only about one out of fifty interviewers comes to "go after" you, either by order from their editors— which I've never personally experienced—or because they think it will be more "interesting," or because they just don't like you. On those very few occasions, I'm very polite and try to get the hell away from them as fast as possible.

To this day, about eighteen years later, whenever I'm recognized and people start to talk to me, whatever else they say, they often wind up talking about *The Heartbreak Kid*. The movie definitely struck a chord. The number of men, particularly, who tell me how much they loved the movie and how much they identified with the character, while flattering, is also somewhat frightening. I mean, this *is* a guy who leaves his wife on his honeymoon for a beautiful blonde he doesn't even know. I guess it says something about the strong fantasy life of some married men. Of course, the character does wind up with the beautiful blonde. The end of the movie is meant to suggest that he's going to be just as unhappy as he was with his first wife. I guess if there's an underlying message in the picture, it's not "Let's leave our wives for beautiful blondes," but "Be careful of what you want—you may get it." Or maybe, on a deeper level: "Look at yourself for your problems." Having written this, somehow I feel fewer men will be telling me how much they loved the movie.

I suppose it's inevitable for the public to identify the screen character of the actor with the personality of the performer in real life. It's almost impossible for the moviegoing public to imagine that James Cagney was not "James Cagney," that Spencer Tracy was not "Spencer Tracy," that Gary Cooper or Humphrey Bogart were not "Coop" or "Bogie" off-screen as well as on. Of course, certain characteristics might be similar, but as far as "What is so-and-so really like?"—that, of course, is entirely different from what you're seeing on the screen. Once that screen persona is really stamped on the public's consciousness, however, it's rare that any performer is accepted in a totally different light. When one of them has tried to break a screen image—for example, Henry Fonda or James Stewart as a villain—it's almost as though the public has stood up as one and shouted: Stop that! So, even though it might be a while, if ever, before Charles Grodin would be doing any public-consciousness stamping, I was aware that the identification of Lenny, the Heartbreak Kid, with Charles Grodin had happened to some degree. Having taken this long to get here, I was going to make sure that the next character I played wasn't going to beat his dog or anything.

The success certainly felt better than rejection, but it didn't bring any particular change in my personal happiness. The expectation that life was going to be total euphoria was never in my mind. So when life went on and the offers were just bigger and better, with their own sets of problems, it was what I unconsciously expected. I happily avoided the disappointment when the ecstasy wasn't there. It was nice to have a success—but life was still life, and that was just fine.

I Could've Gone Back to Pittsburgh

The warm reception I received for *The Heartbreak Kid* made me feel an added responsibility for the next movie I would do. I felt there were some people who would actually come to see me in my second starring role, so not only was I looking for the right part, but it had to be in a movie that wouldn't disappoint people as well.

For six months I read and turned down every movie that was offered. Some were never made, none was successful, but some did benefit the leading actors, because they were good parts and the actors were good in them. But as long as I wanted both the part and the movie to be very good, my judgment had been right. Of course, I later understood that looking for both an excellent role and script might mean a wait of three years or so, which is exactly what some actors do. I also felt that the success of *The Heartbreak Kid* would sustain this ongoing industry interest in me. Finally, someone said, "You really ought to do something because the way Hollywood works, while you're waiting, another new actor comes along."

Eventually, a script was sent to me called *11 Harrowhouse*. It was based on a popular adventure novel about a jewelry robbery in which all the jewels are sucked up from a vault by a vacuuming mechanism through the ventilation system of a building. The thief, played by me, would be on the roof of the Diamond Headquarters at 11 Harrowhouse. By the time the robbery occurred, the audience would be rooting for the guy to succeed, as by then the diamond establishment had done sufficiently bad things to him. The cast included James Mason as the inside man; Sir John Gielgud as the arrogant head of the diamond cartel; Trevor Howard, who plotted the robbery with me; and Candice Bergen as my girlfriend. It seemed to have a lot of elements going for it, not the least of which was that I didn't do anything bad to anybody but the bad guys, and that I didn't leave my wife on our honeymoon.

The Heartbreak Kid had given me power. Gordon Stuhlberg, the president of 20th Century-Fox, told Elliot Kastner, the producer of *11 Harrowhouse,* that the studio wasn't interested in making the movie unless Elliot could get me to star in it. I was given my choice of about half a dozen leading-lady stars, and even before they hired the English stars they checked with me. I said I'd be delighted if they could get Candy Bergen, whom I'd met once and liked; and the English stars were among the best actors in the world.

I went to London for the filming. On one of the first days on the set at Pinewood Studios, I was especially looking forward to meeting Sir John Gielgud, who would be working that day. As I walked over to shake hands with him, before I could get a word out about how much I admired him, he said, "Oh, you were so wonderful in the Elaine May film." I muttered some thanks, then tried to talk about him, and he quickly changed the subject. At lunchtime, we looked at the previous day's rushes. I asked him if he'd like to join me even though he wasn't in the footage. He was very shy, but came with me. In the theater, before the film started, he very self-consciously and apologetically called out to the director, Aram Avakian: "Aram, Chuck said it would be okay if I came along." He was shy and deferential except when he acted, and then he was a powerhouse.

I had always been a big admirer of Trevor Howard, and I was thrilled that he was in the picture. It was not exactly a secret that Trevor had been known on occasion to have a drink or two. Since most of his scenes were with me, I asked if the drinking was an issue. I was assured that whatever drinking Trevor did, he certainly didn't do it while working, but only afterward, which, in my experience, put him in the overwhelming majority of the human species. I was told that he would be quite happy to meet with me at the studio before shooting began. I thought that was a useful idea since there wasn't going to be any rehearsal.

I was already filming on the picture for a few days when the time came for Trevor and me to meet. At some point in the shooting, I was told that Trevor had arrived a bit early and was passing some time in the cocktail lounge at the studio. Aram assured me that Trevor probably felt the meeting was really about his sobriety, so we needn't worry, wherever he was waiting. We completed shooting, and I returned to the main hall of the administration building, where we were to meet Trevor. No one was there. I glanced down the long hallway just as Trevor appeared, having just come out of the bar. Well . . . "come out" isn't exactly what he did. "Lurched out" would be a little closer to the truth. I began to smile: What a great gag he's pulling! He knows we want to see him sober, obviously, and he's doing a great drunk bit as a gag.

As he approached me down the long hall, he acted as though he literally had to balance himself on one side of the wall and then the other. I almost laughed out loud at his brilliant, ironic wit. Of course, as he came closer, it was obvious that this was no performance. I had now been joined by Aram and Candy Bergen, and the three of us smiled weakly at Trevor as we all shook hands. We moved toward a flight of stairs that led up to a conference room where we were going to read over the scenes Trevor was in. I felt terrible as I watched Trevor shakily make his way up the stairs. I didn't see how he could possibly read over anything. Inside the room, we all took seats. I wondered what was going to happen. I assumed that Trevor, having had to wait for us, had given in to the temptation to steady his nerves at being looked over. Since I had had a lifetime of being looked over and rejected, I felt nothing but sympathy for him.

Suddenly, Trevor picked up his script and began to attack it. "It's not James Bond," he said. "It's not *The French Connection,* either. It's somewhere in between—and where's that?!" he demanded to know, somewhat angrily. Well, he was right about the script, in a sense: It wasn't James Bond. This movie's budget was about two million dollars, a small fraction of a Bond movie. The book, *11 Harrowhouse,* had been a success, and if they actually had filmed the book it would have cost what a Bond movie cost but the studio wasn't ready for that. It didn't have the excitement of *The French Connection* either, but, of course, that criticism could be applied to 95 percent of all the adventure movies made. Also, I had been hired to do some work on the script within its two-million-dollar budget confines, so his outburst against it offended me more than it otherwise might have. On the other hand, at similar meetings I've seen actors attack scripts in which I've had nothing to do with the writing, and I'm always offended. I always think, If you didn't like it, why did you agree to be in it? Anyway, all this passionate criticism coming out of Trevor, who was slurring his words pretty heavily now, really made me angry. Then I did something that I don't think I've ever done before or since; I committed a consciously mean act. I suggested we read over the scenes, knowing that would be fairly close to impossible for Trevor. Aram and Candy were just staring at me now. Trevor announced grandly that that was a good idea, and began to read his first scene. I instantly felt terrible. It was impossible, of course. I just gazed at Trevor as he tried to navigate his way through some long speech, which he gave up on halfway through, and began to attack the script again. Suddenly, his eyes shot up from the table and quickly peered at me looking at him. I don't know what he saw, but his eyes burned into mine. Without a word, he struggled to his feet and started to come around the long table toward where I was sitting. I had no idea what he was doing. I rose as he stumbled toward me, prepared for anything, including a punch in the face; I couldn't tell. As he got close he threw his arms around me and gave me a big hug, and then announced to everyone that he liked the look on my face that he'd caught while I was watching him. Fortunately, he'd seen me at a compassionate moment. The meeting broke up after that. It was decided, in spite of everything, to go forward with Trevor in hopes that that wouldn't happen again. It didn't, ever, and he ended up being brilliant in the role.

About three weeks into the filming of the movie, I was having lunch with the producer, Elliot Kastner, and he said quite casually, "You know, the studio really wishes they weren't involved with this movie."

"Really?" I said, trying to sound just as casual. "Why is that?"

Elliot, not a man of great tact, said bluntly: "They don't like you in it."

"They don't like me?"

"Right."

"What about Candy Bergen, James Mason, John Gielgud, and Trevor Howard?" I asked.

"They like them. They only don't like you."

I got through the rest of the movie, trying, with only partial success, not to be demoralized by my conversation with Elliot. This was difficult, because after our lunch he virtually stopped speaking to me. He seemed desperate to ally himself with the studio. On hearing of my experiences, a friend who had earlier worked with him shook his head knowingly and said, "You were Kastnerized."

Elliot Kastner is a man whose name I haven't been able to say out loud indoors all these years. It's only very recently that I've been able to say his name outdoors—and rarely. I was told of an Englishman who says, "I just saw—you should pardon the expression—Elliot Kastner."

Elliot's idea of a good time was attempting to grab my or Aram Avakian's scrotum on special occasions—the first day of shooting, important conferences, et cetera. I'm not saying he'd want to do anything with these scrotums if he got hold of them: Apparently just reaching for them and catching a little feel was enough.

When it seemed likely that the movie wasn't going to be successful, Elliot did everything he could to remove himself from any responsibility for it. Ever since my lunch with him I had been wary, but I wasn't fully certain of what he was up to until I got back to America and got a call from a journalist who said he had wanted to interview me in England but had been told by the producer that I didn't allow any interviews—of me or anyone else. Of course, it was all made up. Perhaps Elliot figured that if he could paint me as being difficult, it would take the focus off him as a producer, which is what he seemed to want.

I'm pleased to say that after thirty years in this profession he is the only person I hope I never encounter again. If you took a vote in Hollywood on which producer is best avoided, I'd put my money on Elliot to win. If he didn't, I sure wouldn't want to meet the one who did.

As far as the studio not liking me in the part, that had nothing to do with Elliot. I have to take responsibility for it. My choice in how to play the role would have been perfect if I had been Clint Eastwood. Probably in an overreaction to the aggressive nature of the character in *The Heartbreak Kid*, I played the role in an extremely passive manner.

After I finished filming I went back to New York and started to hear terrible reports about the movie. There had been a sneak preview of it out in Los Angeles, and it got a 50 percent favorable and 50 percent unfavorable response—which made it barely releasable.

I went out to California and saw it; it was very, very slow. As I've said, I came off extremely laid-back. It just didn't come over. So I talked to some friends, particularly Elaine May and Herb Gardner, and we came up with the idea of doing a narration for the movie—like in the old Bogart pictures where you hear him talk to the audience to let them know a lot they wouldn't know without it: "She was the kind of dame . . ." Herb and I went to the studio and persuaded them to let us do this, which wasn't difficult because they were so unhappy with the film. Herb had had a previous experience with the studio president, Gordon Stuhlberg, who had once headed another studio; it had gone out of business, and the newspapers had reported the movies it had done. Among them was a picture Herb had written called *Who Is Harry Kellerman, and Why Is He Saying Those Terrible Things About Me?* His movie was listed next to a failed John Wayne picture called *Big Jake*. Herb, who is one of the wittiest people in the world, said that his movie, with its long title, listed next to the short title of *Big Jake*, kind of made it look like he was at least five or six times more responsible for the studio's bad fortune than the makers of *Big Jake*.

We put the narration together from the beginning of the movie to the end. The studio never checked to see what we were doing. Only once, an extraordinarily cheerful man I never saw before or since came in, nodded for a few minutes, and said casually that it looked good to him. There were long silences in the movie, so there was a lot of room in which to say things. I, as the main character, talked to the audience in the silence and kind of made jokes and told them more about what was going on. The studio took the movie out and sneak-previewed it again, in San Diego. Elliot Kastner, Aram Avakian, a lot of 20th Century-Fox executives, and I were all there. The audience loved it! They laughed at everything in the narration (which was extensive) and it warmed them to the whole picture. They cheered and applauded throughout the movie. They filled out preview cards at the end and gave it a 93 percent favorable reaction—which almost set a record. The studio executives were jumping up and down. Guys in suits and ties who had barely been speaking to me were literally hugging and kissing me in the lobby of the theater. They had thought they had a barely releasable picture, and now they felt they had a hit. There was actual awe in their eyes as they looked at me. They couldn't believe it. The next night, they took it to another theater in San Diego, and the same thing happened. Elliot Kastner was there in the middle of all this gleeful preview-card counting. He managed to look up at me once and say softly, "Nice job."

Next, they were going to have a trade screening, meaning they would present the picture to be reviewed by *Variety*, the most important trade paper, read by everyone in the profession. The picture wasn't going to be released for a few months, so the *Variety* review was very significant. Theater owners all over the country would read it and decide, based on what it said, if they wanted to play the picture. The *Variety* reviewer came to see the picture, and he hated it. Absolutely hated it! He didn't see it with an audience, by the way, which is crucial to a comedy. Sometimes in reviews you might see a paragraph in black bold print. This guy had black bold print all over the review—big black letters that said, in effect: I HATE THIS MOVIE! There was only one thing he hated more than the movie, and that was me. And the only thing he hated even more than me was that narration. "This might have been a good movie without that narration," he said. And he knew I did it. So all this big black bold attack print was for me.

The other trade paper, *The Hollywood Reporter*, also slammed the movie, thereby supporting the *Variety* critic's opinion. That critic also saw the picture without an audience. Amazingly, the studio executives, rather than believing their own eyes and ears at the sneak previews, believed the reviews. Maybe they knew what an uphill battle they faced with the theater owners all over the country who primarily read the *Variety* review. Maybe they were men in a tough business who weren't particularly looking for trouble. Whatever the reasons, their enthusiasm for the picture disappeared when the reviews appeared. The executives who before we started filming had been so warm, and then so cold after the picture was finished, and then so warm after the sneak previews, now were cold again. Worse, the rest of Hollywood, who hadn't, of course, seen the picture—only the review—believed it. People believe what they read unless they have a reason not to believe it. Even gossip columns are believed by people who really should know better. Once it says that Sylvester Stallone will get $12 million for a movie, and it's true, people will believe anything. I like Stallone's work; I'm just saying that once someone gets $12 million, people will believe anything. I once read an April Fool's version of a news column aloud to a friend, and although my friend did a "take" at each item, she believed it. It had items like: "Paul Anka will do the life story of Gertrude Stein." She believed it. People believed the *Variety* review.

I read the review in Los Angeles. My mother had come to visit, and she'd seen the picture and liked it—which wasn't automatic, by the way. I'd say she hasn't liked about half the pictures I've done. Here was a perfect example of how the repression mechanism works. I read the review, with all its big, black, bold attack on me, probably went numb, put my body on hold subconsciously, finished reading it, started to chuckle, and said: "Hey, Ma, listen to this." I read it aloud to my mother, who also probably went numb, because she chuckled too. It was like we were both mildly amused. It seemed odd for the critic to write so viciously about such hard work that an audience really enjoyed. That kind of detached amusement has been my attitude on the subject of what happened with *11 Harrowhouse* all these years. I also think part of my body is still "on hold" on the subject. Mother's forgotten it, anyway.

All of a sudden, everything that had taken twenty years to get to with *The Heartbreak Kid* was over. Absolutely over. Nobody wanted me. All calls stopped immediately. I had just lost in a few days something that had taken me a career to achieve. I'm sure that on some subconscious level I once again felt kicked out, pushed away—the Pittsburgh Playhouse was having the last word, the people responsible for firing me from *Steambath* were having the last word.

I don't mean to suggest that on a conscious level I felt nothing. I certainly experience success and failure differently. I just never soar to the heights or crash to the depths. I do remember sitting around my apartment in New York late one night during this period, wondering if this business—show business—was ever going to get any easier. I walked into the bathroom and splashed some cold water on my face, when suddenly I heard a loud voice say: "You want to know who's had it tough? Chuck Grodin had it tough." I honestly thought I had suddenly lost my mind or was having a heavenly visitation. Then I realized, without being aware of it, I'd flipped a radio on. It was the voice of Barry Gray, my favorite radio talk-show host in New York, chatting with some actors. Barry went on to talk about how I'd driven a cab and been around for about fifteen years before I'd "made it" with *The Heartbreak Kid*. Certainly, Barry didn't know I'd just "unmade it." Show business can be weird this way. Nobody but you and your agent really knows what's going on in terms of demands for your services. The public seems to believe that anyone who's famous is always in demand. The epitome of how untrue this is was shown years ago when Bette Davis took out a full-page ad in *Variety*, saying, in effect: EXPERIENCED ACTRESS NEEDS A JOB.

At the time, Harry Ufland, who was still representing me, called a producer about my playing a part in a movie. The answer was: "We saw the review." They didn't see the movie, just the review. In fact, the movie, when it came out without much support from the studio, didn't do too bad. It's amazing it did any business at all, because in some cities they actually released it on a double bill. It didn't make any money, but it was not a disaster; and, in fact, it got a lot of excellent notices and never got another review like the one in *Variety*. I've been surprised over the years at how many people have written me or told me how much they liked the movie. At the end of the *Variety* review it said: "It would be sad to think that an acting career lay ahead for Mr. Grodin. Fortunately, he's also a writer and director." I could have quietly gone back to Pittsburgh, and no one would have noticed.

Of course, along with being a writer and director, I had something even better: That finely developed skill at dealing with rejection served me once more. I'd spent all but six months of my life not being a movie star, so I wouldn't be one again.

How long this defense system would continue to work, the future was going to reveal; and when it wouldn't any longer, a different person would emerge, but that was a while away, and, of course, I had absolutely no inkling of it.

The Other Side
of Show Business

After *11 Harrowhouse,* which pointedly showed the whimsical ways of Hollywood, something happened that showed the other side of the profession called show business. As someone I knew once said to a complaining artist: "Hey, what do you expect? They call it show *business,* not show *art.*" And yet there was another side.

I got a call from Marlo Thomas, who by this time had become a close friend. Our mutual friend Herb Gardner had a play in trouble out of town, called *Thieves.* It had opened to poor reviews in New Haven, and then again in Boston. The star had gone, and the understudy was playing out the run; the director, Michael Bennett (who a year later would direct *A Chorus Line;* this was 1974), had gone, saying he had done everything he could; and the producers had one foot out the door. Herb had asked Marlo if she would consider taking over the starring role to try to help turn the situation around. Herb said she would do it if I would come in as the director. We both knew Herb had worked on the play for a long time, and I'd read it and was surprised to hear of such a negative reception. I agreed to fly to Boston to look at it and give my opinion. The situation already was fairly unusual. Shows that are greeted that poorly in two cities, especially after the star and director have gone, aren't usually looking for

■ 217 ■

opinions. But this was Marlo and Herb, and "giving up" comes at the bottom of their list of things to do.

I sat next to Marlo, seeing the play for the first time. About ten minutes into the show people started heading up the aisles, and by the end of the evening a significant portion of the audience had left. I didn't speak to Marlo throughout the show. I saw her looking at me out of the corner of her eye. To put it gently, I did not like the way the play was being presented. For reasons I'm still not sure of, it was fairly dark onstage (the play took place at night, but still . . .), and most of the cast was too far away from the audience, to whom they were directly shouting (another idea I had trouble with). Somewhere in all this darkness and distance was Herb's play. After the performance, I told Herb and Marlo and the producers that I didn't know how good I could help make it, but I knew how to make it better than it was. Herb seemed heartened, Marlo, who has an indomitable spirit, was ready to go in, and the producers headed out the door.

I now became the director and the producer, along with my old friend Dick Scanga, who flew up to Boston to help. Because the production was losing money, Dick worked for no salary, as did, of course, Herb and I. The actors had to be paid. Marlo worked for a small fraction of what she normally would get and then gave it back to the production to be used as needed. I began to split my time between working with Herb on the script and directing Marlo into the part. Also, I had the lights turned up, moved the cast closer to the audience, and asked everyone to talk to each other and not to us out front.

I sat in the back of the theater with Herb every night watching the play, with the understudy playing the role Marlo would eventually play. One evening, when the performance was over, two ladies came up the aisle, the last to leave. They spotted Herb and me sitting in the back of the theater with our yellow pads and assumed we were involved with the production. They started to laugh, and in a ridiculing whisper exclaimed: "They're trying to fix it!"

It never occurred to me not to try to fix it. I've seen so many people over the years run in or out the door, depending on which way the wind was blowing, and I didn't like the look of that, so I continued to work with Herb.

A few nights later, there was Marlo, with only four days' rehearsal, sitting in her dressing room about to go on for the first time. I went back to wish her well, and I saw a look of such terror on her face that I burst out laughing . . . because I knew exactly how she felt. It was one thing for me to be sitting in the dark theater trying to help; it was another for her to step into the bright lights and do it. I mean, it's no fun to have a lot of people turn and walk out when you're up there.

The play starts with Marlo lying on a bed. Marlo later said her heart was thumping so hard she was afraid the audience would hear it. I remembered my *Armstrong Circle Theater* television debut, when I feared viewers would hear my heart thumping and adjust their television sets. The performance began with our changes and Marlo, and nobody seemed to be leaving. In fact, people seemed to be enjoying it. We were thrilled! It was as though a corner had been turned. The audience loved Marlo, and the changes in the script seemed to be helping as well. The play continued to get better every night. After about five days, we invited the critics to review it again. They did, and this time, amazingly, they liked it. Instead of people walking out, people were lining up for tickets. Herb and I would sit in a restaurant across the street from the theater and stare at each other in astonishment as the lines formed. The turnaround ranked right up there with the *11 Harrowhouse* narration sneak preview. Experience told me to await Broadway cautiously.

Not that there were no bumps in Boston. One night after the performance, Marlo and I were leaving the restaurant across from the theater when a man began to follow us down the street, calling after Marlo: "You should be embarrassed, Miss Thomas, appearing in this play. Your father'd be ashamed of you! It's not what I would expect from you, Miss Thomas." It seems that the guy was a big admirer of Marlo from her *That Girl* days, and came to the play expecting more of the same. While *Thieves* would not have shocked your average theatergoer, it was not *That Girl*. I felt that we'd all been through as much stress as we needed to get this far, and I didn't need anyone shouting after Marlo in the street. At first I ignored him, but when he persisted with his "Shame on you!" I told him to knock it off. He didn't, but kept after us with more of the same, and louder. I had had very little sleep (this was another one of those round-the-clock jobs) and I sure wasn't in the mood for this character putting I-didn't-know-what into Marlo's head.

I turned and started toward him, surprised by my anger. I told him that if he didn't lay off, I would get him to in my own way. He started to back up. Suddenly, I was on him. I didn't really hit him, but drove him back. He took off into the night.

Marlo watched, open-mouthed. I said that I was sorry for the outburst, but I didn't want her mind to be messed with. She laughed and said it had no effect on her at all.

As I lay awake in bed that night, I realized it had been twelve years since my last "fight" in Boston, the one where the sailor had punched me in the stomach. I was now one win, one loss, with no plans to continue my pugilistic career.

In New York, the original producers, without our knowledge, had let our theater parties go, which were just about our whole advance sale. They hadn't believed we'd make it to New York, and wanted to protect their theater-party contacts. Outrageous! But here we were—coming after all. We were to play some previews in New York before opening night. At the opening preview, the audience went absolutely bananas for the play. They laughed and applauded and cheered wildly throughout. I had never seen anything like it. It was more like a religious event than a show. It was never received like that again, nor has anything else I've ever seen. I went backstage afterward and told the cast that, while I was happy too, we certainly in no way should be looking for that reception again, and not to be disappointed when it didn't come. I believe what happened that night was that a lot of people who love to root for the underdog heard about this play that wasn't supposed to come to town, whose theater parties had been canceled, that was just supposed to close—and here it was, and they came to cheer.

Later that night, I joined Herb and Marlo for a drink with the president of Paramount Pictures, who had financed the play, a man named Frank Yablans. He was very complimentary to me ("You can feel there's one controlling hand behind the production"), but basically he reminded me of a momentarily friendly wildcat. Although he was charming, you just couldn't tell when he might turn into something else you might not want to see. I had no way of knowing that night that years later Frank Yablans would have a major impact on both my professional and personal life.

The show opened to mixed reviews in New York—not really

good enough to run. I think the Boston critics gave it better notices when they rereviewed it because they had seen how far it had come. Of course, we got no points for that in New York. But we had been through too much to just pack our tent and go away, so we decided to stay and try to carry on, hoping the audience would like the show enough that maybe we'd catch on.

One Saturday morning shortly after the show opened, Herb called to tell me that William Hickey, who was playing the part of the old alcoholic bum in the play, had badly hurt his ankle and couldn't go on for the Saturday matinee. I asked Herb who the understudy was, and he replied that there was none. In all the confusion of getting the show in shape and on to New York, the subject had never come up. I had just assumed that all that had been done before I arrived on the scene since the play had already played in two cities. It hadn't.

Herb said, "Either you or I will have to go on."

I said, "What do you mean, 'you or I'? You're not even in the union." I couldn't say he wasn't even an actor, because even though Herb's a Tony Award—winning playwright (*I'm Not Rappaport*), he's also a wonderful actor. But there was no question, union regulations being what they were, that when the curtain went up and the old bum came out that Saturday afternoon, it was going to be me.

The part wasn't very big. I quickly went into my closet and found the oldest, most beat-up–looking clothes I had. Since I rarely got rid of old clothes at that time, I had a selection. I put them on and jumped into a cab.

Herb was standing in front of the theater when I arrived. He looked at me semiapprovingly and began to pick up I-don't-know-what from the street and put it all over my clothes and face. An hour later, as the curtain went up, there I was lying in the gutter as the old bum. Later that night I thought about this year, in which I had gone from being one of the most sought-after young leading men in Hollywood to being a drunken old bum on Broadway.

With the enormous skill of our general manager, Jim (Keep on Truckin') Walsh, pulling one rabbit after another out of the hat, the show ran for eleven months and became the longest-running play on Broadway that season. We never made a dime; we even lost some money. But we won the war. The audience had liked the show and was allowed to see it, and they came. It remains the most gratifying experience I've had in the theater. I've always measured the quality of my show-business experiences not on whether they were successful, but by what the actual experience of doing them was like. While every career needs a certain amount of successes just to sustain itself, the actual human experience is what really stays with me. By that standard, *Thieves* was a big hit. To join forces with Herb and Marlo and Dick Scanga and Jim Walsh and the whole cast and make it go was the best side of the profession. Sometimes show business isn't necessarily show *business*.

Broderick Crawford

Meanwhile, as far as the movies went, all remained quiet on the western front. It was as though *The Heartbreak Kid* had never happened. I'd always known how rough show business was, but this was a surprise even for me.

Putting the difficulty of the last one out of my mind, I agreed to direct another television special—this time with Renée Taylor and Joe Bologna starring as well as writing. The show was called "Paradise," and it was set on a tropical island. Because it was less expensive, we filmed in a studio in Toronto, Canada, in the wintertime.

I experienced something on this special that I have experienced many times over the years in television, the theater, and movies. Putting it broadly, I've worked with two different kinds of people. There's a group that aspires to make every project wonderful, the best it could possibly be. There's no sacrifice in time or effort too great. This attitude applies to all aspects of the work: preproduction, production, postproduction. Everything else in their lives takes a backseat to this goal of trying to achieve something absolutely memorable. They may fail, but never for lack of effort. Then there's the other group. They want to have a success. They want it to be very good. But they're also aware of life itself outside the project. They too work hard, but they consider life demands just as seriously as work demands. They certainly are not willing to work years on a project, like the other group, or even into the night. On most of the projects in which I've been involved, these two groups work side-by-side. The group that's aspiring to make it the greatest thing since the wheel eventually looks at the other group more or less as hacks, or, at best, as laggards. The group that would like to have a life along with a job eventually looks at the no-effort-is-enough group as nuts. When that moment comes, when people begin to reveal which their group is (and it's usually early on), then the eye-rolls and the friendly digs begin. How these two groups constantly work side-by-side is one of the miracles of show business, but they do. It's done with disdain and tolerance, with ridicule and acceptance. Sometimes it seems to be done with mirrors. As is probably obvious, I've always been part of the no-effort-is-too-much group. And I've had the success and lack of personal life to prove it. I've never looked at the other group as hacks or laggards, but more often with a feeling of "I wish I was in your group." In recent years, I've tried to find a third way: Aspire to do something wonderful, and also have a life. That seems the most difficult goal of all.

As was usual with Renée and Joe, we had a tremendous amount of laughs, and, while I skipped the pain, gin, and hospital, once again it was twenty hours a day on a short schedule and a highly ambitious special. No Emmy this time, but a nomination. Also, I had a reunion with my old pal Ted Knight, now a television star on *The Mary Tyler Moore Show*. He was a lot easier for me to direct than to act with. Ruth Buzzi, from *Laugh-In*, was in it too. I remember her quite seriously and intently sweeping up the rehearsal hall when no one else seemed to be going to do it.

One of the other guest stars on the special was Broderick Crawford, an Academy Award–winning actor probably best known to the public as the gruff, tough cop on the old television series *Highway Patrol*. Mr. Crawford was to play Joe Bologna's gruff, tough father in a very good piece about a son who had dragged his father down to an island vacation spot. The father was unable to relax and enjoy himself, and therefore so was the son.

When Broderick Crawford arrived on the scene, I introduced myself as the director, and he gave me a slight, wary smile. I then proceeded to give the dumbest direction of my life. I told Broderick Crawford that the father was very disgruntled about being there. Well, the one thing you didn't have to tell Broderick Crawford to be was disgruntled. He was an actor of considerable talent, but disgruntled was as natural a part of his makeup as the drawl is to Jimmy Stewart. When rehearsals began, he was so intensely disgruntled, it really wasn't funny. I made a few comments, such as, "Pull it back a little, Brod." Nothing changed. I tried: "Be a little warmer, Brod." Nothing.

We had an angry scene with no laughs, and I was already calculating in my mind if the show would be long enough without it. At lunch break, I decided to have a chat with Mr. Crawford, no easy task since he hadn't exactly seemed the chatty type. I tentatively knocked on his dressing-room door, identified myself, and was greeted by a growl that sounded like "GRR-RUGH-RIF." But the door opened.

I went in and said, "Brod, I've come to apologize. I really feel I've misled you into playing the part too disgruntledly."

Brod said, "GRR." The tension in the room rose considerably.

I said, "The father really loves the son and just wants the best for him."

Brod said nothing. The tension rose a little higher.

I further explained: "We really need to feel the warmth of the relationship under all the disgruntledness. Otherwise, the scene runs the risk of being a bit too angry."

Brod glared and said nothing.

I went on in this fashion for a few more minutes, thanked him for all his good work, and said I was sure it was going to turn out really well.

Brod said nothing.

Eventually, I got up and left.

Over the next few days, the scene warmed up just a touch. At the end of the shooting, I went over to Brod once again and said, "I just want to thank you for your excellent work, and I'm sure you'll be very happy when you see it."

Brod said, "GRR." I began to nod my head, searching for something to say to get me out of there. After several nods, I came up with nothing, so, backing away from Brod as if he were royalty, I repeated, "Yes, I think you'll be very happy." Brod stared. I backed out the door into the hall and began a serious re-evaluation of my interest in being a director that continues to this day.

Bob Hope
Was in the Balcony

I went out to Hollywood to finish editing the special. From time to time, Renée would look in and suggest that I use a close-up of her for this shot or that. I went along with her suggestions since she and Joe had written as well as starred in the special, and I felt she deserved a chance to see the show as she envisioned it. I finally showed her the version of the show with all her suggested close-ups. About halfway through the screening, she looked at herself talking in a big close-up and yelled out: "Oh, shut up!" We went back to considerably fewer close-ups.

Just as I finished the special, I received a phone call from a director I knew in New York, Gene Saks. He said he was about to direct a Broadway play with two characters, and asked if I'd be interested. I said I would never go to see a two-character play, and given the world of the Broadway musical as competition, it was always hard for me to understand why anyone would. He then said, "It's about a couple who are having an extramarital affair who meet one weekend a year, and the changes they go through over a period of twenty-five years."

The idea of playing someone over a twenty-five-year period immediately appealed to the character actor in me. I had always played different kinds of people, but the idea of playing the same person over a twenty-five-year period was really interesting. I read it, called him immediately, and said: "I never have any idea what critics might say, but I think audiences will really respond to this play. And I'd love to do it."

It was called *Same Time, Next Year*.

I met with the playwright, Bern Slade, a distinguished-looking Canadian with the glint of a hunted fugitive in his eyes. Bern had great success as a television writer. He created and wrote a lot for shows like *The Flying Nun*. It was considered a good idea to leave most of his career out of his bio, as theater critics are thought to be particularly disinclined toward writers who have primarily written for television situation comedies. I'm not sure exactly why, since a lot of successful Broadway shows, such as *Barefoot in the Park* and, more recently, *Social Security* and *Rumors,* are good situation comedies. In any case, Bern was redefined as a guy who had mostly written plays for Canadian repertory companies, which probably represented less than 5 percent of his writing efforts. So the guy who had the look of a hunted fugitive had to come to Broadway with a kind of alias.

Ellen Burstyn was already set to play the woman, and all that was needed was for Ellen and me to meet and like each other. That was quickly arranged. Ellen, who lives in upstate New York, drove down to Manhattan, where I live, and took me to her home. She wore no makeup at all to our meeting, which instantly impressed me—I'm not sure why. It ended up being part of the overall package of who Ellen Burstyn was. She was completely straightforward, said exactly what she meant, and played no games. She could also put a female George C. Scott move on you if she didn't like something. We spent about six hours together that day. We liked each other very much (still do) and, equally important, had similar backgrounds. Ellen was a devoted acting student of Lee Strasberg. (She later became the head of the Actors Studio after Lee's passing, as well as the head of the stage actors' union, Actors Equity.) Ellen thought it would be a good idea to take the play into the Actors Studio and "work" on it. That would mean improvise, make changes, add, and cut. I said, "Bern Slade I'm sure wrote his first Broadway show, among other reasons, so it wouldn't be rewritten." In television, the writer is constantly rewritten by other people. But the Dramatists Guild for the theater, as I've mentioned before, doesn't allow one word to be changed without the writer's approval. I told Ellen that if we even suggested taking *Same Time, Next Year* into the Actors Studio, Bern Slade would feel mugged. She dropped the idea.

Most all of my personal and professional success with Ellen was based on her finding me funny. That sounds immodest, but let me mention the other side. Once the play was running, at least a couple of times a week Ellen would say to me: "You didn't make me laugh out there as much tonight, Charley." (Friendly George C. Scott—slightly threatening.) Frankly, I liked everything about her.

We went into rehearsal, and Ellen and I began stumbling along, trying to find our way through twenty-five years of life changes in six scenes, starting as young, nervous lovers in their twenties and ending as a couple in their fifties who had experienced a lot of the blows life had to offer.

There was a moment in the play where the script called for me to put my hand on Ellen's breast. After a couple of weeks of rehearsal, when I still hadn't done it, everyone felt it was because I was self-conscious. I said I wasn't, but the more I got involved in the play, the more it seemed a bad idea. In my opinion, for the play to work it always had to be about love, not about sex. After all, these people were married, not unhappily, and having an affair. Ellen, Gene, and Bern still felt that the real reason for my attitude was a discomfort about putting my hand on Ellen's breast. I said again that had absolutely nothing to do with the question, and, to make my point, put both my hands on Ellen's breasts, obviously without any discomfort, putting the "breast" question to a close.

It was a tough play to master in three and a half weeks, which is what we had before we were to open in Boston. Out front during rehearsals, the looks on the faces of Gene Saks and Bern Slade seemed to say to us: What are they doing up there? It was a fair question. We were building this slowly, carefully, as we understood it . . . so slowly that Bern Slade, in obvious torment, would at some point each day just bolt from the theater when it got too difficult for him to watch. Eventually, he would peek in from time to time through a slight crack in the doors at the back of the theater. I understood his plight: He was more used to the short television schedules, where the whole show was finished in a week and you'd often show up and perform full out right away. Finally, Gene called me over one day and said that Bern felt he'd just as soon not open the play if it weren't going to be . . . At that point, Gene threw his head back and searched the ceiling looking for the right words to be delicate. Gene Saks, aside from being one of the funniest men I've ever met, is a master director, but he was watching two performers who weren't performing, and that does give even a master pause—especially with the Boston opening about a week away.

I explained that it was all very complicated, as he knew, and that I felt we could make everyone a little happier very soon. Ellen and I worked all day at rehearsal and all evening drilling the lines. We loved to work with each other, but when we arrived in Boston a week later and stood on the stage of the fifteen-hundred-seat Colonial Theater, a theater often used more fittingly for musicals, we had a little bit of the Christians-and-the-lions feeling. The theater seemed huge. It was difficult to imagine how two people could go out there and . . .

An elderly stagehand watching me from the wings came over and said: "Don't worry, Mr. Grodin. The first laugh you get will be one more than the show that just closed here got." I'm sure the remark was meant to encourage me, but it just heightened my doubt about the massive size of the theater.

Opening night came. The show was sold out. Within the first minute, the audience started to laugh, and they never stopped. It was a sensation! The curtain came down, and immediately after many curtain calls Gene Saks, Bern Slade, and the producer, Morty Gottlieb, were in my dressing room embracing me. Not since the great sneak preview of *11 Harrowhouse* had I been so hugged, but this time there was no *Variety* review to reverse the reaction. The reviews were just sensational. There were no negative reviews at all—not in Boston and not in New York. It was an out-and-out smash hit. People were actually having fistfights on the long lines, pushing for their place to buy tickets. It became a standing-room-only show instantly and stayed that way for every single performance. Every night there was a standing ovation.

Ellen and I stayed with the play for seven months. The enthusiastic response never changed. Bob Hope came to see it and the producers struggled to find him a seat in the balcony. Secret Service agents and plainclothes security police were often around the backstage areas because government officials and foreign dignitaries were regularly in the audience. Celebrities poured backstage every night. Carol Burnett came, knelt, and said: "I come to pay homage." It was funny and thrilling. Gregory Peck filled the opening of the door and said, in perfect Gregory Peck style: "I enjoyed it very much." Burt Lancaster was flattering, and then told me the story of his experience watching the play: "When it begins, you think, Hey, this is just another light comedy. What's all the critical fuss about? But then, all of a sudden, you're unexpectedly moved." Walter Matthau came back. He was sarcastically complimentary: "You were okay." Matthau had told Elaine May after seeing *The Heartbreak Kid*, "He's too good." None of us could figure that one out. Jack Lemmon came with Matthau. Jack, who everyone who's ever met him knows is one of the kindest men in the profession, just kept chuckling through his compliments. Mike Nichols said, "You had a triumph." My old boyhood hero, Ralph Kiner, the Pittsburgh Pirate home-run hitter, came back to meet me. Sir Laurence Olivier came backstage, paid me a compliment, and then was interested only in talking about the various types of wigs that were used. The list of people coming back was endless.

Maybe the most appreciated comment was from the first person backstage on opening night, Lee Strasberg, with a simple: "You were very good." Shortly after Lee's visit, I received an invitation to join the Actors Studio, something I later learned is almost never extended. I accepted happily. It was twenty years since I had first climbed that narrow staircase for that nerve-shattering audition under the spotlights.

One evening about a month into the run of the play, after everyone had left, Ellen came to my dressing room and said she had to talk to me. It was clear from her attitude that something was wrong. She said she had just learned that she was nominated for a Tony Award and I wasn't. Instead of getting tense, I relaxed because I had thought someone had died. Ellen was always outspoken in her praise of me. She felt, prior to the opening, her reviews would say she was capable in her support of me. In fact, we had both received glowing notices. She seemed stricken that I wasn't nominated. It was Ellen at her heartfelt best. I reassured her that I was fine, and said that I also hadn't been nominated for *The Heartbreak Kid* when people felt I would be. And while it was always nice to be nominated, not being nominated for an award wasn't very high on my list of bad things that could happen to you. After seeing I was fine, she added: "It's worse than that. It's not just that you weren't nominated; everyone else involved with the play was: Bern Slade, Best Play; Gene Saks, Best Director—and every other category as well." After just the tiniest of pauses, I reassured her again that I was fine—and I really was.

I learned the next day that I was in excellent nonnominated company, including Rex Harrison. These omissions, by the way, happen regularly every season when you have categories filled with possibilities. Morty Gottlieb, the producer, was so concerned about my reaction that before he spoke to me he called Herb Gardner and asked his advice on how to handle all this. Morty feared I'd just break my contract and leave. Herb laughed and correctly predicted that no one would have anything to worry about. I personally went around the next day and ressured everyone not to worry a moment about me.

That night I couldn't resist a great chance for a gag. Just before each night's performance was to begin, Ellen and I would get into bed onstage, which is where we were when the curtain rose. We would both go onstage prior to curtain with our robes covering our underthings: Ellen in a slip, me in boxer shorts and undershirt. Our dressers would accompany us. The night after the nonnominated day, I got a black mourning band and wrapped it around my upper arm under my robe. When my dresser, a wonderfully sensitive fellow named Lee Austin, removed my robe, everyone spotted the mourning band. There was a moment of silence from Ellen, her dresser, and the stage managers, and then one of the best laughs I've ever gotten in my life.

Ellen won the Tony as Best Actress, and she and I won the Outer Critics Circle awards as Best Actress and Best Actor. After the play was bought by the movies for one million dollars, we were told we would be asked to star in the movie. I went to a celebration party shortly after that. The party was given at the apartment of one of the co-producers, Dasha Epstein, a lovely, helpful woman whom I've always liked. Jill Slade, who is playwright Bern Slade's wife, was there and came over and sat down next to me. I asked her where Bern was, and she very easily said, "He's off meeting with an actor who everyone desperately hopes will star in the movie of *Same Time*." I didn't know what to say. My feelings were hurt by the news, but I think I was more hurt by the cavalier, joyous fashion in which it was delivered to me. I should have asked her if she was at all aware of her insensitivity. Instead I attempted to inquire casually who the director was . . . anything to change the subject a little. She enthusiastically said, "Oh, anyone would direct it if we got this certain Mr. X to star in it." All references to the star Bern was meeting with now became "Mr. X." As I started to stand to move away for a drink, Jill said: "Oh, and that's not all. We think Ellen may be interested in starring in the movie." I quietly asked, "Why wouldn't she?" "Oh, you know," Jill said, "sometimes when someone does the play, they really don't want to do it again in the movie"—introducing a show-business phenomenon I'd never heard of, which, of course, also doesn't exist. I wished Jill well with Mr. X and the lucky director, and slunk away.

I know Jill was used in some sense as a model for my unseen wife in *Same Time, Next Year*. In the play, the offstage wife has a bit of foot-in-the-mouth disease, so I chose to take it all as that and not as the out-and-out hostility it felt like. I always liked Jill—she's warm and attractive and very sweet—but to this day, I duck just a little when I see her.

For seven months the bravos and standing ovations never stopped, and in those seven months I got no offers at all from Hollywood—not for the movie of *Same Time, Next Year,* not for the movie of anything. That was some Harrowhouse, that *11 Harrowhouse,* I thought.

Back in the Movies:
King Kong's Left Leg

It had been over two years since that *Variety* review of *11 Harrowhouse* had totally silenced any communication from Hollywood. This was 1976. Harry Ufland, who was still representing me, said he had never seen anything like it. He felt that along with the lack of success of *11 Harrowhouse*, there remained a slight uneasiness about the character of the Heartbreak Kid. "A lot of people aren't quite sure what to make of Charles Grodin." Since I never lived in Hollywood except for my cowboy period almost ten years earlier, no one really knew me. They had only what they saw on the screen. It would have been to my advantage to move to Los Angeles, where 95 percent of the film actors live. I've always found people on both coasts the same overall, and I had as many friends in Los Angeles as in New York. But I couldn't move there. There was a simple reason.

In New York I was living in the world. In Los Angeles, I would also be living in the world, but too much of the world seemed to be centered around show business. It was reflected more on the local TV news and at the newsstands and supermarkets, where they sold the show-business trade papers. Given my inclination, the "work" had taken my concentration just about every waking hour. I wasn't looking for more show business in my surroundings, so I stayed in New York and decided just to let career issues fall however they might.

Then I had an unforeseen surprise—this time, a happy one.

After my run in *Same Time, Next Year,* plans were forming for the movie version of—of all things—*Thieves.* Those two women who laughed, "They're trying to fix it," would never have believed it.

Marlo was to star in the movie, and the male lead was offered to Peter Falk, who turned it down, and then to Gene Hackman, who turned it down. One day I was with some of the people involved in the movie who were trying to figure out whom they could get to play the male lead. I cleared my throat a little louder than necessary, and I was back in the movies.

Some two years after the *Variety* critic had said of me: "It would be sad to think an acting career lay ahead," a big smiling, full-page picture of me appeared in that paper for the new, about-to-be-released film *Thieves.*

The ad appeared on a day when the flamboyant Italian movie producer Dino De Laurentiis was in the midst of making plans for his spectacular remake of the classic film *King Kong.* However, Universal Pictures was also making plans for its own spectacular remake of *King Kong.* All interested parties felt that two *Kongs* at the same time was one *Kong* too many. It was complicated and heading toward the courts in a battle over rights. Dino felt he might cut through the whole legal mess if he went ahead and started his *Kong* while everyone was arguing. All this had to be done in a big hurry before anyone could figure out a way to stop him and before Universal could rush ahead with *its Kong.* He had to get his leading lady and his two male leads cast as fast as possible.

He saw this smiling picture of me in *Variety* and started asking people, "What about this guy, Charles Grodin?" He heard that I had just won a Best Actor award on Broadway, and he and the director, John Guillermin, met with me. Quickly, because they were racing against time, they decided they wanted me. It was only a question of which of the two roles I was to play. One character rescued Jessica Lange from King Kong; the other was in charge of the expedition looking for oil, and was ultimately responsible for Kong's death.

When I was a little boy my favorite movie was the original *King Kong.* I used to dream about King Kong beating up all those giant prehistoric animals in the jungle. Now, forty-three years after the original movie was made, I was being asked to star in the remake—as the man responsible for the beloved Kong's death.

This was only three years after *The Heartbreak Kid,* so I knew clearly how the audience identified the actor with the character.

"No, no, Mr. De Laurentiis," I said, "I don't want to be responsible for Kong's death! I want to play the other part, the guy who rescues Jessica Lange. I would much rather rescue Jessica Lange than kill King Kong. After all, not only was Kong a childhood favorite of mine," I said, "he is a childhood and adulthood favorite of millions of people all over the world. He is one of the most beloved animal figures in the movies, right up there with Lassie and Bambi, and I don't want to kill him—for personal as well as professional reasons."

But Dino De Laurentiis wanted Jeff Bridges to rescue Jessica Lange and he wanted me for the killer.

Fred Wilson, whom Dino wanted me to play, was an executive for an oil company who travels halfway across the world to Skull Island. He has maps and charts that show there would likely be enormous oil deposits at Skull Island. As it turns out, there were no enormous oil deposits—but an enormous ape.

In trying to persuade me to his point of view, Dino reasoned that the audience, in the spirit of the American free-enterprise system, would identify with Fred Wilson, who, not finding oil, decided to bring the ape back and exploit it to his oil company's advantage.

Dino is about five feet four and has a thick Italian accent. "You come to look for oil," he said. I nodded. "You no find oil. *But* you find a big ape." I nodded again. "What you going to do?" He said it as though *anybody* who went to look for oil, and didn't find oil but found a big ape, would take that big ape and bring him back to New York City and try to make as much money as they could off him. He said: "Everybody in America believes in free-enterprise system. They all identify with you. This the great part."

I reasoned that Dino was putting a little too much emphasis on the audience's identification with the free-enterprise system and not enough emphasis on the audience's identification with the ape. But Dino made his points with a lot of passion.

He is a salesman, and he was in a hurry to cast his movie. I had to decide quickly. I couldn't ignore the "audience hatred" factor of playing the part after *The Heartbreak Kid*. On the other hand, I wasn't *that* much back in the movies. And this was one of the two male starring roles in a big-budget remake of a classic movie. Of course, everyone knew who the real male star of this movie was, but still . . .

Dino signed up Jessica Lange, Jeff Bridges, and me. It was a little harder to get old Kong to report. In the rush to begin production, two huge right hands were made by mistake, and the picture had to be delayed a month because neither worked. When one finally did and we began to film, a stand-in for Jessica Lange was lifted high and dropped. She wasn't badly hurt, but it made a lot of nervous people more nervous.

Jessica emerged from ten months of shooting significantly bruised from Kong, who, squeezing too hard on occasion, caused her to cry out for help. Since the script called for her to cry out for help, there was real tension and confusion around some of those calls. Once, Kong cracked her on the head with a huge iron finger that seemed bigger than all of Jessica when he just meant to fool around with her dress a little. These mistakes happened, of course, because of the human factor. All of Kong's big hand moves were under the control of several tense Italian technicians who were frantically pushing and pulling a lot of levers this way and that.

I had been part of some of the worst trouble of all. It happened in a sequence where hundreds of extras were supposed to flee in panic when Kong broke loose from his cage in a stadium. When the cue came for the extras to flee, they did. Some of them accidentally tripped, causing others to fall over them; as a result, several people were actually trampled to various degrees. The extent of the injuries was kept from me, but I knew lawsuits were pending. On the first take that night I had been accidentally lifted off my feet and carried through the air by the force of the crowd. Veteran of the movies that I now was, by the second take I had four stuntmen forming a protective wedge around me as I began to flee Kong. The movie company was very careful with me for the remainder of the night's filming. There's an old adage in the movie business: Never crush your leading man until he's finished on the picture.

Several weeks later I came to my last night of filming. This was to be the moment in the picture when Kong, having escaped from his cage, attempts to stomp me personally to death—and misses. I wondered why this shot hadn't been done weeks ago as part of the whole sequence in which Kong escapes from his cage. I quickly told myself that the reason for the delay had nothing to do with any movie-company nervousness about their ability to do this shot without accidentally crushing me when I was still needed. I told myself that there was probably a very good reason to have delayed my last shot, and that it most likely had to do with some complicated scheduling. That's what I told myself. But my self decided to keep a keen eye out, remembering all the earlier injuries and everything I had seen and experienced, starting with being thrown out of the car years ago in *Man Against Crime*.

As I arrived at the MGM back lot that final night, there were two hundred extras already on hand to re-create the background for this attempted-stomping-of-me shot. I looked around the large field, but Kong was nowhere to be seen. A fifty-foot Kong had been built at the cost of one million dollars. He had actually appeared in the earlier scene when everyone had fled. All he had done then was stand there and look around. Any real moves he made had been done by a huge remote-controlled arm or hand. When you actually see all of him walking down the street or swatting at airplanes, that's a fellow named Rick Baker in an amazing ape suit—which, incidentally, was so hot that he had to be fed oxygen constantly through various hidden openings. It was pretty complicated, and even though I was there for nine months, I couldn't really tell how it all worked.

My last night, as I arrived, I knew it wasn't going to be Rick stepping on me, since he was about five feet eight and that wouldn't look quite right. I was hoping it wouldn't be the fifty-foot guy either, because the night when he was just standing around our eyes met—and I'd just as soon not do that again. I have a fairly good imagination, and I swear he looked like he really had it in for me.

As I was trying to figure out what was going to happen, a large van arrived and about twenty men carried out King Kong's left leg, which was about ten feet tall and massive in circumference. The leg was made of steel and, of course, covered by fur.

It must have weighed tons. The first assistant director, a very nice low-keyed fellow named David McGiffert, came over to me and explained that the shot would be done by Kong's left leg running across the field from one direction and me running from the other in panic, and somehow we'd collide and I'd get knocked down. Kong's leg would then attempt to crush me, and miss. I nodded easily, resisting an almost overwhelming urge to get the hell out of there.

Instead, I went off to get into my costume—kind of a great-white-hunter bush outfit with a big wide-brimmed hat. When I returned about a half hour later, the director, John Guillermin, had arrived.

After months of filming, John Guillermin could, more and more, be seen gazing off vacantly at some distant, unseen point in space. This had been a particularly grueling picture, and John had already been through enough grueling pictures for any human before this one. His previous movie had been *The Towering Inferno,* in which massive fires had been set every day. (They certainly had their share of injuries on that one.) And so John, for many reasons, was given to a lot of blank staring by now.

John was French but had been raised in England. He was lean and wiry, and looked like a former RAF pilot, which he was.

I first noticed this staring thing of John's months earlier, when we were down at the beach one night for a sequence where all of us were to arrive in little rubber boats to go ashore in an attempt to recapture Jessica, who had been kidnapped by the natives and given as a sacrifice to Kong.

That night at the beach I went over to say hello to John, whom I liked enormously, particularly for the brave way he always pressed ahead, no matter what, but John wasn't so much pressing ahead as he was staring out to sea. There was something in his look that had me put my hello on hold. I joined the little group of assistants standing beside him and waited for John to speak. Finally, when it seemed that wasn't going to happen, one of the assistants said (I had the feeling not for the first time): "John, the men out at sea would like us to put the actors into canoes and row them out to the rubber boats."

John waited a long moment, looking at the crashing surf, and finally spoke in his crisp English accent: "Are they boatmen?"

The assistant meekly said: "I beg your pardon, John?"

"Are they boatmen?" John repeated. "Are they experienced boatmen?"

"I'm sure they are," the assistant responded.

"Are you?!" John asked in a tone that made everyone wish they were somewhere else. This time John continued. "I can't put the actors into that sea—they'll drown. Any experienced boatman would know that." John then turned to look at the assistant and noticed me standing there for the first time. "Oh, hello, Chuck," he said, and flashed me a wide grin.

I said, "Hi, John. What's going on?"

John said, "You might as well go home, Chuck. I'm not putting you into that sea. If it calms down much later and we make the shot, which I seriously doubt"—and here he flashed the assistant a very strange look I can only describe as annoyed astonishment—"we'll do it with a double for you bringing up the rear echelon."

I said happily, "Sounds good, John. Thanks," and quickly left, wishing everyone a good-night.

Now it was months later as I stood in my bush outfit watching John stare off into space again. There was no question that John's stare had deepened in intensity over the months. There had been so many mechanical breakdowns of Kong and his parts along the way that the picture was now months behind schedule and millions of dollars over budget. Even though John had no responsibility for making Kong work, somehow a director gets blamed for everything that goes wrong on a movie. John was certainly blamed for everything on this one (not in public, but you got the feeling). I had witnessed one event where the tension between John and Dino surfaced. Dino had sent some of his people to Hawaii to persuade John that it would be perfectly safe to have Jessica running through actual Hawaiian woods fleeing Kong instead of the way John wanted to do it—in a more controlled studio situation where the movie company would create the woods, without any hidden rocks or anything to injure Jess. Dino's emissaries asked for a nine P.M. meeting. John asked Jess and me to accompany him, I think for moral support. When the meeting got a little tense, John suddenly announced quietly to all that it was perfectly within his capability to kick Dino's emissaries in their faces. There was a little throat clearing after that, and the meeting came to an abrupt end. John and Dino had an ongoing tug-of-war.

By the way, John directed the sequel, *King Kong Lives*, for Dino. About halfway through the filming of *King Kong*, Dino had approached me about doing the sequel, *King Kong Lives*, as well. I said, "But Dino, how could King Kong live after he falls off the World Trade Center?" After the shortest of pauses, Dino said, "All right, we make him Kong's brother or nephew." I must have had some look on my face, because Dino uncharacteristically let it drop.

As I stood beside John on this, my last night, I became aware that the feverish activity usually surrounding the working part of Kong was more than normally feverish. A dozen Italian technicians were pushing and pulling and probing endless levers, but Kong's left leg wasn't moving.

John wasn't looking at any of this but at a point way off in the distance beyond it all. Two assistants stood near John, who was sitting on a very tall director's chair placed on the back of a truck, causing him to tower over everyone.

After several moments of silence, I looked up and ventured a "Hi, John."

He turned, flashed me his grin he could still muster, at least for a second, and gave me an unusually hearty: "Hello, Chuck!" Then he quickly turned back to fix his gaze at that far-off distant spot, saying nothing further.

I got the message and drifted away and sat in a chair of my own.

One of the assistants soon came over to me and explained that they were having trouble getting the leg to move, let alone do its thing, which he said was to run across the field and smash into me. He started to explain the shot in detail, waiting for my horrified reaction. But I casually said I knew the shot and "I'm ready whenever you are." I watched him walk away in admiration for my macho move as I trembled inside.

Two hours went by as the technicians continued to work frantically on the leg, their exclamations of Italian profanity piercing the night air. I watched John stare into space. It was fascinating to see how long he could do it, never once even glancing at the Italian technicians or Kong's leg.

Finally, around midnight, the longest limousine I've ever

seen in my life drove onto the field, and Dino De Laurentiis bounded out, dressed in a natty dark-blue suit and surrounded by four Italian associates, also in dark suits. Without even a look at John, he went straight to the leg and began to speak quietly in Italian to his technicians. He and his associates stood there as the technicians continued to push and pull and probe. After about forty-five minutes, the leg began first to move a little, and then actually to hop around, as the extras cheered.

Dino announced with great flourish, in a voice loud enough for all to hear: "Finally!" He then headed back to his limo with his men, and was driven off into the night.

Through it all, John Guillermin never took his eyes off that distant point in space.

Five minutes after Dino's car drove away, the leg stopped moving. The extras moaned; John continued to stare.

Finally, after fifteen more minutes of remarkable pushing and pulling, the leg was hopping around again, looking like it was raring to smash into yours truly.

The first assistant director, David McGiffert, approached me to say that they wanted to test the shot of the steel-fur leg running in one direction and me in another, colliding in midfield. As I shakily started to get out of my chair, David stopped me, saying the idea was for him to try the rehearsal just to see what would happen before they put me in there. David was ten years younger and twenty pounds leaner than me. What a good idea, I thought.

The leg started at one end of the field and David at the other. David kind of ran sideways, not seeing the leg, and the leg clomped across the field. They collided. David fell backward and immediately leaped up, as the extras applauded and cheered. He went over to confer with John for a moment, and then came over to me. "We're not going to do the shot that way," David said.

"Why not?" I asked, relieved and curious at the same time. "It looked great!" I said.

"I almost broke both my legs," David said.

"Uh-huh," I nodded.

The idea now was for me to run into a stationary leg. "Let's do it," I said immediately, and trotted into position, as the extras cheered again. It wasn't as hard, of course, to run into a stationary leg, but I was happy that John thought the first take was just fine.

The second and last shot of the night and for me in the picture called for me to lie on the ground while Kong's leg was raised high, slams down, and just misses me as I roll away at the last minute.

John came over and assured me that the leg would miss me by plenty. In spite of John's assurances, we got some pretty good photographed fear out of me. But, again, we did it in one take. I was through with the picture—and alive. John announced that it was my last shot, and all the extras cheered again, even though I'm sure most of them had no idea who I was. John and I exchanged warm good-byes, I wished him well, and he flashed me that haunted grin once more.

Six months later, when the picture was sneak-previewed for the first time and Kong went to stomp me and missed, the audience groaned in disappointment that the ape hadn't killed me. *Me*, the guy Dino said they'd identify with! At the next preview, they reedited the movie to make it look like Kong killed me—and the audience cheered.

NBC had a big party for a live TV special called "The Big Event," and *King Kong*'s opening was one of the big events that night. The party was in a spacious glass room at the top of the Gulf & Western building (they own Paramount Pictures, which financed the movie), bordering on Central Park. Outside, on the sidewalk, Leonard Nimoy, in a tux, was interviewing celebrities as they went into the building. I came up in my rented tux. He stopped me and said, "Here's Charles Grodin, one of the stars of the picture. Charles, how are you tonight."

"I'm okay. But I just left Kong in the park, and he's a little pissed he wasn't invited to the party."

Leonard Nimoy nodded. "Thank you very much. That was Charles Grodin."

Inside, at the party, Lauren Bacall was hosting our segment for NBC. I'd been there for about an hour when I realized I had no seat assignment. There were only a certain number of chairs, and some of us had to wander around with our plates all night long, like nomadic tribes of old. For hours I continued to wander, nodding at people I knew who were sitting at tables, celebrity friends who *did* have seat assignments. I'm sure they assumed I had one too, being, as Leonard Nimoy had said, "one of the stars of the picture." But I didn't.

Eventually, a table of people in advertising became suspicious when I hovered near them longer than anyone would who had a seat assignment, and they asked me to join them. So I did—most thankfully.

All this time, Dino and seven other executives had been at a table up on a pedestal in a corner with Jessica Lange. It looked so unwelcoming, I didn't even go over to say hello to Jessica, who by now was a pretty close friend—close enough to caution me that she had heard that Dino and Paramount were going to sell the movie, promoting her and the ape (they were on the cover of *Time* magazine together), and leaving me and Jeff Bridges in the dust, promowise (which I personally thought was a good idea). Only a close friend and good person encourages you to try to take away some of their publicity. I had stayed away from that table all night long; I never hovered once. Suddenly, someone from NBC was ushering me over there, as Lauren Bacall was about to interview the *Kong* group live on NBC. As I sat down, Dino's mouth dropped open. Charles Grodin wasn't in his sell-*Kong* plan: You could see it on his face. He quickly leaned toward me and whispered intensely: "Talk about *Kong*!" I have no idea what else he thought I'd talk about, but of course I did talk about *Kong*. I think I redid the joke that Leonard Nimoy didn't get. Jessica laughed anyway.

She was glad to see me, as she had been alone with Dino and the executives all night and probably hadn't heard too many jokes. After the TV show was over, I stayed right there at the table as though I had come into my rightful seat assignment.

King Kong opened, didn't take in the $200 million they'd hoped for, but did bring the movie company $90 million, which put it right up there, anyway. I always felt that it was particularly appreciated by the people who disliked the character in *The Heartbreak Kid*, as they got to see me squooshed.

Heaven Can Wait

A couple of months later I was out with a group of friends, among whom was David Geffen, a highly energetic, bright guy who can get people to challenge him to a duel easier than most because of his strong opinions. I had first met David when he was a young agent at William Morris. At that time he told me I should go out to Hollywood to sit on the set watching Carl Reiner direct the Dick Van Dyke TV series. He felt I'd end up being a comedy director long before I did. Anyway, I didn't really feel like flying out to watch Carl direct Dick, although for someone else it could have been the opportunity of a lifetime. David went on to fame and fortune heading company after company, culminating in Geffen Records and Geffen Pictures.

David Geffen likes to know everything first, so he delightedly slid up to me at some point in the evening and casually dropped: "Warren wants you for his next movie, you know." I *didn't* know. I didn't even know Warren was making a movie. I really didn't even know *Warren*. But it was nice to hear.

Warren did eventually call me, even though I'd only met him casually a couple of times. He doesn't go through agents—only at the last second, when he absolutely has to, when the talk is of money. When it's of anything else, he's talking to you. He asked my opinion on everyone's acting, from Julie Christie to

President Reagan. I had heard that it was tough to pin Warren down on start dates of movies, so I asked him when he was going to start his movie. He asked me how I felt about Jessica Lange's work. I asked him when he was going to start his movie. He kept telling me he was going to start his movie any second. (Any second means at least four months.) He asked me what I thought of Dyan Cannon for her part. I said I didn't think she was right for it. He asked Dyan Cannon what she thought of me for my part. She told him she didn't think I was right for it. Luckily, he ignored us both. All these preliminary conversations with Warren made working with him more like a relationship than a job.

From the very beginning of the experience, I could tell the movie was something special. This was to be the third picture Warren produced. His first two, *Bonnie and Clyde* and *Shampoo*, were big successes, and Warren, while known to the public as a romantic movie star, enjoyed a reputation within the movie industry as an outstanding producer. One of his unique qualities, which permeated *Heaven Can Wait*, was his absolute and remarkably thorough attention to each question—particularly those of casting. He spent months trying to persuade Cary Grant to be in the movie at a time when any other moviemaker had long since believed Mr. Grant was retired. Warren's original idea for casting the movie was Muhammad Ali in his role and Warren in James Mason's role.

During the filming, Warren asked me to tell him if I ever saw him looking at the love interest, Julie Christie, below the neck, as it was very important to the tone of the picture that it be love interest and not sex interest. (It reminded me of my unwillingness to put my hand on Ellen Burstyn's breast for the same reason.) It was ironic, these heterosexual leading men never looking below the neck and fighting tooth and nail never to touch a breast.

When the filming was over I sat with Warren at a music-recording session. This is where the musical technicians spot the places music would start in the picture and for how long. They seemed annoyed at Warren's reluctance to commit to exactly where these cues would come. Finally, Warren, sensing the men's impatient attitude, said, "You know, we're not making hamburgers here." And, boy, we weren't!

He brought an enormous amount of patience and care to the

movie. I saw this first on the day the whole cast gathered to read the script. I went over to the studio where underneath the logo reading PARAMOUNT PICTURES, I saw two guys holding a big white sign Warren had made that said HOME OF CHARLES GRODIN. I'm not sure why he did that. *Rosemary's Baby*, *Catch-22*, *King Kong*, and *Thieves* had all been Paramount Pictures, but I doubt Warren knew that. In any case, he did it, and I walked into that first reading feeling really special. It wasn't until years later that it occurred to me that there were probably two guys holding HOME OF . . . signs for everyone.

For me, all movies have interesting casts one way or another, but *Heaven Can Wait*'s, maybe because of the wide variety of people in it, seemed unusual. It was particularly fascinating to be around the elegant James Mason and the streetwise Jack Warden. Jack is considered in the show-business world to be as entertaining a man as there is. For me, he, Albert Brooks, and Mel Brooks stand alone for off-camera fun.

It would take a whole chapter to try to describe why Jack Warden is so entertaining, and even then I doubt I could do it. But there is one famous story about Jack that took place after he was discharged from the paratroopers during World War II. He was in his early twenties, working in a garage and studying acting. He was sent over to meet John ("They make money the old-fashioned way: They earn it") Houseman. Mr. Houseman was a distinguished director in New York then, directing a production of *King Lear*. To arrive on time for his appointment, Jack wasn't able to change out of his greased-up overalls from his job at the garage. John Houseman looked down his nose as Jack entered his office. Mr. Houseman, his voice dripping with disdain, said, "And what part do you see yourself playing?"

Jack, knowing he had no chance for anything, said, "Well, shit, who's doin' Lear?"

The picture allowed me to resume my acquaintance with James Mason, whom I had met about two years earlier on that picture in London that had temporarily ended my career. At that time I had asked him, "What do people call you?"

He said, "Some people call me Mr. Mason, some people call me James, and some people call me Jim." He said this in such a way that I chose never to refer to him at all by name.

Later, I read an interview in which he spoke of me kindly, so this time I dared to call him James.

I had always been taken with James Mason. Since my childhood, it seems, he had been in the movies. I didn't really get to know him when we worked in London on *11 Harrowhouse*. In one of our scenes we were sitting side-by-side on a park bench. I was aware after filming for a while that James never looked at me, only straight ahead. I wondered if that was some particular discovery he had made about movie acting. I couldn't figure out what it meant, but instinctively decided that if he were *never* going to look at me, I would *always* keep my eyes on him. I'm sure there's no great acting lesson here, but the scene was effective. James was very quiet and seemingly always preoccupied with his role or something. There was never any chatting. When I met him again on *Heaven Can Wait*, he behaved exactly the same. One day I passed a doorway to a room in the huge house where we were filming. It was at an estate called Filloli in Palo Alto, California. Warren saw me walk by and called for me to come in. I did, and there were Warren, Julie Christie, Buck Henry, and James. Warren asked if I'd listen to a scene they were rehearsing. When they finished, he asked for my impressions. I had several, and because Warren had asked, I said what I thought for about five minutes, really holding forth. Warren or Julie or Buck would raise a question, and off I'd go again. James Mason never spoke. Finally, after about ten minutes of my carrying on, James interrupted delicately to raise a point. I had been aware that he hadn't spoken at all, so as a joke I turned on him and shouted: "James, will you let me get a word in here?!" He laughed louder than anyone.

There was considerable waiting on *Heaven Can Wait*, and the dressing rooms were nothing you'd want to wait in, so there was a lot of pacing around the grounds. Here's where I got to know James Mason a bit better. I told him, as we paced by each other one day, how much I had enjoyed him in the 1954 movie *A Star Is Born*, with Judy Garland.

He said, "That film represented my unsuccessful attempt at international stardom."

I said, "What do you mean, unsuccessful? The film was

great, you were memorable—how can you say 'unsuccessful attempt at international stardom'?"

He said simply, "That's what it was for what I wanted—unsuccessful."

No one knows better than the actor what a movie did or didn't do for him, so, of course, I took him at his word. I suppose he meant he was after a career with the opportunities of a Richard Burton and he didn't get it. But he was James Mason, and he'll never be forgotten as long as they show movies.

The only difficulty I saw in the movie was between Warren, as director, and Dyan Cannon, with whom I had most of my scenes. Warren had restricted her movement in order to have the lighting work. That's not unusual, but Dyan hated restrictions of any kind, so they were always going at each other. I didn't care one way or another because, restrictions or not, Dyan was going to be an explosive handful in the part, which was just what I wanted in order for me to play my part.

I did have one unpleasant run-in with Warren myself during the filming. There's a scene in which I get a rifle, come down a hall as the camera follows, enter a bedroom, take aim, get Warren in my sights, and kill him. *Heaven Can Wait* is a comedy, and I'm playing a totally comic character, and yet, there sure isn't anything jump-off-the-page funny about me killing Warren, who was the appealing hero of the movie. So I asked if he felt I should possibly try to inject some humor into this killing. "I don't know how," I said, "but should I be thinking about it?"

Warren's eyes narrowed. He suddenly seemed uncharacteristically annoyed, and said: "No, it doesn't require humor. In fact," he said, "one of the two things that concerns me most about the picture is how funny you are in it."

I said, "I don't understand. What's the problem? It is a comedy, isn't it?"

He said, "Sometimes a real funny scene isn't appropriate."

Now I was furious. I thought to myself, If I, as an actor, am being too funny in a comedy, then it's the director's responsibility to tap me on the shoulder and tell me to knock it off. If there was any kind of problem, why not mention it while we were doing the scene? But standing in the hallway, I said nothing about that. Instead, I asked him what the second thing was that he was worried about, since he'd said there were two things.

He said, "My own performance." He was worried that he had to concentrate so much on all his different responsibilities on the picture that his performance might not get enough of his attention.

I nodded and walked away. I was still angry about the maybe-I'm-too-funny crack. I had heard that from the same studio during *King Kong*. Ironically, I received some of the best notices of my life for *King Kong* and *Heaven Can Wait*. The problem is never that someone is too funny, only that someone isn't funny enough. I don't mean Warren, because I thought he was wonderful in *Heaven Can Wait*, appealing and funny and all the things he was supposed to be. Within five minutes, I went over to him and said, "I want to talk to you after shooting." He looked startled for a moment (something in my tone of voice probably), and then asked me to meet him in his suite that evening.

I remember trying to form the exact words to describe how I felt about what he did. I think I settled on "cheap shot." I'm extremely fond of him, but I wanted to sting him. I did. He looked as hurt as he had in his movie debut as an emotionally tortured boy in *Splendor in the Grass*, and instantly had me on his side before he even responded. (They don't pay these guys millions for nothing.) He said hurting me was the last thing on his mind, but he did worry a little that maybe the somewhat broad funny scenes Dyan and I were doing weren't consistent with the tone of the movie.

I said I wouldn't worry about that, as I thought they *were* consistent. (That's always an important consideration.) "And if we *are* going to worry about humor, let's worry about getting more, not less. And I mean that for both of us."

He looked at me as uneasily as I had at him when he had said I was too funny. The evening ended at a friendly standoff.

The next morning Warren told me he was thinking of having his cape get caught on the stairwell banister in his next entrance, and asked what I thought. I said, "Good idea." He nodded, walked away, and spent the next few hours getting a hell of a cape-caught-on-a-stairwell shot.

I believe one of the reasons Warren has been successful is that he listens to other people's ideas and doesn't care about ego or whose idea something is, only that it works. He has listened to me and others, and rejected as many ideas as he's accepted. But he listens, and then makes his judgments—in my opinion, excellent ones . . . almost always.

Elaine May had essentially written the script, and Buck Henry was the co-director with Warren, but there was no question that Warren Beatty was in charge of *Heaven Can Wait*. As far as his personal behavior went, no matter how much stress he felt, it was important to him to act like a gentleman. (He's originally from Virginia, and manners mean a lot to him.) He never raised his voice, even with Dyan. Contrary to his well-publicized reputation as a favorite of the ladies, he almost never left his living quarters or had company when he wasn't working. Of course, with all of his responsibilities on the picture, when he wasn't working was virtually never.

Once, toward the end of filming, I spent an evening with him, and he took the opportunity to tell me that he had been reluctant to have me in *Heaven Can Wait* because "I heard you were crazy."

I was shocked, and asked him where he'd heard that. Warren talks to a lot of people, and he couldn't remember. He just knew he'd heard it. I asked him, since he'd been with me every day for months on end, if he thought I was crazy. He said he didn't. We sat there silently and nodded for a while, thinking the whole thing over. Finally, he said, "Maybe it's because you're an actor, a writer, a director, and a producer, and anyone who does all that would have to be a little crazy."

I said, "*You* do all that."

He said, "That's how I know."

When *Heaven Can Wait* opened, the success was enormous. All the movie people who had been interested in me after *The Heartbreak Kid* were interested once more, except this time they included offers to write and direct as well as act. As the success of the movie grew, I was even asked to make my own movies, which put me in a very small group of people. I had no way of knowing that from this elite position I was about to encounter something for which my previous twenty years of trials and tribulations could not even begin to prepare me.

Just When I Thought
It Was Safe to Be Back
in the Movies

Paramount Pictures, in the person of production vice-president Nancy Hardin, called me shortly after it became clear that *Heaven Can Wait* was going to be a success. Nancy asked if I would be interested in writing a screenplay using the title of the best-selling sex manual *The Joy of Sex*. I said, "What?" It seems that Paramount had bought the title for a good amount of money, and had been trying for some time to develop an original screenplay using what they considered to be a highly commercial title. A few people had already tried to do this, and evidently the studio wasn't pleased with the results. I told Nancy that if I were going to write an original movie, why be burdened with having to call it *The Joy of Sex*? She repeated that the studio considered the title a big advantage, but that the movie could be about anything. I thanked her for her interest, but said no thanks. A week later she called again, asking me to reconsider. Again, I said no thank you. A couple of weeks later she called again. I had never been so wanted. This time I said, "Let me think about it."

The only thing that interested me about it was that the studio was in this situation. The idea that they had paid a lot of money for a famous title of a sex manual and now didn't know what to do with it seemed part of what makes Hollywood Hollywood. So I started to think, What if I write a movie about a studio that buys a famous title of a sex manual and doesn't know what to do with it? It seemed like a promising beginning, but what exactly was the movie?

One day I was skimming through an old magazine and came across an interview with Robert Evans, who had been head of Paramount Pictures. It gave him a lot of credit for the *Godfather* movies and *Love Story*, among others. It said he always had the biggest house, the most beautiful wife or girlfriend, the biggest pool, et cetera. It was a story describing a guy on top of the world. At the end of the long article, almost as a throwaway, it mentioned that the interview had been conducted over a period of several days, during which time Mr. Evans had been confined to a special bed due to a chronic back condition.

Having battled a back condition myself, and watched numerous other Hollywood producers, directors, writers, and actors fight all kinds of physical ailments caused by working in a profession that demands the longest hours and as much stress as any field, the last paragraph struck a chord.

A week later I was sitting at Paramount in a meeting with Nancy Hardin and Michael Eisner, the head of production. I made a proposal for a screenplay for *The Joy of Sex*, saying that if they liked it, this is the movie I'd like to write.

It would be the story of how a studio buys the famous title of the sex manual *The Joy of Sex* and doesn't know what to do with it. Michael and Nancy stared at me, wondering, at least for a moment, I think, if an insult was in the air. The head of the studio decides it should have something to do with love, and goes out and gets a writer and a director to help him make it. As the story unfolds, we see that these three people are trying to make a great movie about love while their own love lives are falling apart. There would also be a subplot that would deal with all the physical ailments they were coping with due to the stress of their own lives and the demands of trying to make a movie. As I told the story, Michael and Nancy at first watched me with quizzical interest; soon, they were smiling; and by the time I finished, they enthusiastically told me to go and write it. Contracts were drawn that arranged for me to direct and star in it as well—in other words, to make my own movie. It had been about three years since *11 Harrowhouse* had run me out of Hollywood.

I went back to New York and spent the next four months

writing the movie. I felt it turned out a lot better than I had described it. I immediately sent it off to Paramount, expecting they'd be throwing a party for me. Right around party time, I got a call from my representative telling me that Paramount had "passed" and put the script in "turnaround," a word that means: We don't want it; you're free to take it elsewhere. Or, more bluntly: Turn around and get out of here with this script. I was told the script had been read by Don Simpson, a senior executive at the studio (who later left to produce *Flashdance* and *Top Gun*, not to mention *Beverly Hills Cop I* and *II*). Simpson, who hadn't been at the meeting in which I described the story, had made only one comment that got back to me: "Everybody gets sick in this movie!" He didn't find the plight of the studio executives humorous. Nancy Hardin later told me she completely disagreed with the decision and loved the script. I was disappointed and completely surprised by the Paramount reaction. I had believed that the worst thing that could have happened (and it would have been a good thing) was that they would meet with me to suggest changes. That is what I would have expected, since most scripts are rewritten quite a bit before they're filmed. This outright rejection was baffling since the script was almost exactly what I had described in the meeting, except, in my opinion, funnier.

Still in New York, I decided to put together a cast of very good actors and invited half a dozen people to hear the script read. It was very well received. Some people have said: "What kind of test is that, to invite friends?" Well, even friends don't fake laughter, and since some of these readings of plays and movies are received considerably better than others, I take the results seriously. Besides, I have highly critical friends. Some people in New York laughing at a script, however, doesn't ensure anything other than some people in New York will laugh at it. The taste of the country really varies, and what some will laugh at in cities is different from what others will laugh at in the country, or, for that matter, in other cities. At the first preview of the first Marx Brothers movie, the audience watched in silence. The next night, at a second preview a few blocks away, the audience laughed throughout. The reasons for that vary, anywhere from the temperature in the theater to one bad cougher, but, really, no one can explain it. In any case, it's sure not like selling ice cream.

Still, I was fortified by the New York greeting that I was not alone in my appreciation of the script. I headed to Hollywood to see what I could do to get it made somewhere other than Paramount.

Frank Price, then head of Columbia Pictures, quickly read the script and wanted to make the picture. I was invited to a meeting at Columbia Studios to talk about it. Well, that wasn't so bad, I thought. In no time, somebody else wants it. I showed up at the meeting at Columbia, and there were three other executives sitting with Frank Price. However, I soon realized that this was not a meeting to discuss how I wanted to make the picture, but to determine *if* Columbia wanted to make it. Obviously something had happened between Frank's enthusiastic response and this meeting. Suddenly I was being asked questions by the other executives.

"What's the movie like?" I had no answer. They tried to help me: "Is it like *Network* [Paddy Chayefsky's exposé of the TV industry]?"

"No," I answered.

"Is it like *All That Jazz* [Bob Fosse's look at the life of a Broadway director]?"

"No," I answered again, feeling like I was failing a test.

"Do you think the audience will be interested in a movie about people who work in Hollywood?"

"They will if the audience can empathize with them," I answered. "The humanity of the characters of any story can transcend the milieu." I thought that was a pretty nifty answer. They seemed unimpressed. They said they would think it over and get back to me.

I went home and called Peter Falk, who had agreed to play the leading role. I said, "I think they were more interested in the picture before the meeting. Maybe we ought to keep me out of those meetings." Peter said he would see what he could find out. He made a call to a Columbia executive he knew who had read the script but wasn't at the meeting. This fellow was wildly against the picture and tried to persuade his friend Peter to get away from it. "It's all about greed," the executive said, "and the character you would be playing is really unlikable." Peter said he didn't see any of what the guy was talking about in the script, but correctly predicted that Columbia wouldn't make the picture.

I called Frank Price, and he was very nice and forthcoming

about the whole thing. Yes, he said, he had wanted to make it, but found himself to be the only one at the studio who did. Frank said he felt the script was accurate, incisive, and "it was like you had a tape recorder at our meetings." On the other hand, the other executives felt the script attacked them, and "people will think anyone could be an executive at a movie studio, and why should we finance something that attacks us?" I thanked him for being straightforward with me and said good-bye.

It was time to try the next studio to see if they felt they were being attacked. In quick succession, Warner Brothers and Orion Pictures joined Paramount and Columbia in saying no. However, in a few weeks I was told that David Begelman, the head of MGM/UA, had read the script and wanted to make it if it could be done for under eight million dollars. He authorized a budget to be made; it came in at seven million one hundred thousand dollars. Okay, I thought, that wasn't so bad. Suddenly, I read in the papers that the executive from Columbia who thought the script was about greed was now working over at MGM. I waited. Soon, I got a call that MGM wasn't interested. This fellow, I heard, had written his "greed" assessment of the script and had it circulated all over the studio. I asked to see David Begelman. I was greeted in his office by the "greed" guy who had just shot me down for the second time. We exchanged friendly nice-to-see-yous. Neither of us mentioned the word *greed*. Eventually, David Begelman arrived, and the three of us cordially discussed the movie. They made a case against it, dissecting all aspects. I just listened. I finally said, "Look, you just don't want to make it, and you're making your case against it. If you wanted to make it, you could just as easily make your case for it." That was greeted by an uncomfortable silence. I then made my passionate case *for* the picture. They said they'd be in touch. I heard a couple of days later: "Because of Chuck's passion for the project, we'll make it for five million." Since they had a week earlier told me it would cost over seven million, it sounded like they'd prefer it if I went away. So I did . . . believing the seven-million-dollar budget was absolutely necessary to make the movie.

Time began to pass. The script was submitted to all the remaining major studios. Everyone turned it down. One main reason given was: "Too inside. People aren't interested in Hollywood." I argued that one by saying, "People are interested in anything if it's done well. People said boxing movies would never make money, and they hadn't before *Rocky.*" I had an answer for every objection, but still they all turned it down. The biggest complaint was that the plot didn't go anywhere. By accepted standards, it didn't; but that was the point. The three main characters—the studio head, the director, and the writer— are all trying to make a great movie about love while they have nothing but trouble at home, so they can't make a great movie about love. That was the idea, but it was an ironic idea, and in the Hollywood of *Animal House* and *Rambo,* irony wasn't in demand.

Months turned into years. The script was being submitted to every independent financing source. In all, counting studios and independent sources, it was turned down about fifty times. It was now about five years since I had written it. It was becoming increasingly obvious that I couldn't take no for an answer. I guess by now "no" just meant detour, turn right or left rather than stop, since I never had. Of course, if I had accepted no for an answer, I would have stopped trying to do anything in this profession by the time I was twenty and leaving the Pittsburgh Playhouse. Anyway, I thought the script was good, and I was determined to continue. In the movie, the character of the writer I was going to play learns that everything is a much greater struggle than first meets the eye. I was living the part in absence of playing it. Of course, my decades of experience in dealing with rejection was serving me well and sustaining me. I wasn't really hurting at all . . . yet.

As time went by, I started to do more writing. I even wrote a special that got wonderful reviews and very high ratings, and participated in writing a Paul Simon special, for which I won an Emmy. I told my agent to tell the people he was sending the script to that I'd just won an Emmy. No one cared.

After about six years, I decided it was time to try a new tack. I was going to phone the different heads of studios I knew and offer to come over and read them the script aloud in their offices or in their homes, acting out all the parts. It was a highly unusual idea, but I offered and they accepted. My agent said he felt I was possibly demeaning myself, but I just saw it as "giving it my best shot."

I went over to see Sherry Lansing, who was the head of production at 20th Century-Fox. She had agreed to hear me read the script. When I arrived for our meeting, she told me she was sorry, but something had come up and she only had one hour, not two. After a moment's consideration, I decided to read her the first half rather than the whole thing fast. I never saw anyone laugh so hard at a script. She said she'd read the second half right away. She did and didn't think it was as funny. I felt that if I could have kept her there for the whole thing, she would have made the picture. She was very nice, but she said no.

It's a crucial skill for movie executives to be able to say no to projects and retain the good feeling of those they're rejecting. Since economics dictate that they have to say no almost all the time, it becomes absolutely essential to do it with warmth, charm, and friendship, or else you eventually alienate most of the movie community. Since there are several studios to go to for financing, you tend to go where you like the people the most, the money being the same. So charm and warmth become a prerequisite for studio executives. Some people never say the word *no* at all; they say it without saying it. It comes out something like: "I'd really love to do something with you someday." Or they just never give an answer at all. Of course, while "no" is tricky for an executive, "yes" is really dangerous since most movies fail, and when they do, the powers that be at the studios start looking around for "Who was it who said yes to this one?"

The next time out, a couple of months later, I was reading the script alone to Ned Tanen, who is now head of Paramount and was then head of Universal. He didn't laugh once. Evidently, any story that included a studio head who had a heart attack on the job wasn't that funny to Ned Tanen, who, as a studio head, had had a heart attack on the job. About halfway through, when I realized this, I wanted to stop playing the fifty parts I was playing, but pressed ahead. He was extremely nice, but "No thanks."

Around this time, my agent got the idea to have me read the script to Frank Yablans, who was no longer the head of a studio, as he was when I met him during the *Thieves* experience. When he'd been president of Paramount, he also, like Robert Evans, took credit for the *Godfather* movies and *Love Story*. Frank was between studio-head jobs and was now an independent producer at 20th Century-Fox. I went over and chatted with him about the project, and the next night I was in his big house in Beverly Hills reading him the screenplay. Since he wasn't running a studio now, Frank didn't seem like such a dangerous character, but more like a clever fox who was angling to *become* a dangerous character once again. I began to read, and Frank seemed instantly interested, but by the end I thought he was dozing off a bit. (Personally, you couldn't pay me to listen to someone read their whole screenplay aloud.)

When I finished, Frank expressed great admiration and enthusiasm, and from his remarks it was clear that he hadn't been dozing. He was now going to become the producer and spearhead the effort to get it made. First, though, he had some thoughts and ideas on what should be in the script. Since the story was taking place largely behind the scenes in a movie studio, and Frank had been president of Paramount, his input was invaluable. We worked very well together for a few weeks.

Suddenly, *S.O.B.*, Blake Edwards's movie about Hollywood, opened, and wasn't really a hit. Frank said that would make it even harder to have a studio want to make ours. Over the next few months, it was becoming increasingly clear from the time he took to return my phone calls that Frank was no longer the producer.

In the six years since I had started taking the script around, the heads of some of the studios had changed, so I made return engagements now reading the script. I went over to United Artists to read it to Steve Bach and Anthea Sylbert, two people I had worked with on *The Heartbreak Kid*. Steve had worked for the producer, Edgar Scherick, and Anthea had been the costume designer. They were now studio executives. They seemed to like the script, but Steve kept having to leave the room because of a picture he was in charge of for the studio, *Heaven's Gate*. As *Heaven's Gate* and its director, Michael Cimino, brought United Artists, and specifically Steve Bach (among others), untold grief, I sensed a preoccupation there.

In the meantime, I acted in a production of *Charley's Aunt* for cable. This time I wasn't calling out "Jack, my dear boy" as Sir Francis Chesney (although my age was now closer to his); this time I played the leading role of the college student at Oxford who dresses up like a woman. So when I was college-student age at the Playhouse, I played middle age, and when I was middle-aged, I played the college student. I got on very well with the director, Bill Asher. Aside from his talent, I was also impressed that no matter how long we worked, Bill never seemed to need to sit down, which is no small gift in this grueling profession. I showed him my screenplay, now called *Dreamers* (Paramount retained the original *Joy of Sex* title). Bill loved the script and said we could make it for two and a half million dollars if people would defer their salaries. So now Bill was co-producer with me and the director. For the first time, I had a real ally.

Michael Brandman (my pal who, way back, had thought the Tarzan-was-Jewish monologue was so funny), who was now an executive at Lorimar, put together a drinks-and-hors-d'oeuvres afternoon where I would read the screenplay to about twelve of their people to see if they'd make it. Bill asked, "You're going to get up in front of a dozen people and read a one-hundred-thirty-five-page screenplay with you playing fifty parts?"

I said, "This has become my thing. I could tour with it."

Bill sat nervously munching near the hors d'oeuvres table as I read. They loved it. But there was a big surprise: The only two men with the authority to say "We'll make the movie"—Lee Rich and Merv Adelson—weren't there. Lee Rich read it after his people recommended it, and turned it down because he thought the leading character wasn't likable. It amazes me to hear people talk so much about whether a character is likable. There are certain star actors—always have been—who are very likable. It doesn't make a huge difference who they play: The guy comes out likable. I mean, the character generally can't do something that would make the *National Enquirer*'s cover, but short of that, they're likable. You get one of these guys in the part, and your leading role is likable. Remember how likable Jimmy Cagney was in those prison movies? He'd kill a couple dozen cops a movie at least, and he was still likable. For the longest time, the script mostly had Peter Falk attached to it. Peter Falk—likable? Lovable! Without even trying. He's a real favorite of mine. I think what I've always liked the most about Peter is his capacity to engage in any subject that's brought up. Once, at a little dinner party with Peter and his wife, I said, "Driving over here, I was trying to remember exactly who Chicken Little was."

Peter's wife, Shera Danese, a boisterous, vulnerable woman who always makes me feel good, said, "Come on, Chuck, you can't expect us to discuss *that!*"

Peter jumped right in, already deep in thought. "Chicken

Little," he said pensively. "Let's see. I know Henny Penny said the sky was falling. Or was that Chicken Little?" Pretty soon, he was more interested than I was.

It seemed, even for the low price of two and a half million dollars, I wasn't getting any takers. By now the script had the reputation of having been rejected by everyone, and no one wanted to try to be a hero.

I went back to New York to continue life. I got a call to have lunch with a financing film team, two producers who had been wanting to do something with me. I said, "Would you take a couple of hours and let me read you a script?" They agreed. The next day, at their suite at the Sherry-Netherland Hotel, I read it to them. They loved it. They wanted to do it. They were heading back to Hollywood, and we would draw up contracts. When they got back and announced to various people, including the studio that distributed their pictures, that they were going to do this with me, they learned that everyone in Hollywood had turned it down—and then, quickly, so did they, not wanting to go against the flood of the mainstream. I called one of them from New York and said, "I thought you said you were going to do it."

The producer said, "When I said we were going to do it, that didn't mean that we were going to *do* it."

I hesitated a moment, wondering if I had just heard right. "What did it mean?" I asked.

He said it meant they'd do it if the studio wanted to distribute it and if . . . and if . . . and if . . .

"Oh," I said.

So there was still no heroic figure on the horizon to swoop down, champion the picture, and get it made.

The most precarious job in Hollywood is head of production of a studio. In the seven years since I had begun the saga of *Dreamers*, a.k.a. *The Joy of Sex*, many studio heads had come and gone. Then, a change took place that seemed to promise, finally, that there could be a breakthrough for *Dreamers*. Frank Yablans had become the president of MGM/UA. I decided I would make him an offer he couldn't refuse. The script had now been around so extensively that it would take something really special to make it work, even at two and a half million dollars. I began to send the script to various actors I knew.

When I called Frank Yablans, I offered him the movie for

two and a half million dollars plus a cast that included, among others, Steve Martin, Gilda Radner, Penny Marshall, and Tyne Daly, along with me. All of these people had agreed to work for the least amount of money the union allowed because they liked the parts. Steve Martin, as an act of friendship, bless him, agreed to appear without even reading the script. Frank said, "If you can deliver those people for two and a half million, you have a deal." I called my agent, a man named David Wardlow, and told him to call Frank (who was a good friend of his) to make a contract. David called Frank and confirmed our conversation. I was ecstatic. I called Bill Asher. He couldn't believe, after all these years, that it actually had happened. We were thrilled. The next day I got a call from David Wardlow telling me that in today's conversation with Frank Yablans, the budget was referred to as "two million," not two and a half. Everyone doubted it could be done for two and a half, and *no* one felt it could be done for two. I asked David what had happened. He said there was no question that the figure had been two and a half yesterday, but no matter what David said to his good friend Frank, it was now two. Yablans denied it was ever referred to as "two and a half."

Because the picture hung in the balance, I flew to Hollywood to see Frank directly. He welcomed me into his new, huge studio office with a big hug. Even though I felt there was a knife hanging out of my back, I still had great affection for Frank. He might have been trying to do me in in the Hollywood game, but no one else was even playing the game with me. I had done a lot of work on the script since he'd seen it, and I told him all about it as we sat around his coffee table. I told him how exciting it was going to be, with all these people involved. He seemed very happy about everything. At the height of his happiness, I hit him with: "But, Frank, I can't do it for two. I have to have the two and a half we discussed." He vehemently denied that we'd ever said two and a half. But there, in the middle of the denial, he casually slipped in what had happened in about three quick sentences. Apparently, after he made the deal with me, he told his associates, who were upset that he'd done it on his own. So when he got to the part about the two and a half, in order to make it easier for them to swallow, he made it two. Since at that time the average picture cost around eight million dollars, I don't know why they couldn't have swallowed two and a half. But that's what happened.

Looking Frank deep in the eye, I said, "You don't want us to make a movie that would have to be sold straight to cable. I've got to have the two and a half."

Frank, who, like most politicians, always likes to appear he's winning even when he's conceding something, snatched up a legal pad and dramatically listed all the promised stars in the picture, almost shouting: "I'll give you two and a half, but I want Steve Martin! I want Gilda Radner! I want Penny Marshall!" And down the line. I nodded. He then picked up the phone and called his main associate, Freddie Fields, who had earlier been one of my agents (I'd met him once), and said, "You don't want us to make a movie that will have to be sold straight to cable," and got agreement on the two and a half.

The contract MGM made with what was now called The Dreamers Film Company, which consisted of Bill Asher and me, was about the worst it could possibly be and still be legal. However, everyone in my life felt it was a miracle that after seven years we were actually doing it. David Wardlow was right in the middle of working out the bondage (as someone called it) deal with MGM when Frank Yablans offered him a job—which he took—as one of the two heads of United Artists, which was controlled by MGM. After assuring me I now had a friend at the studio, David put me in touch with a man named Frank Wulager at the agency who would continue working out the details for our side. After about a month, Frank Wulager happily told me he was no longer an agent, but was now a production executive for the Mirish Company, an independent film company. Frank said I now had a friend at the Mirish Company, and put another agent in touch with me. By that time, I decided to let our attorney, David Nochimson, handle everything, after he promised me he had no ambitions to be a movie executive.

Bill Asher put together a production team for the picture, and the process finally began to move ahead smoothly as we neared the beginning of shooting. One nagging question was, How was a movie that was originally budgeted at over seven million dollars going to look when it cost two and a half? We planned to shoot it in five weeks, not ten, but I was all for that; I always found the slow pace the hardest thing about making movies. Bill assured me I wouldn't know the difference. If that was the case, then I had to assume most movies had considerably inflated budgets.

We were now only four days away from beginning. There were a few bumps here and there, but the whole project continued to move ahead amazingly smoothly. It seemed incredible that, after seven years of rejection, a wonderful cast would be bringing this story to life after all.

Bill called a meeting of all our department heads to go over every last detail of the script—what we would need from costumes, props, set dressing, etc. With a short schedule, it was crucial that we be completely prepared. I had never been to a meeting like this. We started on page one and worked our way through the whole script, under Bill's supervision. He seemed a bit preoccupied, but I figured he just had a lot on his mind. When we finished several hours later, Bill and I went back to his office, and he shut the door and asked that we not be disturbed. He said he had some bad news. I almost held my breath as I waited for his next sentence. Our leading actor, the one who would play the studio head (Peter Falk by now had other commitments), hadn't passed his insurance physical and, even though he eventually would be okay, was not going to be able to be in the picture. I'm not mentioning this actor's name because, even though today he is fine, he doesn't need me to say he once didn't pass a physical (the movie business being as nervous as it is). He is one of our best character comedy stars and was replaceable (for studio acceptability) by only two actors in the whole industry— both of whom were unlikely to be available on four days' notice. The picture again hung in the balance.

I called David Wardlow and told him of the crisis. The deal with MGM was what is called "a negative pickup," meaning they guarantee a bank loan, then they pay the bank after the picture is delivered. A lot of money had already been spent. It only became MGM's responsibility when and if the picture was finished and delivered. The movie was insured, and the completion-bond company would have been responsible if we had just folded our tent and given up. No one, including David, seemed to want that. Everyone at The Dreamers Film Company was very nervous and depressed as word got around. Things looked bad, but there was an ace in the hole.

A few months earlier I had been to a gathering and ended up at dinner afterward with Peter Falk and Walter Matthau, whom neither Peter nor I really knew. Peter was telling Walter about the script and what a wonderful leading role it had. Walter, quite a wry character in life as well as in his movie roles, said, "If it's so good, why don't you do it?" Peter said he had a long-standing commitment to do a picture that was actually starting the same day we were. The role was cast, I said, but Walter was curious, and asked to read it anyway. I sent it to him, and the next day he called me, announced himself as Konstantin Chernenko (then the general secretary of the Soviet Union), and talked wittily for about half an hour about any number of subjects, never once mentioning the script till the end of the conversation, when he asked me some question about the plot.

Still, now three months later, there was no question in my mind that if Walter were available and MGM and his agent could get together, Walter Matthau would play the starring role in this movie.

I called him immediately. There was an answering machine. I left a message, asking him to call me whenever he got in. Around midnight, he called. As usual, he launched into an anecdote that made me laugh. I really learned something about myself that night. As important as it was to get Walter into this movie right away, his anecdote reminded me of one of my own which I couldn't resist telling him. It became clear that no matter how crucial the professional issue, I evidently was the type of guy who couldn't pass up an opportunity for a good laugh first, or maybe I was just delaying the possible rejection, which would have been particularly rough under the circumstances. Eventually, after exchanging a few more stories, sitting in my dark living room, I told Walter what was going on. The next day MGM and Walter's agent made a deal, and Walter Matthau became the last-minute star of the movie. Everyone began to breathe again. We were heading into the weekend before the Monday start.

Sunday night around seven o'clock I got a call at home from the production manager telling me that the woman who owned the house we were going to shoot in on Monday was claiming that thirty thousand dollars' worth of jewelry had been stolen from a secret hiding place in her bathroom. I gazed into the night for a moment. "What do we do about that?" I asked, trying unsuccessfully to sound calm.

"Well, we're discussing it now with the police," was the answer.

"Uh-huh," I said. "Does that mean the police will be on the set tomorrow when we begin to film this comedy?"

"We'll try not to have that happen," was the answer.

(I don't know what happened about the jewelry. I never mentioned it to anyone, and, happily, no one mentioned it ever again to me.)

I quickly decided to go to bed. As I went to unplug the phone, it rang again. It was one of the stars of the picture telling me "they" (I'd like to protect this person's identity) wanted out. They were convinced they weren't going to be any good in the part and just wanted out. All the stars were necessary to obligate MGM to honor the contract. I didn't say that; I just talked nonstop for the next twenty minutes about how terrific this person would be in the picture (I meant every word). After I finished, they seemed reassured, and said to forget they called. I hung up and dived to unplug the phone before it could ring again.

The next morning I got up at five A.M., and soon was driving in darkness on mountain roads toward the ocean, where we would first be filming. The seven-year saga was over. In my wildest imaginings, I couldn't have foreseen what lay ahead.

As I arrived at the location, a woman I hadn't met before who was working on the technical side of the picture asked to speak to me. She wanted to let me know that she wasn't used to working at this salary, and even though she had agreed to it and would stay, she wanted me to know she wasn't happy. I thanked her for the information, and walked away to get into my clothes for the first scene, which, conveniently, was a really explosive one in which my character had to express a lot of built-up frustration. It went well.

Things moved very smoothly under Bill Asher's expert guidance. He had directed a lot of pictures, and was really prepared. Friendliness and cooperation pervaded the set. When Walter Matthau arrived on the scene, the whole picture took on a specialness. He was enthusiastic and warm toward everyone. Even though he was a last-minute replacement, he came in totally prepared. Not only was he solid on his lines and on what he was doing, but he also kept a string of anecdotes rolling, to everyone's amusement.

Steve Martin, who was playing a legendary screen idol, arrived for some makeup tests. He had to have rubber makeup applied in order to look eighty. After a couple of hours of makeup, he came on the set so we could run some film. Steve is as witty off-screen as he is on. He was there for sixty seconds. As he left, he announced in a loud voice: "This is the finest crew I've ever worked with in my life."

The filming continued with good humor. I recall only one day when we had some difficulty. We had rented a large suite of offices in downtown Los Angeles to be the headquarters of the film's movie studio. The man responsible for renting the space seemed to have an endless set of rules for where we could go or not go, sit or not sit. Finally, Bill had the inspiration to put him in the movie to get him off our backs. All he had to do was lean over a secretary's desk as though he were pointing out something to her on a piece of paper. Since this was now to be his motion-picture debut, all his energy seemed to go into his part, just as we'd hoped. It was a rather difficult shot: The camera had to move on tracks down a long hallway and through one door and then another. After eight tries, we hadn't gotten it, and had to break for lunch. By that time, he was fed up with being an actor and quit the movie. He reverted to his office manager's identity, but since he'd now had a personal taste of how demanding moviemaking is, he seemed to lay off us a bit.

Shooting continued to proceed smoothly, in spite of the fact that our cinematographer (the man who's basically responsible for the look of the picture) caught a cold and wanted to quit the movie (unheard of). He missed a few days before Bill got him to return. I think it was more exhaustion than a cold that got him, as he'd just finished another picture before coming to us.

In any case, the daily film was looking very good. It seemed like a ten-million-dollar movie. With a cast filled with well-known actors, it was hard to imagine it wasn't. I regularly received phone calls from David Wardlow telling me how wonderful and funny it all was, and how happy the studio was about everything. One slight bump came along when I was told one day that we couldn't use the title *Dreamers*. It seemed that 20th Century-Fox had done a picture years ago called *Dreamer*, and we were too close. *Dreamers* was an accurate title for us, but now we had to come up with a third name. I went to a book of quotations and found the phrase "movers and shakers," which was first used in a nineteenth-century poem. I was having lunch at the MGM commissary with Irv Ivers, the head of publicity and marketing for the studio, one day, and Frank Yablans was sitting at an adjoining table. "What do you think of the title *Movers and Shakers*?" I called out to him. "Terrific title!" he responded. So we had our new title. *Joy of Sex* had become *Dreamers*, and *Dreamers* had become *Movers and Shakers*. MGM did a survey, and learned that 85 percent of everyone questioned on whether they'd like to see a movie called *Movers and Shakers* with our stars in it said they would. That was very high. Later, they did another survey that revealed that about 70 percent of the people questioned had no idea what "movers and shakers" meant. But we stayed with it. Since 70 percent of the people questioned didn't know what it meant, let me define it here. Movers and shakers are the people who get big things done in the world; and, since our movers and shakers didn't get anything done, it was an ironic title. I later learned that 75 percent of all people questioned didn't know what "ironic" meant.

While it seemed strange to be on our third title, it was less strange than the fact that we were making the movie at MGM for $2.5 million—MGM, from whom I had earlier turned down an offer of $5 million after they, of course, said it would cost $7.1 million.

Robert Towne, the acclaimed screenwriter (*Chinatown, Shampoo*), was working as a creative consultant to MGM. Frank Yablans, at a social gathering, had offered him a sizable sum to pass judgment when the studio wanted his opinion. He was also an old friend of mine, and one day I called him to ask if he would intercede with Frank to get us enough money to use a Kem instead of a Moviola in editing the picture. To put it simply, a Kem lets you look at the picture as though it were on a sixteen-inch TV screen, against a Moviola, which is more like two by three inches. This was a huge distinction, since one of the major considerations in editing is determining the size of a shot in a picture: Do you want to be on a full shot, showing lots of people at a particular moment, or a close-up? There are hundreds of those kinds of questions. Using a Moviola when ultimately the movie will be shown on a huge screen can be very misleading to a lot of people working in film. I'm certainly one of them. Bob asked Frank about this at a breakfast meeting. Frank issued a lot of profanity in my direction, but agreed to give us more money, not only for the Kem but so everything wouldn't have to be done under such tight circumstances. We were on an extremely short schedule for all the key postproduction activities, such as editing, putting in music and sound effects, and mixing all the elements together for the final version. Bob got Frank to give us fifty thousand dollars so we wouldn't be working under those kinds of pressures. I should say Bob got Frank to *say* he'd give us fifty thousand.

Time went by, and we completed filming. We asked for the promised fifty thousand for the Kem. David Wardlow, who knew of the fifty-thousand pledge, told us to prepare a thirty-minute reel of footage from the picture since Frank, with all of his duties, still hadn't seen any of the movie. This amazed me since it was actually his project. It made me wonder how he spent his time. But according to David, we'd get our fifty thousand once Frank saw this reel. Bill Asher and I stopped editing for a few days to prepare it. We worked carefully and meticulously on it. Frank still couldn't find the time to look at it. He never saw it. At this point, I possibly should have called Frank myself, gone to his office, hugged him, thrown him to the floor, and sat on him until he coughed up the fifty thousand. But at the time I couldn't help but be aware of two things. One was that MGM/UA, under Frank's control, was putting out one picture after another that was failing at the box office. As the string of pictures that weren't successful grew longer and longer, approaching record proportions, I wasn't that eager to confront Frank about anything. I always liked him, but found him more than a little explosive under the best of circumstances. Also, we were doing great in the editing room, and I figured the more I called Frank or MGM, the more they might call me. While Frank had been very helpful a few years back when he was the producer, I hadn't heard any wisdom coming out of MGM/UA for some time. Since it was their bat and ball, and if they talked I had to listen, I chose not to call.

We became the invisible unit; we even avoided going to the commissary lest some executive see us and want to talk. MGM/UA continued to release one picture after another that disappeared in record time. Their big picture, *2010*, a sequel to *2001* but not made by Stanley Kubrick, was supposed to be their Christmas blockbuster, the one that would turn everything around. It didn't. Tension grew thicker at the studio. We slunk from the parking lot to our editing room, ducking so as not to be seen by any MGM executives.

Finally, the day came when we were finished enough with our work that we could show it to Frank, who would be seeing it for the first time, along with his associates David Wardlow and Jay Kantor, a film executive who excels at making you feel good, which I always appreciated. Jay had come over from the Ladd Company, which had recently ceased its activities after the unexpected lack of success of *The Right Stuff*. I thought we would be seeing our movie with the MGM group, but we got a last-minute message from David saying: "Frank wants us to see it alone. I'll call you afterward." We sent the picture over to the executive screening room and waited in our editing room for their response. "We" were Bill Asher, me, our editor, Tom Benko, and our location manager and postproduction supervisor, Pete Ware, whose goodwill and spirit made him seem like a religious figure in our midst. We needed him. Frank Yablans was viewing this movie while he was on the ropes. He had been fired from Paramount years earlier, despite a string of successes, after publicly attacking Charles Bludhorn, the chairman of the board of Gulf & Western, which, as I've said, owns Paramount. Now he had a string of failures, and rumors were heavy that he was about to be fired again.

Ironically, *Movers and Shakers*, with our cast, produced for $3.5 million (it went from $2.5 million to $3.5 million because we paid Walter Matthau $1 million, which was half his normal fee at the time), couldn't possibly lose money. This was because of the value of its cable and cassette rights. But still, Frank Yablans was under a lot of stress while he was looking at it.

On the other hand, I reminded Bill and Pete and Tom that Frank had at one point been the producer of the movie. He had actually contributed valuable material and insight to it, and now he was seeing it with an all-star cast. How could he not like it? The minutes dragged as our group paced around our small editing quarters. We were trying not to look at our watches while we were waiting for the phone to ring. The time they should have

finished seeing it came and went without a call. "They're probably talking a while amongst themselves," I said. Someone took an
Alka-Seltzer. A half hour after we expected a call, the phone
rang. I picked it up as everyone stared at me.

"Chuck?" David Wardlow's deep voice soberly said on the
other end.

"Yeah?"

"Wardlow. It did *not* go well." (He said it with the stress.)

I did *not* feel good. "It didn't?" I asked, trying to think of
what to say.

"No. There was some sporadic laughter for the first two
thirds of the movie, then nothing."

"Uh-huh," I said. He expressed his sympathy, and seemed to
be bringing the call to a close. I said: "Well, wait a minute. I'd
like to come over and see you." We fixed a time and hung up.

I turned to Bill and Pete and repeated the conversation.
They looked very depressed. We had all worked so hard for so
long (months of sixteen-hour days), and now all we heard was: "It
did *not* go well." Translated to us, it felt like *we* did not go well,
we were not accepted. I said, "I'll go over and see what I can
learn," and left for David's office.

When I arrived, David's secretary, a friendly woman, gave
me her usual warm greeting tinged with a bit of sadness. She's
heard, I thought. David's office had a huge famous portrait of all
the stars of MGM in the forties: Gable, Tracy, et cetera. Movie
executives, particularly ones who haven't achieved anything,
often surrounded themselves with portraits of past glories of their
studios.

David told me he too didn't find the picture funny.

I said, "It's very difficult to make a judgment of a picture
alone in a screening room." David said he felt he could make that
judgment. I said, "By what qualification?"

He said, "I've seen a lot of movies."

I said, "I have too, but only an audience can tell you what an
audience feels—and not just one audience, either, because even
audiences disagree." He said nothing. I said, "What happens
now?" He said he'd be in touch. I went back to the editing room
and repeated the conversation to Bill and Pete. A lot of profanity
and slamming of doors followed.

After a couple of days of silence from the studio while Bill

and I tried to keep busy with this and that, David called request-
ing a screening of three sequences that we had chosen not to
include in the picture. I showed them to David and Jay Kantor,
and explained why we had left them out. Jay seemed to agree;
David partially did. No conclusive decision was made. We began
a series of screenings of different versions of the picture for
David. No one else seemed interested enough to come. We
seemed to be going in circles.

We screened the picture for Robert Towne and Elaine May
and a series of friends to get reactions. Bob, Elaine, Steve Martin, and Peter Falk were particularly helpful. Bob and Elaine became champions of the picture. We made editing changes and
reversed the order of some scenes based on their suggestions and
showed the picture to David again. He thought it was greatly
improved. So did we.

Finally, I decided to call Frank Yablans, as we were ready to
finish the picture. He was extremely friendly. He said he felt the
picture just missed, but a miss was as good as a mile. I thought
that was a lot warmer than "It did *not* go well." We discussed the
whys and why nots of some possible changes, and the whole situation was again turned over to David Wardlow. He asked for a few
more changes; we made them. He said, "Okay, finish the picture." We did. We put the music in and completed all the finish-
ing processes. Our money had just about run out when we
delivered the picture to MGM on the designated day.

I went back to New York and waited to hear what MGM's
plans were for the release of the picture. After a week of silence, I
called our attorney, David Nochimson, who told me MGM had
requested an extension of the deadline to pay the bank. I asked if
that was unusual. David, a gentle man, hesitated, then said, "It's
not the first time I've heard of it."

"What does it mean?" I asked him.

"I don't know," he said.

A week later we knew. MGM, instead of paying for the picture, was claiming they weren't accepting the picture because "it
was not of first-class technical quality and the photoplay [the
movie] does not reflect the screenplay." No one knew what they
were talking about. It was clear they were trying to get out of
paying. It was confusing, because even if they didn't like the picture (which, of course, we had to assume), with our cast, as I've

said, they could have easily gotten their money back from cassette, cable, television-syndication sales, and foreign rights.

I was living in Connecticut at the time. I took a walk late one night along the water to try to figure out what was happening. I couldn't. I was furious. I had worked for two years on the picture for virtually no salary—no salary as a producer, no money as a writer, and the minimum allowed for five weeks as an actor. I had earned about five thousand dollars for two years' intensive work. I had been unavailable to work in a lot of other movies I had been offered. MGM couldn't lose, and yet they, in effect, wanted to go to court. Now, for the first time, all the lessons I had learned about dealing with rejection failed me. Too much time and effort had gone into this, and too much meanness was coming back our way for any of my old methods of "getting through" to work. It was time for some new strategy, for some new "creative survival" methods—and I didn't know what they were. I don't remember ever feeling that bad since I'd gotten into the profession. Even the *11 Harrowhouse* experience seemed to pale in comparison. I felt that *I* was finally becoming a little bit of a "dangerous character," somebody it wouldn't be good for certain people to run into. Possibly, all the early career abuse and indifference was coming to the fore now and adding to what I was feeling. I've obviously done better than most who've gone into this profession, but anyone in it can tell you, no matter how well you've done, it's always hard. I mean bring-you-to-your-knees hard.

I decided to fly back to Los Angeles to confront Frank Yablans personally once more. When I got there, he took my call immediately and made an appointment to see me right away. I drove the forty-five-minute trip to MGM. My mind was racing. The malice I had felt for the *11 Harrowhouse* producer would have to take a backseat to what was going on toward Frank at that moment. I parked my car in their lot, and as I walked toward the administration building I felt like blowing it up. I walked into Frank's office, and, astonishingly, once more we hugged. I knew Frank was the only one who could authorize a lawyer's letter. Knowing he was behind the stress and grief all of us were feeling, I was amazed that I felt no anger toward him. Whatever else he was, he was still the guy who had made it possible to finally make the movie, and I couldn't forget that. Knowing how rightfully impressed he was with Robert Towne and Elaine May, I told him how much they had liked the picture and how they felt he hadn't even seen the current version he was suing over.

"I haven't. They're right," Frank said cheerfully.

I stared at him. Boy, he really is a number! I thought. I said, "Don't you think it's an okay idea for you to see the picture before you sue me?"

"Absolutely!" Frank said, even more cheerfully.

I said, "Frank, what the hell is going on?"

He said, "David Wardlow viewed the picture and told me it was a catastrophe."

"A catastrophe?" I said, looking him in the eye and wanting to kill.

Probably picking up the glint in my eye, he said, "Well . . . I don't care what anyone says. Let me see it tomorrow, and I'll call you."

"Okay, Frank," I said casually, "give me a call," and got up to leave, thinking I was in a mental institution. At the door I said, "Frank, I'd really appreciate hearing from you as soon as possible, as I'm just sitting around out here."

Frank said, "You didn't fly out here just for this, did you?"

"Yeah, Frank, actually I did," I said, and left.

Two days later Frank called to tell me he completely disagreed with David Wardlow. Forgetting about the technical non-issue (the picture was perfectly professionally presented), he said he thought the movie was much better than the script. In fact, he thought it was a hell of a picture, and he would instruct his people to pay the bank.

I called Bill Asher to tell him the news. There was a long silence on the other end of the phone. Bill had been through the wars, but this was all new to him too. He was as dazed as I was.

The next day I went in to see Frank, as he wanted to discuss a few changes he had in mind. He said David would be joining us, and he just wanted me to know that no one had acted improperly here. I said nothing. David joined us. I felt no anger toward him either, as I know that all that lawyer business was an irrational Yablans explosion. To me, David Wardlow was just another ill-equipped movie executive who wanted to protect his job.

We went down to the screening room. Frank asked for a few changes, which I said were fine. It was all very cordial. He then said he wanted the completion-bond company to pay for the changes. I was suddenly furious. He had been negligent as hell, and now he wanted some innocent insurer to pay for his craziness. "Why should they pay?" I said. "You had plenty of time to see the picture before we finished it. It's not their fault you didn't get around to it." This was the first time I had let Frank see how I felt about all his bullshit.

He became angry instantly. "I never said 'finish the picture'!"

I said, "You didn't say *anything*! We were instructed by David here to finish it. It's immoral to ask someone else to pay for your not doing your job!"

"Don't tell me about morality!" he snapped.

"Fellows," David Wardlow said, as we called each other a couple of names.

As fast as the outburst started, it ended. Amazingly, in spite of everything, we still liked each other. Frank said again that he thought it was a really good picture and he was glad we made it. I said that when all was said and done he was still the guy who made it possible to get it made. We said good-bye and hugged once more.

The changes were finished and paid for by the completion-bond company, who chose to go along to protect their relationship with MGM. Everyone thought Yablans was an aggressive bully, but he was the man in charge of MGM and United Artists.

I wanted the advertising and marketing people at the studio to see this movie about which, by this time, they had heard so much, so I arranged a screening. There were about a dozen people. I sat in the back of the theater. They seemed to be laughing quite steadily. At the end, I walked upstairs with the creative head of marketing for the studio, Greg Morrison. Because of his dry way of speaking as we entered the elevator, I didn't immediately pick up the gist of what he was saying. By the time we reached his office, however, it was clear to me that finally the movie had a champion at the studio. Greg had gone for the picture in a big way. He felt it was going to look good even twenty-five years from now, a classic comedy about the movies. When I reported that David Wardlow had referred to it as "a catastrophe" and that Frank Yablans had tried to get out of paying for it, he looked bemused and just shook his head.

It seemed that now it would be a good idea to meet a man named Richard Graff, who was the head of distribution for the studio—meaning he's the man who persuades theater owners to book the film and arranges the financial terms. I'd been warned by some friends that Dick Graff was a real number, but "he will probably clean up his act for you." I wasn't sure what all that meant, but for years I'd had to deal with different kinds of show-business characters, so I was sure I'd be prepared for Dick Graff. I wasn't.

It's common practice at movie studios to have large photographs from famous movies of the past lining the hallways. The hallway to Dick Graff's offices was lined with such photos, except that the head of Dick Graff had been superimposed over all the heads of the male stars. He was in the outer office when I arrived. He saw me, said, "Charley, come on in," and led the way into his office. He's a burly guy, around sixty, with a lot of energy and a headful of curly gray hair. He was very cheerful as he told me to take a seat. He took a couple of calls as I sat there and listened to him banter wisecracks back and forth with people, not much of it having anything to do with the movie business. He rifled through papers and winked at me as he talked, as though we were sharing some joke. Finally, when the phone calls and the paper rifling were through, he looked at me and said: "I saw your movie. I knew you were coming in, so I saw your movie." I waited. He said nothing further.

I said, "Did you like it?"

With great passion, he said, "Oh, no!"

I was taken aback and angry. He was talking about the movie as though it were a thirty-nine-cent hat. "Why not?" I tried to ask casually.

He said, "People will think we're a bunch of jerks, and that's absolutely right."

I didn't quite understand his answer. I think he meant he thought it portrayed him and his associates as jerks, and felt it was true, but nobody would care. I didn't know what to say.

He said, "Look, I don't have to like it to sell it. We'll sneak it somewhere and see what happens. I hope I'm surprised."

I went home with my mind spinning.

I next was told they were going to sneak-preview the movie in a place called Goleta, a suburb of Santa Barbara, California. They put it in a large theater near an airport. I drove up with some friends. The people from marketing were there, including the movie's MGM champion, Greg Morrison. The picture received a fair amount of laughs, but afterward, in assessing the preview cards, the results weren't very good. The idea of a movie about three men failing to make a great movie about love because of their own lack of a love life struck the Goleta crowd as something considerably short of *Star Wars*.

Everyone was very depressed. The next day Bill Asher and I showed up at Greg Morrison's office. Greg told us that his teenage son had been there, and had liked the picture, but felt the audience wasn't really in on it enough, "and why couldn't Charles Grodin kind of lead people through this kind of unusual movie?"

"How would I do that?" I asked Greg.

"What about a narration?" he said.

Bill and I had earlier discussed that as a possibility. I thought about it some more and decided it could work. I started to write it and figure out how to place it in the picture when I got a call telling me that Frank Yablans had just been fired as head of the studio.

The board of directors was saying that under Frank's regime they had lost record amounts of money. Frank called me the next day to say good-bye. He jokingly said it was because of the Goleta screening, and then went on to say that, as far as he was concerned, he had primarily been responsible for a lot of hits at the studio, and all those other pictures that "hadn't performed" and lost MGM all that money were someone else's fault. He didn't say whose. I said good-bye to Frank, thanked him for all his support, and was actually sorry to see him go. I'm sure that if I had been there with him, we would have hugged again.

It wasn't until much later that I understood how Frank could institute a lawsuit to get out of paying for a picture he knew would be profitable to the studio. At the time, he probably knew he wasn't going to be at the studio much longer, so he could afford these irrational emotional indulgences. He certainly couldn't care less that MGM would make a profit after he'd gone. He wouldn't get any credit for it anyway.

The new head of the studio was Alan Ladd, Jr., or Laddie, as he is affectionately known. Laddie has a reputation as a straight-shooter and, while not the most talkative man in the world, he is thought to be trustworthy—which, for Hollywood, probably will qualify him for a statue someday.

I had dealt with Laddie about ten years earlier when he had been a production executive at 20th Century-Fox during the whole *11 Harrowhouse* saga. Laddie had been very pleased with my narration abilities in the seventies; now here were the eighties. I hadn't seen him in all these years. I called him; he was very friendly. I brought him up to date on all that had happened. I then said I felt that it was narration time again. Laddie said he hadn't seen the picture, but would, and we would meet. When we did he told me he thought the movie was "special, very, very special." I think that was Laddie's polite way of saying he thought it was too inside and inaccessible for the general public. I then began to recite my narration for him. First he looked a little surprised that I was doing it right in the middle of our conversation, and then he looked a little more blank than I would have liked as I was reciting. When I finished, he looked unimpressed, but said he felt it couldn't hurt, and go ahead and do it.

Over the next few days I put it in the picture. Greg Morrison said that if it worked, we should print T-shirts that said: I SURVIVED GOLETA. People working with me at the studio felt it helped the picture's accessibility immeasurably. The new version was sent to New York and shown at small media screenings, and seemed to be playing much better.

Dick Graff was now screening the movie for exhibitors. The idea was to find one small theater in New York and see what would happen. He called me one day and asked if I had a match.

"A match?" I asked him.

"Yeah," he said. "If you have a match, burn the print. No one wants to play it."

"No one?" I asked, trying to get my bearings.

"No one," he said. "You made a home movie. You should have thought of that when you were making it."

I said, "Do you mean that theater owners like every movie they play?"

"Yeah," he said.

I said, "Well, then they're wrong most of the time,

since most movies aren't successful, and maybe they're wrong here."

He didn't quite know what to say about that, so he said he'd see what he could do, and be in touch.

After getting Frank's lawyer's letter and hearing Dick Graff tell me to burn the print, I found myself thinking about issues of mortality on a regular basis. Even though I had occasionally felt upset with MGM over what had taken place, I hadn't really allowed myself to feel it consistently. Now all this meanness was once more starting to push me over the edge. I called Laddie and said I found talking to Dick Graff really depressing, and asked him if I were wrong in assuming the studio would make money no matter what. He said I was right. I then said I'd prefer it if I wasn't told to burn the print. It might make life just a little bit more pleasant and get my mind off thoughts of death. Soon afterward, Dick Graff called to apologize, saying that was just his sense of humor. I asked him what he said if he wanted to hurt someone. He chuckled and asked me how I'd like to go into Cinema II on the East Side of Manhattan. I felt that was the ideal theater for the picture: It was perfectly located, and had only three hundred seats. He said the theater had another booking, and we could only be there for three weeks. (I know he felt three weeks was plenty long to establish that no one wanted to see it, but he didn't say it.) Laddie's call to him, I'm sure, was still ringing in his ears. I asked him, "What if people want to see it after three weeks?"

He paused (probably censoring a whole lot of zingers), and said; "If people want to see it, we'll find a place for it."

I thanked him and started to arrange some screenings for critics.

A movie opening in one theater on the East Side of New York City must have some critical acclaim, because it's perceived more or less as an art film; and if at least some critics don't like an art film, then no one comes.

The critics in New York—or elsewhere, for that matter—have always been extremely supportive of me as an actor; but here was a whole movie, and I really didn't know what to expect. The reviews were surprising. They ranged from "You'll laugh till you cry" to "There's absolutely not one funny thing about this movie." One critic said it was good enough to be put in a time capsule; another wondered why it was made. One paper gave it a very bad review, and then a little later forgot it had reviewed it, and reviewed it again with another writer, who gave it a very good review.

We opened at Cinema II to okay business. Since movies almost always do their biggest business in the opening weekend, it looked like Dick Graff was right about the three weeks being plenty. Then a funny thing happened: The second-week business went up, not down. Then an even stranger thing happened: The third-week business went up again—almost unheard of. Somebody was liking the movie. Three weeks turned into three months at Cinema II; during some of that time, it was grossing more than any other movie playing at a single theater in Manhattan.

Greg Morrison was delighted. Dick Graff had no comment. But I was informed that the picture definitely would open in Los Angeles, with a full-page ad. The same thing happened all over again with the critics. Gary Franklin, who was the CBS film critic in Los Angeles and now is the ABC film critic, gave the picture a 10 on a scale of 1 to 10. He called it the funniest intelligent movie of the year. A critic for a Santa Monica paper said: "If you want to know what it feels like to die sitting upright in a theater, go see this movie." Clearly, the picture wasn't for everyone. Still, it ran for two months in Los Angeles.

In both cities I did publicity and made sure the letters weren't falling off the marquees at the theaters. (They constantly did in Los Angeles.) I met with Laddie, who said, rather than continue releasing the picture around the country, with the summer's big-budget movies and their big-budget advertising campaigns coming upon us, he would release it in some select theaters in the fall.

When the fall came and it went out to a few other cities, I was absorbed in something else—I think much to the studio's relief. It did okay. I made some calls and learned that very little advertising money was behind it; in the case of one city, it had no ad at all by the second week.

I have learned that MGM will end up with between one and two million dollars' profit on *Movers and Shakers*. It didn't make any money in its theatrical release, but, then, neither do most movies. As I've said, it will make its profit from the ancillary rights—cassette, cable, regular television, foreign rights, et cetera. So *Movers and Shakers* will be a profit picture for the studio (which clearly puts it in the minority of movies anywhere)—the studio that tried to go to court to avoid accepting it. What were they doing or saying to all those people who were making those big-budget movies that lost all the money and cost Frank his job? I shudder to imagine.

By the way, at this writing, Frank is living in Italy, where he is the president of Empire Pictures. David Wardlow is, once again, an agent. The blows delivered by Frank have permanently changed me. I have learned that in the movie business "yes" means "maybe," and "maybe" means "no"; that people can threaten to sue you, even if they will make money and you won't; and that they will say "burn the print" and expect you to laugh. I've had to become tougher. Since the business is filled with people who are charmers in those early, trouble-free stages of a movie, it has become important for me to know before I work with anyone what they will act like when it's *not* smooth sailing, when there are problems, since it's clear that, sooner or later, there always are.

About a year after all this I was at a party, and a woman came up to me and excitedly said: "I'm selling your movie."

I had no idea what she was talking about. "You are?" I said. "What movie?"

"*Movers and Shakers*," she said. "I just sold it to a prison."

"A prison?!" I said. "Boy, that seems like an unlikely audience. That's the best we can do, a prison?"

She said, "Not a prison, *Prism*, which is the largest cable outlet in Canada."

"Oh," I said, "did they see it?"

"Yes, of course," she said.

"Did they like it?" I asked nervously. (Remembering Dick Graff's "Oh, no" response to that question, I was ready for her to tell me, "We *made* them buy it.")

"Of course," she said. "They wouldn't buy it if they didn't like it." She said, "Call me at MGM on Monday, and I'll tell you all about the other places we're selling it."

"Great," I said. "Thanks a lot."

On Monday I called, eager to hear about all the cable and cassette and TV sales. She didn't return my call. I tried three more times over a period of a couple of weeks. It was clear she was ducking me. Finally, I called and she got on and said she was sorry she had spoken so soon, as she realized that she wasn't permitted to give this information to me.

I said, "I'm not asking about money, just where it was sold and when it will be shown."

She said she was sorry, but she couldn't tell me. She did say it was sold in the United States to a prominent cable system, but if I wanted to know where or when, I would just have to check my local listings.

Midnight Run

Given my experience over the years, I've always tried to come up with any idea I could to protect myself—emotionally. After much consideration, my list has all of one item: I've asked the people who represent me to tell me about a project only if I'm definitely wanted for it. I don't want to know about "interest," because more often than not, "interest" leads to nothing.

The "interest" calls are more dangerous than first meets the eye. Once, I met with a producer who was "interested" in doing the movie *Fletch* with me (which Chevy Chase later did). The producer was "sure" he wanted me, but he wanted to hear my opinion of whether I felt women would be attracted to me. At the time, I was seeing a woman who was a world-known beauty, but I could only mutter softly, "I think so." He apparently didn't, and I didn't get the role. I try to remember that exchange as funny—I don't quite succeed.

Shortly after the *Movers and Shakers* experience, I had a rare "interest" lunch with a man whose company had a deal with HBO and really wanted to work with me. Since HBO also had said they really wanted to work with me, it seemed fairly safe to have the lunch. The guy talked about several different projects his company was developing with HBO and with movie companies. I would be great for all of them, he said. First, I felt good;

and then, as he got to project number four, I began to hyperventilate. I had no idea what was going on. Here was a man offering me starring role after starring role—"You're the guy!" "You're the one!" "You'd be great!"—and I thought I was going to faint. This had absolutely never happened to me before. I couldn't figure out if I should go to the men's room, have a drink, go out, get some air, say—what? I just couldn't bring myself to say, "Excuse me, I think I'm going to faint"—not me, not this guy who had just been offered five starring roles. So I simply sat there, nodding and gasping—not too noticeably, I hoped.

When I got home, I really thought about it. I fancy myself pretty decently developed in the psychological insight department, but I drew a blank. Later, on reflection, I think I had an anxiety attack because I felt I was being set up for many rejections all at once, and it was too big a blow, particularly after *Movers and Shakers*. I felt the fellow meant everything he said; but, ultimately, when he got back to his company or HBO or the movie studios, nothing would happen. And that's what did happen—nothing. I never heard another word about any of it for a couple of reasons. Most of the projects were dramas, and people perceived me as a comedic actor. Also, each of them was the starring role—and that week I wasn't considered a star. I knew it and he'd find out. If he'd have talked to me after *The Heartbreak Kid* or *Heaven Can Wait*, I probably would have ordered dessert. But that week it was fainting. So I never want to hear about "interest."

It was the spring of 1987 when my friend and representative, Jim Berkus, called to tell me there was "interest" in me for a picture called *Midnight Run*. I quickly reminded Jim of our understanding. He said he felt compelled to make the call because this was an over-$20-million movie directed by Martin Brest, whose last picture had been *Beverly Hills Cop*. *Midnight Run* was basically a two-man picture. The other man was Robert DeNiro, and there was serious "interest" in me. I thought a moment, then said, "How serious?" He said he had been involved with it for weeks: At first it had been serious, then less serious, then more serious. He said that it was a great part, that movie stars were auditioning for it, and that I would have to audition for it (something I hadn't done for years, which is one of the most important tangible rewards of being recognized). Jim said again that they were very serious, but he would call Martin Brest to see if he could figure out *how* very serious. He called me back the next day to say they were coming to New York to see "some" people, but were really *very* serious about me, and if I'd come in it would just be Martin Brest, DeNiro, and me in an office on a Saturday in the Gulf & Western building, which was closed—implying no one would see me go in. It felt like a drug transaction.

I asked Jim to send me the script. He overnight-expressed it and I read it right away. It was clear immediately that if I were offered the part it would certainly be the best one I had ever played in the movies. The Heartbreak Kid was obviously a great role, but Jonathan Mardukis, "the Duke," was more dimensional, more unexpected, and more human than any part I'd yet done.

I drove in from Connecticut on Saturday and went to the closed Gulf & Western building. I went to a suite on a high floor and was met by Bonnie Timmermann, a New York casting director I knew from my auditioning days. Fighting a feeling of regression, I was introduced to Michael Chinich, who I thought was the producer but was actually a Hollywood casting director. He then introduced me to Robert DeNiro. We shook hands and nodded familiarly to each other as though we'd met before, but we hadn't. I then shook hands with Martin Brest. We greeted each other cordially.

I had met Martin Brest once before at a party at Paul Simon's apartment. I was seated between him and a New York film critic on a sofa. The critic whispered in my ear that she felt very uncomfortable because she had just panned Marty's first movie, *Going in Style*. I whispered back, "Why'd you pan it?" She whispered: "Do you want to watch three old men sit on a park bench, walk down the street, eat lunch?" (I made a mental note to see the movie because it sounded pretty good to me. I later did and really enjoyed it.) I managed to stay between Marty and the critic that night, trying to keep the discomfort between them at bay.

This afternoon I spent three hours with the group at the Gulf & Western building. Robert DeNiro and I read over all of our scenes together, which was most of the movie. Then Marty Brest asked us to improvise on every scene. I had earlier been told he would do that, and it was one of the reasons I was willing to audition. The ability to improvise was one of my main assets and really the only one that might get me the role over a big movie star. When I left, Bonnie Timmermann and Michael Chinich were beaming; Robert DeNiro said good-bye in the same amiable manner he'd said hello; and Marty Brest said he appreciated my coming in. That sounded pretty close to a kiss-off phrase I remembered from my old auditioning days. Still, I felt that if they were actually going to cast this part from an audition, and not by giving it to a nonauditioning big star, I had a good chance.

Monday, Michael Chinich called Jim Berkus to say they were really interested. Of course, I asked, "What does that mean?" Jim is too much a pragmatist to give in to idle speculation, so he said, "I have no idea."

I went back to my life. Two weeks later Jim phoned to say the choice was now down to Robin Williams and me, and they wanted one more session with me. They had just come from two full days of auditioning with Robin in Los Angeles, so Jim and I figured that if they were ready to fly in to see me after that, it was certainly worth another trip down from Connecticut. I drove in and did another three-hour version, similar to the first—this time in a suite at the Sherry-Netherland Hotel. The same people— Bonnie Timmermann and Michael Chinich—were beaming. Michael even threw out a "You were superb" as he walked me to the elevator. Martin Brest had a hint of a smile. Robert DeNiro again greeted me and said good-bye in the same amiable fashion. It was impossible not to like him on sight. He was all about "work," plain and simple, and being with him felt like breathing pure oxygen.

I drove back to Connecticut feeling I would get the part. I mean, you always have to consider that Robert Redford might call up and say he read the script and wants to do it—and then you're out. But I somehow didn't see Redford doing that. I enjoyed the drive home.

Every couple of days for the next two weeks Michael Chinich would call Jim Berkus to say they were "really interested." Jim would report that to me. I would again say, "What does that mean?" and Jim would again say, "I have no idea." After a few weeks, though, Jim said he had heard from a couple of different sources that I was in the movie. Nobody connected to the actual movie had said that to Jim, but he was "hearing it around." The reason he was hearing it around was that Marty Brest had gone to Ned Tanen, the head of Paramount Pictures (who was financing

the movie), and said, "I want to do this with Charles Grodin."
And Ned Tanen had said, in effect, "Not at these prices." The
movie, as I've said, was figured to cost just over $20 million, and
for that kind of money they wanted box-office names: Robert
DeNiro and Dustin Hoffman, for example. They even suggested
making the part of the accountant, who learns one day that he is
working for the mob and embezzles $15 million from them and
gives it to charity, a woman—Cher. Cher read the script, tried to
envision the whole thing, and told Marty Brest it seemed like a
much bigger deal than just changing the name from Jonathan to
Joanne. Marty quickly agreed. He made his Charles Grodin case
again. Ned Tanen, who had just a week earlier offered me a role
in a John Travolta movie (which I turned down), stood fast. And
Marty Brest decided to take the project to another studio, which
was his right. Within two days, Universal Pictures said they
wanted to do it and told Marty he could make the movie with
whomever he wanted. Marty, first and foremost a careful man,
decided he wanted me—to audition again.

Jim Berkus called to inform me, and I stared out the window
for a moment. I said, "I've spent six hours on this. What is it he
wants to see me do he hasn't seen? I'll need to hear that from
him, and I need you to see if you can make a deal with Universal." An objective bystander might say: "Why wouldn't you be
able to make a deal with Universal?" But, remember, I was the
guy who turned down *The Graduate* "offer." I was having a wonderful life in New York and Connecticut, writing all kinds of
things, and, every so often, being in movies, and watching sports
on television a lot. I have a reclining chair, a Stratolounger, that I
spend a startling amount of time in. The script called for me to be
thrown from moving trains, go down some rapids (without a boat),
be hit on the head several times, and be shot at endlessly. I know
it's a movie and they use doubles, but, believe me, you could
definitely be sorry you were there.

Universal wanted me, *if* they wanted me, for about five
months. It was going to take more money than they probably
imagined to get me out of the Stratolounger and into the rapids—
no matter how good the part was.

Marty Brest called me from a plane that was flying from Chicago to Los Angeles to answer my question about what else he
wanted me to do. It was my first phone call from an airplane. If

you could have had Orson Welles calling from an airplane on a conference call, and speakerphones on earth, it would have been like God calling from the heavens about your career. With Marty and me, there was just basically a lot of static.

He shouted: "Chuck, it's Marty!"

I shouted back from my Stratolounger: "Hi, Marty!"

He yelled, "I'm in a plane, flying from Chicago to Los Angeles!"

I hollered, "This is my first phone call from a plane!"

He said, "Can you hear me all right?!"

I yelled, "No!"

He shouted, "What?!"

I yelled, "I can't hear you!"

He hollered, "I'll call you right back!"

He did. We chatted a very short while, and I said, "What is it you'd like to see you haven't seen?"

He said something through a lot of static.

I yelled, "What?"

He said something else.

I yelled, "What?" again.

He said, "I'll call you right back!"

He did. He said something. I said, "More vulnerable?"

He hollered something I just couldn't quite hear.

I said, "More sympathetic?"

He said, "No."

I said, "What is it you want? I'd be happy to take a shot at it, but what *is* it?" The connection never cleared up enough for me to hear what it was.

When Marty landed in Los Angeles, the studio told him they couldn't make a deal with me. Tom Pollock, who's the president of Universal, said to Jim Berkus: "I won't be able to justify that much money to Sid Scheinberg [who's Tom Pollock's boss]." Marty Brest called from a land-based phone and said, "Universal is telling me they can't pay you what you're asking. Would it help the situation if we forgot about the third audition and I just say, 'You have the part'?"

I said, "It certainly would help the situation."

We made a deal with the studio shortly after that. It was only when Marty said "I want you" that I allowed myself to feel how much I wanted it. At that moment, I would have stepped right out of my Stratolounger into the rapids fully clothed—which is pretty much what I actually did several months later.

In choosing me for *Midnight Run*, Marty Brest, a thirty-six-year-old director with only two feature movies to his credit, bucked the system. It's the conventional wisdom in Hollywood that people who star above the title in big-budget movies are hot numbers coming off recent hits. Marty had a different way of looking at it. He wanted who he thought were the best people for the parts because he felt that's how he could make the best movie. It doesn't sound that daring, but the only other time it had ever happened to me was with Elaine May in *The Heartbreak Kid*.

We began with two weeks' rehearsal, which included virtually no rehearsal. Since Marty had seen Bob and me read the script over several times, he chose not to keep doing that. We all knew there would be improvisation used throughout and decided to hold it for the filming. The time was used carefully, going over the rather intricate script, being sure we all agreed just where each necessary piece of information was revealed. This is not usually done with the actors, but it had the effect of forging a unified-team feeling about the whole picture that was unique.

Robert DeNiro had already been working on his role as a modern-day bounty hunter for some time. He had been going around on actual drug busts with teams of detectives, sometimes wearing a bulletproof vest as required. He had befriended a Los Angeles homicide detective who had killed several people in the line of duty and kept us regularly informed on the daily L.A. homicide rate: "There were two shooting murders and a stabbing fatality downtown last night." DeNiro had traveled to Chicago, since that's where his character had originally been a policeman, and went around with the police there, putting himself in Chicago danger.

In my research for the role of the accountant who embezzles $15 million and gives it to charity, I placed one ten-minute phone call to my business manager, Ralph Goldman, to ask how such a transfer would technically be done. It was a pleasant chat.

Bob DeNiro and I remained cordial and slightly bemused toward each other. I think both of us were waiting for the other to reveal himself so that we could get a clearer sense of what this experience of just about being handcuffed to each other six days a week for five months was going to be like. It had to be a relationship . . . but what kind?

Our first actual filming together was done late at night on a residential street in Brooklyn Heights. For about four hours we shot a scene where he hustles me down the street and throws me into his car. He had just nabbed me upstairs in a house. I was to be handcuffed behind my back. In the picture there were three kinds of handcuffs used—steel, rubber, and plastic. It was very dark. We were walking toward the camera, so you wouldn't actually see my hands in the shot. I suggested I just hold my hands behind my back and not use cuffs. Marty Brest suggested my arms would only look exactly right if I had cuffs on—rubber ones, since they wouldn't be seen. Bob asked if I would mind wearing the steel cuffs. I looked at him a moment, smiled, and said, "Sure." He smiled back. Neither of us knew what the other was thinking and didn't ask.

A couple of hours later, having been taken on the walk to the car and thrown in by Bob about fifteen times, I could really feel the cuffs on my skin, adding to the depth of my performance in the scene. Bob asked again if I minded. I said, "Not at all," and smiled again; so did he. I was enjoying the nonverbal repartee between us so much, I really didn't mind the cuff discomfort.

Finally, at around three A.M., Marty felt it was as good as we could do it. Since I would be wearing handcuffs throughout the picture, I went home that night curious about what my wrists would look like in four months. I never saw that first night's shooting, as it wasn't in the movie.

We moved on to Chicago shortly to film a big shoot-out in a bus station in the heart of downtown. Bob and I would arrive on a bus, get off, and the FBI would come screeching up in several cars and spread-eagle us against the bus. Then the mob would start firing at us from nearby rooftops and the FBI would shoot back at the mob. Explosions were going off for days. They weren't real bullets, but whatever they were, they could put your eye out. Bob and I went through some real jeopardy over the next few days, and, like people who go through anything together, we grew closer. Not as close as I had hoped, though.

The next shot called for Bob to drag me away in the confusion of the shoot-out—up a ramp, over a wall, under a truck, and into an empty police car, which he then steals. Bob thought it would be good to do it without rehearsal—let the camera see what happens the first time we actually try it. We headed up the ramp, but since Bob is up every morning working out at four-thirty, he moves a little faster than I do. As he pulled me up the ramp, we got some great realistic shouts of pain from me as the steel cuffs dug into my wrists. We got over the wall reasonably okay, although I quite sincerely improvised, "It's way too high." When he dragged me under the truck, I realized that unless I fell flat on my back I would crack my head on the truck's underparts. Bob can crouch lower than I can too, so I quickly went on my back. He dragged me under the truck, threw me head over heels into a police car, and then sped away. At the end of the first take, he stopped the car and looked at me. "You okay?" he asked with genuine concern.

I looked at him for a long moment, and then said: "Let's talk."

The only thing I felt had to change was that we had to stay closer together with the handcuffs going up the ramp, in deference to my limited blood supply. The rest I felt I could do again—just. We did the whole scene about ten times more before we called it a day. I still have the scars.

In spite of the shoot-outs and the handcuffs, I was having a good time. I wasn't looking at the daily film, but everyone who was seemed very happy, and that was good enough for me. I used to go see the dailies every day in movies, but over the years I found that that extends a twelve-hour working day by about two hours. I figured that in this film I was better off going home and resting up to be shot at the next day.

When a movie feels good, every home feels good. It wasn't hard to like a suite at the Ritz-Carlton Hotel in Chicago overlooking Lake Michigan, but I even enjoyed the Copper Hills Inn in Globe, Arizona, our next stop. I had a tiny room literally thirty feet from the train tracks—happily something I noticed on moving in, or I would have thought the world was coming to an end that first night around two A.M. when the first train rolled by. The train was in back of the inn. The front faced enormous slag heaps of copper waste that looked like pyramids for giants. The place was run by a grizzled old guy called Danko who had been a pall-bearer at John Wayne's funeral. We had come to this area for some car-chase sequences that would climax with us going over an embankment and smashing into a stone pillar of a bridge. Sometimes in chase sequences the car with the actors is towed by a camera car. I like it that way because the other way the actor is actually driving the car around hairpin curves or wherever. In this case, the actor/driver was DeNiro. Before beginning the movie I had read a magazine article about Bobby in which Shelley Winters was quoted as saying she was terrified in a movie she had done with Bob when he was at the wheel of a car. I saw myself as someone a little more easily terrified than Shelley Winters, so my head really shot up when I heard that today Bob would be at the wheel in a desperate getaway attempt. I will take no credit for any acting in those chase scenes. A guy who goes on real-life drug busts wearing a bulletproof vest also drives a car at top speeds as he's trying to get away. The man made no concession to anything. Confronted with that much dedication to reality, I couldn't bring myself to say, "Take it easy," or "Slow down," but expressed myself again through improvisation with some pretty good heartfelt attacks on him. He had earlier proven that he could gain and lose a hundred pounds or so, but nowhere in the deserved great-actor literature on DeNiro does it say he's a great driver. I would rate that whole chase experience as a little worse than being shot at.

We had an outstanding supporting cast on the picture, including an odd couple more odd than Bob and I. The mob boss was played by Dennis Farina, who was actually an ex-Chicago police detective turned actor. One of his two henchmen was played by Richie Foronjy, an ex-convict turned actor. Both men are extremely talented. Richie, about twenty years ago, had served time in Sing Sing and Attica, among other places, for robbery. He had turned away from that life simply because he was tired of serving time. ("If you can't do the time, don't do the crime.") It was fascinating to watch the ex-cop, Dennis, watch the ex-con, Richie, talk about his past, kind of like a cat and mouse who had called a truce. Richie told me that the best thing you could possibly rob—should you ever be interested—is a trailer truck full of razor blades. When I looked uncomprehendingly at him, he explained, "Do you realize how many razor blades you could put in a trailer truck?"

There was an elderly man I had seen walking around the streets of Williams, Arizona, where we were to shoot a scene in which Bob and I pretend to be FBI agents in order to claim some "phony" twenty-dollar bills in a bar so that we can get some money for food. I first saw the man as Bob and I were driving through the town on the way to the bar. I learned he was with us, an extra, and asked that when we do the bar scene he be placed on a stool next to me for some possible improvisation. He looked very much at home on a barstool in the morning nursing a drink and sucking on a cigarette. I told him that in the middle of the scene I was going to look at him suspiciously, and ask if he'd seen any suspicious characters around here. We were supposedly looking for a ring of counterfeiters. He was to simply say, "No." Then I said I'd ask him if *he* lived around here. He was then to say, "Yes," and I would look at him with extreme suspicion. We incorporated it into the first take. Marty Brest and everyone else loved how he did it. As the day wore on, I suggested to him more dialogue to do with me. At one point I told him I'd ask him if he'd ever done any time in prison. He was to say, "Yes." I'd look at him accusingly and ask, "What was the charge?" and he was to say, "Murder—but I didn't do it." After that, the guy was being celebrated as the hot new find of the picture. Everyone thought he was making up his lines on the spot. By the end of the day I think he was receiving more applause and approval than he'd gotten in his previous eighty years. But suddenly all the attention seemed to be too much. He had an uncontrollable coughing fit. His blood pressure shot sky-high and he had to be raced to the hospital, all the while resisting: "I want to work, I want to work." I later learned that, although he looked eighty, he was the same age I was. The next day he was back on his stool to finish out the sequence.

As we were getting ready to move on to our next location, Bob sidled up to me and whispered, almost like a racetrack tout, that if I was smart, I'd stay at the such-and-such hotel in the next town. Normally, I just let the company book me where they chose, but Bob evidently had made a reconnaissance trip to the next area and scoped out this place where he'd be staying, and he strongly suggested I go there too. "Listen to me on this one. You won't be sorry," he assured me.

I said, "We're working day and night. How can you possibly get away to check out different hotels in other towns?"

He shot me a mysterious smile and just said, "You'll like this place."

Since I already knew he was up at four-thirty every morning, I guessed he really had somehow checked out all the next town's possible inns. He's a man with enormous energy who moves at a rapid pace. I could visualize him doing a pretty good surveillance of a town during a lunch break.

When we got to the next town, I moved in where Bob had suggested. After about a week of shooting, he came to me and said he'd found another place, even better, that he had somehow initially overlooked and he'd be moving there tonight. Why didn't I move there too? I thought a moment, decided I'd stay put, and promised I'd visit him at his new spot. We spent New Year's Eve at his new place, and he was right: It was a knockout. A place in the side of a mountain, owned by the former great quarterback Y. A. Tittle.

It was ironic. I was someone who had been seen in movies often playing more sophisticated, worldly people than Bob, who often played a man of the streets, known for strapping weapons to his body so that he could dispatch you unexpectedly. In fact, as I've said, in life—as a teenager, anyway—I would sometimes have a knife strapped under my pants leg while making my way through rough areas. Even though it was never used, I had been a strapped-knife type of guy. Bob (in the movies, Mr. Hidden Weapons), in life, was a connoisseur—not just about where to stay, but about where to eat and what to drink once you got there. Somehow he would find the most elegant French restaurants hidden away in the least likely backwoods spots. He seemed to know wines even a little better than the tuxedoed French maître d'. He also liked to make toasts. As time went by, more and more he began to resemble the Godfather. Once it came out that Bob was going to be having some dealings with a show-business character I had dealt with a few years earlier with slightly unpleasant results. He listened to my story and then formally asked my permission to speak to the man about it. I could just visualize the scene: "I would like to ask you why you did this to my friend Charles Grodin." I decided the slight was too insignificant to bring up, and, besides, I still kind of liked the guy and didn't want to subject him to a Godfather move from Robert DeNiro.

With all the shoot-outs and car chases and jumping onto and getting thrown off moving trains in the picture, there was one upcoming sequence that made all of us involved particularly wary.

It was a scene that called for Bob and me to be swept down the raging rapids in a river—just our bodies, no boat. My normal caution was heightened when I saw that the scene had been scheduled for the last two days of the picture. Experience told me that if there was ever a risk of bodily harm to Bob or me in the movie, this was the sequence. I'm certain that's why it was at the end of the schedule. Naturally, it would be done with great care, but still, over the years, as I've said, there have been thousands of injuries—and, sadly, even deaths—caused by movie companies that had supposedly taken all possible safety precautions. On the other hand, things had gone smoothly enough so far.

When the day came for the rapids, I was not as apprehensive as I thought I might be. Bob and I were outfitted with wet suits under our clothes to keep us warm. The first shot didn't call for the rapids, just for me to be in the water flailing around as the bad guys in a helicopter were shooting at me. Living back in New York, I thought Arizona was warm country, no matter what time of year. That wasn't true. Sometimes it would be snowing, and it was generally much colder than I would ever have expected. This was January. I was led down the side of a mountain to the river's edge, where a stuntman dressed like me was standing. I was wearing my movie costume—slacks, shirt, sweater, topcoat—with my wet suit underneath it all. Someone came over and put some webbed flippers on my feet.

The stuntman said, "We'll put you in a boat, take you out to the middle of the river, and then lower you over the side into the water to start flailing. He said, "We'll be in a boat close by. If you feel anything is wrong, signal us right away, and we'll come over and get you." That was the first time in twenty movies a stuntman had said anything like that to me, so I quickly asked, "Wrong? Why? What would be wrong?"

He said, "Well, if anything doesn't seem right to you."

I said, "I've never done anything like this before. How will I know if it's not right?"

He stared at me a moment, clearly searching for a better way to put it. "If anything unusual happens." I stared back. He added, "Anything that you feel you're not comfortable with."

I could see we were going in circles, so I tried to help him out. I said, "I assume it's going to be cold [I hadn't even stuck my hand in]. But what else should I be on the lookout for in the unusual department?"

He said, "Anything at all."

I saw he either didn't know a better way to put it or just wasn't going to, so I said, "Fine. Let's go."

As I moved toward the boat, he said, "Just touch the top of your head as a signal to us if there's trouble."

I spun around. "Touch the top of my *head*?! Why? You're going to be about ten feet away—right?"

He said, "Yeah."

I said, "Well, I'll just call out."

He paused the briefest of pauses and said: "Call out or touch the top of your head—whatever."

He was a nice guy, and I knew him pretty well by now, so I got into the boat. Marty Brest and the camera crew were set up about seventy-five yards away on the edge of the river. My guy took the boat out to the middle of the water, then said, "Okay, you get out here," walked over, and lowered me over the side of the boat into the river. Within half a second I knew I'd made a huge mistake. Wet suit, shmet suit, it was like being submerged in ice water. Actually, it wasn't *like* ice water, it *was* ice water. The water temperature was in the forties: ten degrees less, and it's not even water. In a second, my topcoat felt like it weighed four hundred pounds, and I was on my back dropping like a mob victim. Within two seconds, using my old deep voice from the westerns, I shouted: "Okay, I'd like to come out right now!"

The boat quickly moved in, the stuntman pulled me out, and I stared numbly as we went back to shore. Marty and the camera crew were baffled, and some heavy walkie-talkie action quickly ensued. Marty asked, "What's the problem?"

Someone handed me a walkie-talkie. I reached out with a blue hand and took it. "Marty," I said, trying to stay calm, "I felt I was going to sink like a rock." Some people had taken my coat off and were wringing it out. Out of the corner of my eye, I noticed that it took two men to lift it.

Marty said, "Glen [the second-unit director] says the coat will serve as a flotation. You won't actually sink. How's the water temperature?"

I said, "I really wasn't in long enough to see if I would freeze; I was more preoccupied with sinking."

Someone suggested finding a spot where I could stand on the bottom and flail, so we'd only be dealing with the freezing issue, not the drowning issue.

Marty, still on the walkie-talkie, said: "How would you feel about trying that?"

Everyone was looking at me, so I said casually, "Sure, let's do it."

Within ten minutes they found a spot and lowered me over the side; my feet gratefully touched bottom, and I began to flail. I found that if I could keep the water off my bare skin, my hands, I could handle the cold—kind of. Between takes, I held my hands up in the air. After about ten minutes, Marty felt they had what they needed and said I could come out. As I reached the shore, bluish and shaking, Bob was coming down to do his end of the shot, which was to dive in and swim about fifty yards. "How was it?" he asked.

I said, "Try to keep your hands out of the water when you swim."

He laughed and dived in. Two hours later we were both still shaking. The company ran a test on the water temperature and decided that if we did the rapids part of the sequence here, neither one of us would be available to go to the premiere. A search began to find a location for warmer rapids that could reasonably match the mountainous terrain where we'd been shooting. Absolutely none were found in America, but soon an ideal matching location with warmer raging rapids was found—in New Zealand.

A few days later a column appeared on the entertainment page of the *Los Angeles Herald-Examiner*. It said, in effect, that Robert DeNiro and Charles Grodin were heading to New Zealand to film a scene in the rapids because "Charles Grodin had put his toe in the water, found it too cold, shouted out, 'I'm drowning!' and refused to go back in—hence, New Zealand." Ah, the accuracy of the press!

Happily, a brother of the entertainment editor of the paper had been one of our assistants on shore helping to lift my topcoat. He quickly called his brother, who printed a letter from me saying, in essence: If I had that kind of power as an actor, I'd never get near rapids anywhere—especially in New Zealand—and where the hell was it, anyway?

It turned out that New Zealand was just about as far away as you could go. It was farther than Japan. In fact, as I understood it, the only place farther was a country called Tonga.

Bob and I and his eleven-year-old son, Rafael, set out one night from Los Angeles to New Zealand. Marty Brest and a few other people would be on a later plane. We flew through the night for five hours on a 747 to Honolulu, where we changed planes. It was about three A.M., somebody's time. We waited in a lounge to board our next plane, which would take us in nine and a half hours to Auckland, New Zealand, where we'd take another plane to Queenstown, New Zealand, where we'd take a van to some other place where we'd stay, about forty minutes from their rapids.

Bob left the lounge to make a telephone call. He was regularly excusing himself from wherever he was to make a call. Sometimes he'd disappear for shockingly long periods of time, and sometimes he'd *never* come back. I always felt he could be running an international ring of some kind in addition to gaining and losing hundreds of pounds and going on drug busts with bulletproof vests. It was interesting to me that a man of so few words in person would be so comfortable on the phone. In the Honolulu lounge, he'd been gone about fifteen minutes when I looked at Rafael, who was sitting on a suitcase, and said: "I know why I'm here. But why would a bright kid like you be here at this time?"

He gave me a broader version of his father's mysterious smile.

Eventually we boarded our plane to Auckland, where we were met by some very friendly people and taken through startlingly green, rolling countryside to a hotel and a nap. A few hours later, Bob; Rafael; Marty Brest; the executive producer, Bill Gilmore, a former minor-league catcher; Don Thorin, our cinematographer; and I boarded the kind of small plane I've sometimes flown in for twenty minutes. This was a three-and-a-half-hour flight to Queenstown, and it was a ride like I've never had before. The weather wasn't ideal, and we bounced around the sky just a little slower than a kernel in a popcorn machine. All of us men were too macho to scream, but some very serious looks were exchanged. Marty Brest kept up a running commentary to the effect that the plane was doing exactly what you should expect a plane to do in this kind of a situation. He didn't exactly define the situation, but used words like *air pockets* and *current* and *wind supports* a lot. I had no idea what the hell he was talking about, but I appreciated every word. Don Thorin, who appears to be an unusually stoic man, told me later that he had been wondering if he should be writing a note of some kind to his loved ones to be found on his clothing.

When we finally got to Queenstown, it was pouring rain and colder than Arizona. Everyone checked into the hotel and gamely set out to take a look at our new rapids. There we were, about eight of us, rain pounding down, shivering in our parkas, standing by these crashing, raging rapids. We'd been told it was the middle of the summer here, with average temperatures around ninety degrees.

Back at the hotel, I unpacked and watched one of Queenstown's two television channels. The program was about a big, fat woman who gets angry at her husband for having an affair and seemed to pretty much turn into a nymphomaniac. At least, that's the impression I got when I intermittently checked it out during our stay.

It rained for a few days, then the sun came out, and word was sent for me to get ready to go into the river. As I was standing in the shower that morning, I began to reflect on the situation. There would be doubles used for the heavy, heavy rapids stuff—young athletes half my age who looked like they breathed, ate, and drank rapids. But Bob and I *would* actually be swept down the rapids—no ropes tied, no trick photography—just us, fully clothed over our wet suits. I took Marty aside in the lobby of the hotel as we were about to head for the river. "How can I be certain that there aren't rocks that are going to gash me under those rapids?"

"You can't be certain," Marty said with great ease. He went on: "Our stuntmen have been over the route several times and assured me it's safe. But there is an element of risk."

Marty's easygoing manner provoked me to a frontal attack. "Can you tell me why, as an actor, I should be put in that kind of risk?" (I fully intended to do it, having already come across the world. I just felt like getting a couple of answers that morning.)

Marty said, "Would you like me to do the stunt to show you it's okay?" Early on, Marty had said he would never ask me to do anything he wouldn't do. Marty is not athletic; he's kind of a slight fellow. But he's a movie director, and since most of them are crazy, his offer never reassured me. Nor had I ever taken him up on it.

I said, "It will give me no satisfaction to see you gashed. Let's go. I'll do it."

When we got to the river location, they took me to a spot where they showed me the side of a cliff I would be put on by a boat. I was then to lower myself into the water. My topcoat had been considerably reduced in weight by removing pounds of top-coat innards. After getting into the water, which they said was warmer here (it was—a little), I was to swim about five yards till I got caught in the rapids, which would take over. After being swept for a while past camera range, three stuntmen would snatch me out, with boats standing by in case something went wrong. I reflected for a moment.

Suddenly, Marty, in a moment of lunatic energy, leaped up from his chair, jumped into a boat, and said: "I'll do it."

"Marty," I called after him, "Marty, that's not necessary."

But there he was, quickly being placed on the side of the cliff, lowering himself into the water, swimming his five yards, getting caught in the rapids, being carried back toward us out of camera range, then snatched out by the stuntmen, and back on shore, thrusting his arms into the air—Olympic style. Everyone cheered.

He later told me that for the rest of the day he had trouble standing.

It was now my turn. With the young New Zealand athletes looking on, I called on long-forgotten macho resources and boarded the boat, went to the cliff, lowered myself in, swam, got swept, was pulled out . . . six times. As I sat there after the sixth time, covered with blankets, overwhelmed with fatigue, and starting to feel dizzy, Marty asked: "Do you have one more in you?"

Something about the way the light hit the camera angle on

my head—something—made them want to do it a seventh time, who knew why? I'd given up asking those kinds of questions years ago. I said I didn't honestly know if I had a seventh one in me since I was basically not a rapids guy—but a Stratolounger guy. I could answer any question in the world about my durability in a Stratolounger, which was considerable. But rapids—who knew?

I did it a seventh time and joyously went back to base camp, passing Bobby, who was heading down for his turn, on the way. "How was it?" he asked. I gave him one of his smiles. He laughed, went down, and did it—probably without a question.

That day at lunch, I asked Bob how he would feel about going first on the next stunt. I had always been going first since, story-wise, I fall in and Bobby dives in after. But when you edit the movie these are separate pieces, and it doesn't really matter who goes first. Bobby quickly said, "Of course," as I knew he would. I mean, he can't fly, but after working out for months at four-thirty A.M., he *is* a man of steel.

Bob and I went up together to check on the next stunt. This one called for us to be pulled by a camera boat through the rapids, holding on to a bar on the boat that would be unseen beneath the water. A stuntman demonstrated it for us. They shot along for about fifty feet, and that was that. It looked simple enough, but we told Marty that Bobby would be going first on this one. A boat took me back to my camper at river's edge while they prepared all the rigging, mounted the cameras, secured the bar, and other things I've never been inclined to learn. Bob stayed on the shore with them.

At the camper I got out of my fins, pants, sweater, topcoat, and wet suit, and put on a nice terry-cloth robe they had provided. I climbed into the top bunk, where I had a clear view of everyone upriver about a hundred yards away, and opened up my paperback copy of Sam Donaldson's *Hold On, Mr. President!* About an hour later, they were still rigging . . . or something. Eventually, I heard gunnings of motors, and three different boats started racing downriver. I put down my book and looked out my window. I had a perfect view of everything, but I couldn't see Bob. Occasionally, I'd see a flash of dark hair, but only a flash. I was surprised to see them blasting by me. The stuntman had gone about fifty feet, but the shot seemed to cover about two hundred yards. I twisted around to look downriver to see it finally come to an end with a lot of boats converging. I still couldn't see Bob. Eventually, he emerged from the river covered with blankets. I saw him say something briefly to Marty and then disappear into his camper. Quickly, there was a knock on my door. An assistant stuck his head in and told me we were leaving this location.

I said, "Why? What's going on?"

Apparently, what Bob had said when he emerged from the river was: "I can't recommend Chuck do this shot." That's the closest Robert DeNiro would come to a complaint, but it was enough for everyone to pack up and forget about doing that shot with me. Bob later told me that the bouncing camera boat kept smashing him in and out of the water, and soon he began to wonder if he should just let go of the bar and take his chances in rough rapids, or . . . He just slowly shook his head.

He's not a man of many words, but I got the point quickly, as had Marty.

The next day, we had a couple more shots to pick up by the rapids. But, of course, there's a hell of a difference between "by" and "in." So, after four months, the filming came to a peaceful end.

Bob, Rafael, and I went out for dinner that night. Bob asked me what I was going to do now. I said, "Go home. Why? What are you going to do?"

He said: "Well, it seems a shame to come all the way to New Zealand and not see Tonga." So I went home to New York and Bob and Rafael went off to Tonga.

About five months later, the picture opened to even more acclaim than everyone said it would. It was called one of the best movies of recent years, as well as the best ever of its kind. The praise came from all over. I had been widely praised before, but playing a leading role in a hit of this size you really feel it. Everyone wanted to talk to me. Articles appeared saying things press agents wouldn't dare write. When I walked down the street, people would call out my name. Secretaries apologized profusely if I was kept on hold on the phone for more than five seconds. Just as after *The Heartbreak Kid* and *Heaven Can Wait*, the offers began to pour in. Once again, I'm being given a chance to write, star in, and direct my own movie.

However, my memories of *11 Harrowhouse* and *Movers and*

Shakers remain vivid. I remember too well Elliot Kastner and Frank Yablans and the *Variety* critic, Art Murphy, who said of me in *11 Harrowhouse:* "It would be sad to think an acting career lay ahead." Or the one who said of *Movers and Shakers:* "If you want to know what it feels like to die sitting upright in a theater seat, go see this movie."

So I am proceeding warily. I know there is a lesson to be learned here somewhere, but I'm still trying to figure out what it is. As I'm sure someone once said: "That's some business, that show business."

Epilogue: "Night of 100 Stars"

The saga of *Movers and Shakers* showed me that I had to rise to a unique position (making my own movie) to experience the most painful rejection. It took another unique event, a glorious celebration, to reintroduce long-forgotten feelings of ineptitude as a performer.

A few years ago, the endlessly resourceful Broadway producer Alexander Cohen was putting together an extravaganza called "Night of 100 Stars." It was to be a television special that would benefit the Actors Fund, a charitable organization for actors in need. In order to be certain he got his hundred stars, Mr. Cohen invited several hundred to participate, and wound up with a night of 296 stars.

He called and asked me to be part of the evening, with Ellen Burstyn. He wanted us to be in the Broadway Legend segment because of *Same Time, Next Year*. He told me he'd already called Ellen, who agreed to participate. I asked what he wanted us to do. He said we Broadway Legends would simply, on cue, step through a huge poster of our show.

I asked, "That's it?"

He said, "That's it."

Ellen and I had been co-chairmen of the Actors Fund during the year we were in the play, so it was difficult to refuse, especially since I knew that Ellen, in spite of our close relationship, sometimes saw me as a little bit of a spoilsport. She had earlier told me that she didn't think I was outgoing enough toward the stagehands on the show, which surprised me because I always thought I was friendly toward everyone. She said she wasn't saying I wasn't friendly, just a little perfunctory in my greetings as I arrived at the theater each night. I thought about it, and figured she was right. I always tended to get a little withdrawn as I approached the place where I had to perform, starting to get into the concentrated state that I needed in order to act. After Ellen commented on my perfunctory greetings, I tried to hold that concentration back, at least until I reached my dressing room, so that I could be friendlier on the way there. As I've said, I've always been crazy about Ellen, and also found her to be someone I'd go out of my way not to mess with. So I quickly agreed to be part of the "Night of 100 Stars" and step through the poster with her.

About an hour after agreeing, I got a call from a production assistant in Alexander Cohen's office telling me to report for rehearsal on Friday and Saturday prior to the Sunday show. I said, "Rehearsal for what? All we're going to do is step through a poster." I figured I could just show up close to air time, and when someone wanted me to step through, I'd step. The assistant said she didn't know anything about anything, but was only giving rehearsal times. I thanked her and immediately called Ellen.

"Listen," I said, "on this 'Night of 100 Stars' thing, I want you to know that I'm not singing or dancing or anything. I agreed to step through a poster, and if anyone tries to make a musical-comedy guy out of me at the last second, I'm not doing it."

"Charley," she said to me, "what are you carrying on about? There's no singing and dancing—we're stepping through a poster! Let's not make a big thing out of it."

I said, "If we're just stepping through a poster, why are we rehearsing for two days?"

Ellen said, "Look, we're not singers or dancers, and you really don't have to worry. They have to coordinate a whole show, and I'm sure that's why they want us there. By the way, I won't be there the first day because I have to appear at a benefit at the Kennedy Center in Washington, but I'll see you at rehearsal on the second day."

Trying not to come off as a spoilsport, I said, as gently as I could, "Okay, but I just want to go on record with you that I'm not singing or dancing."

"You worry too much," Ellen said, and wished me a happy first day's rehearsal.

On the rehearsal Friday, I arrived quite anxious to see just what I'd be rehearsing. I opened the door to the building where the rehearsal hall was located, and there was a young woman sitting behind a desk with a long list. I told her who I was, and she searched the list for my name, asking me to spell it as she scanned. Some star, I thought! Happily I was recognized by someone else, who took me by the hand onto an elevator and up to the third-floor rehearsal hall. As we entered the hall, which was filled with famous faces, two dancers went soaring across the room in an intricate dance step.

"That will be Mayor Koch with a female dancer," the woman with me remarked. "Oh, look," she quickly added, "you're just in time! Here come you and Ellen Burstyn!"

I looked up to watch two dancers soar and twist and turn across the rehearsal stage. "Just a minute," I said. "When you say that's me and Ellen Burstyn, what exactly do you mean?"

"Those dancers are doing what you and Ellen will eventually do on Sunday night."

"Uh-huh," I said. "I think we've got a misunderstanding here. Who's in charge? I have to speak to someone right away."

"Is there a problem?" the woman asked.

Thinking Ellen might hear about my behavior, I said, "Let's not call it a problem. Uh, who's in charge?"

The woman walked me across the room to the dancer who was "me," said, "He'll take care of you," and disappeared.

The fellow told me what a big fan he was of mine, shook my hand, and suggested we go outside the hall so that he could show me a few steps.

I walked out with him, not before noting that not only was the room filled with famous faces, but they were famous faces from the musical-comedy world. Mary Martin, Ethel Merman, and Carol Channing were just a few.

In the hallway outside the rehearsal room, the male dancer instantly started to bound around and dip and show me my moves. When he finally stopped, I said: "Look, it's not your fault, but we truly have a misunderstanding here. I'm not a dancer at all."

He quickly interjected, "These are very simple steps."

"It's not your fault," I said again, "but I'm just supposed to walk through a poster here. I truly didn't come here to dance."

The dancer said he didn't know anything about any poster.

"Look," I tried again, "I'm not a dancer, and I'm deeply uncomfortable suddenly trying to become one in front of millions of people on network television Sunday night."

"Look," the dancer said, "I know exactly how you feel, and I agree with you."

"Good," I said. "I appreciate your understanding."

"Nobody's going to ask you to go out there and dance on Sunday night."

"Good," I said again.

"You don't become a dancer in two days," he said.

"Well, I certainly couldn't," I quickly added.

"No one could," he said, more and more becoming a soul mate to me. "I spent all my life becoming a dancer. It's a very difficult craft to master," he said.

"I admire you tremendously," I said, thinking we were about to go out for a cup of coffee and forget the whole thing, when he suddenly said: "But we're not talking about dancing here."

"We're not?" I said, eyeing him suspiciously once more.

"Not at all," he said.

"What are we talking about?"

"Moving," he said, "just moving," in a tone that suggested, Who could object to that?

I had heard this expression, "moving," before, usually in references like, "Does he move well?" It wasn't dancing, it was true. But "moving," while less than "dancing," was more than . . . moving. I'd say it was somewhere between "walking" and "dancing," and certainly, by anyone's definition, more than "stepping through a poster"!

I wanted to leave. I thought of the Actors Fund. I thought of Ellen and the possibility of bringing out the George C. Scott in her. I stood there as the dancer continued.

"It's just a few steps," he said. "See? Follow me. I'll be Ellen Burstyn."

"Just a second," I said. "I really—"

"Just try it," he interrupted. "You'll see, it's nothing." He then, moving across the hallway, took two steps, then one step, then two steps, urging me to follow.

After staring at him a long moment, with tremendous embarrassment I slowly began to move after him, praying that no one would come out and see me.

"That's great!" he shouted as I made my way after him in anguish. "You studied dance, didn't you?"

"No," I said.

He continued: "That's two steps, then one step, then two steps, then pass me by—"

"Hold it!" I said. "What's this 'pass me by'?"

"It's nothing, it's so simple. Just follow me."

"Look, I really—"

"Come on, you can do it!"

So I followed him—two steps, then one step, then two steps, passed him by—and felt like a total fool. After about five minutes of repeating this over and over, he suggested we try it in the main room.

"You've got to be kidding!" I said. "You've got some of the biggest talents in musical comedy in the last twenty-five years in there!"

"You're great," he insisted. "They'll love you."

I was starting to feel a little crazy. I was not only supposed to dance, which I couldn't, but to do it in front of legends. "What am I doing in this number, anyway?" I asked. "*Same Time, Next Year* wasn't even a musical!"

"Look, I don't know," he said, suddenly revealing a touch of annoyance. "It's a legendary show. Let's go." And he guided me into the main hall.

I stood against the wall and watched Mary Martin sail across the room. By the time my turn came I was feeling so ridiculous that I flew across the room with my "two" and "one" and "two" and "cross." The group, I guess appreciating the effort, applauded. I turned red, smiled at everyone, and "moved" out the door.

Ellen was unreachable in Washington, so I decided the hell with it, and showed up the next day for my second rehearsal. Ellen was there this time and, true to her fashion, adjusted to the new deal. When I reminded her that we were just supposed to walk through a poster, she said, "Charley, we're part of a musical number: Let's get with it."

My mind suddenly flashed to an image of Ellen racing her speedboat from her home in upstate New York down the Hudson River in the darkness for the forty-minute trip to the theater for *Same Time, Next Year;* and then, of course, after the performance, racing up the Hudson River in the darkness once again. Trying to rise to her level of reaching for the gusto, I announced, with probably not believable bravado: "Count me in!"

On Sunday, the day of the taping, which would run three hours on the air, I was told to be prepared for a twelve-hour day. Alex Cohen just felt more comfortable having everyone in the building. What I thought was a one-second walk through a poster was starting to feel like a life's work.

My legendary spot finally arrived around eleven-thirty that night, sandwiched between Carol Channing in *Hello, Dolly!* and Ethel Merman in *Gypsy.* By then, I had pretty much forgotten whether it was "two" and "one" and "two," or "one" and "two" and "one," or what it was, as, holding my hand, Ellen soared across the stage in perfect step. I stumbled after her with no "one" or "two," but basically a rag-doll-being-dragged move, instantly incurring the everlasting displeasure of Alex Cohen and the good-natured ridicule of my old pal Jimmy Caan.

Not since Bill Putch at the Pittsburgh Playhouse gave me a Rorschach test did I feel so out of place in my own profession. Some things never change completely.

As the evening came to a close, I was standing backstage in a corner telling a story. I finished it, and someone listening just behind me started to laugh so loud I turned around to see who it was.

It was Elizabeth Taylor.

When I looked at her, she smiled at me. She wasn't the young girl in the white Cadillac convertible, and I wasn't Montgomery Clift. But it wasn't bad, either. The whole trip from Pittsburgh into show business was so different than I thought it would be. In my imagination, I was thinking love scenes with Elizabeth Taylor; in reality, I ended up almost getting sued by her studio, MGM.

But it hasn't been bad. It hasn't been bad at all.

Index

ABOUT THE AUTHOR

Charles Grodin lives in Connecticut
with his wife and son.